Turkey-Russia Relations in the Twenty-First Century

Turkey-Russia Relations in the Twenty-First Century

Cooperation and Competition amid Systemic Turbulence

Muhammet Koçak

LEXINGTON BOOKS
Lanham • Boulder • New York • London

Published by Lexington Books
An imprint of The Rowman & Littlefield Publishing Group, Inc.
4501 Forbes Boulevard, Suite 200, Lanham, Maryland 20706
www.rowman.com

86-90 Paul Street, London EC2A 4NE

British Library Cataloguing in Publication Information Available

Library of Congress Cataloging-in-Publication Data

Names: Koçak, Muhammet, 1990- author.
Title: Turkey-Russia relations in the twenty-first century : cooperation
    and competition amid systemic turbulence / Muhammet Koçak.
Description: Lanham : Lexington Books, [2022] | Includes bibliographical
    references and index.
Subjects: LCSH: Turkey—Foreign relations—Russia (Federation) |
    Russia (Federation)—Foreign relations—Turkey.
Classification: LCC DR479.R9 K64 2022 (print) | LCC DR479.R9 (ebook) |
    DDC 327.561047—dc23/eng/20220622
LC record available at https://lccn.loc.gov/2022028427
LC ebook record available at https://lccn.loc.gov/2022028428

ISBN: 978-1-66691-573-0 (cloth : alk. paper)
ISBN: 978-1-66691-575-4 (pbk. : alk. paper)
ISBN: 978-1-66691-574-7 (ebook)

To the loving memory of my mother

Contents

List of Figures

Acknowledgments

This book is a product of years of research that began at Bilkent University and continued at Florida International University. Throughout this journey, many people and institutions have facilitated the production of this book.

Before anyone else, I am thankful to my wife, Merve. She moved with me to Miami for my doctoral work right after our wedding, sacrificing her career and comfort zone. Our daughters, Meryem Hanne and Ayşe Saliha, brought me joy that kept me going during the challenging times. The companionship of my wife and our daughters has also been a constant source of *barakah,* enriching our home.

My parents always believed in my potential to achieve great things and contribute to society. My mother and father provided their support, love, and trust as I worked on my book. Without their steadfast support, I could not have come this far in life. I wish my mother had lived to see the end of this project.

I was fortunate to work with excellent scholars throughout my graduate studies and benefit from their passion for knowledge. I laid the foundations of this work in my *alma mater*, Bilkent University. There, I was fortunate to benefit from the mentorship and friendship of Hakan Kırımlı, who introduced me to many aspects of Russia. I was also privileged to work with the legendary scholar Norman Stone, whose astute observations broadened my horizons. At FIU, Mohiaddin Mesbahi encouraged me to write specifically on Turkey-Russia relations and provided mentorship while working on my manuscript. Ronald Cox, Benjamin Smith, and Thomas Breslin also provided valuable feedback to the earlier drafts.

I also relied on the support of many people while working on my book. In Miami, Mirsad, his wife Lenka, and their large family provided loyal support to our family. I was blessed with the friendship of Zeynep, Hami, Dilara, Bill, Orçun, Lena, Onur, and Nika at FIU. Many friends made Bilkent a home for me, including Abdussamet, Ahmet Faruk, Ahmet Sadık, Ahmet Recai, Ali Burak, Ali Cahit, Adil, Ahmet Sami, Bahadır, Emre, Emin, Enes, Esat, Fatih, Fuat, Furkan, Hasan, Hamdi, Hüseyin, İbrahim, Mehmet Akif, Mehmed Sami, Mevlüt, Muhammet, Musa, Ömer, Selman, Seyfettin, Salih, and Yağmur. They were there whenever I needed them.

Diana, Nora, Sara, İkbal, Gaye, and Deniz read my work and made me aware of several issues I might have missed. Bilgehan, Gloria, Zeynep Büşra, and Ömer shared their expertise whenever I needed it. Alperen Vural helped me with the drawing of the figures. I am thankful to all of them.

Last but not least, I thank the staff at Lexington Books, notably associate editor Trevor Crowell, for working with me on this project. Their cooperative attitude made it easier for me to make this book ready for publication.

Abbreviations and Acronyms

A2/AD	Anti-Access/Area-Denial
AK PARTY	Justice and Development Party
Akkuyu NPP	Akkuyu Nuclear Power Plant Project
BLACKSEAFOR	The Black Sea Naval Cooperation Task Group
BOTAŞ	Turkish Petroleum Pipeline Corporation
BP	British Petroleum
BS	Baku-Supsa Pipeline Project
BSEC	Black Sea Economic Cooperation
BTC	Baku-Tbilisi–Ceyhan Pipeline Project
BTE	Baku-Tbilisi-Erzurum Pipeline Project
CAATSA	Countering America's Adversaries Through Sanctions Act
CHP	Republican People's Party
CIS	Commonwealth of Independent States
CNN	Cable News Network
Comintern	Communist International
COVID-19	Coronavirus Disease 2019
CSTO	Collective Security Treaty Organization
CUP	Commitee of Union and Progress
DPR	Donetsk People's Republic
ER	United Russia Party
EU	European Union
FSA	Free Syrian Army
GDP	Gross Domestic Product
GNA	Government of National Accord of Libya
ISIS	Islamic State of Iraq and Sham

KY	Kirkuk-Yumurtalık Pipeline Project
LNA	Libyan National Army
LPR	Luhansk People's Republic
MHP	Nationalist Movement Party
Narkomindel	Commissariat of Foreign Affairs
NATO	North Atlantic Treaty Organization
Nazi	German National Socialist Party
NEP	New Economic Policy
NGO	Non-Governmental Organizations
NPR	National Public Radio
PKK	Kurdistan Workers Party
PYD	Democratic Union Party
RSDLP	Russian Social Democratic Labor Party
SCO	Shanghai Co-operation Organization
SGC	Southern Gas Corridor
SNC	Syrian National Council
TANAP	Trans Anatolian Pipeline
TCP	Turkish Communist Party
TGRT	Turkish Gazette Radio Television
TIKA	Turkish Cooperation Coordination Agency
TRNC	Turkish Republic of Northern Cyprus
TRT	Turkish Radio Television
Turkic Council	Cooperation Council of Turkish Speaking Countries
TURKSOY	International Organization of Turkic Culture
UACV	Unmanned Aerial Combat Vehicle
UAE	United Arab Emirates
UAV	Unmanned Aerial Vehicle
UK	United Kingdom
UN	United Nations
UNSC	United Nations Security Council
US	United States of America
USSR	Union of Soviet Socialist Republics
YPG	People's Protection Units

Introduction

WHAT THIS BOOK AIMS TO ACHIEVE

This book explains Turkey-Russia relations in the twenty-first century. Turkey and Russia are two of the most significant powerhouses in Eurasia. They are close neighbors, each with a strong influence on multiple regions, including the Middle East, the Black Sea, and the Caucasus. Two countries' increasing strategic presence in Syria, Libya, the Caucasus, and several other hot spots are cases in point. Moreover, both countries' revisionist language towards the current global political system makes Turkey-Russia relations even more critical and interesting.

In the past, the Russian Empire played a significant role in the collapse of the Ottoman Empire, and during the Cold War, Turkey took part in containing the USSR as a NATO member. However, in the twenty-first century, Turkey and Russia invested in bilateral trade and established partnerships in the defense and energy sectors. The two countries also worked together to resolve several regional conflicts, including the Syrian Crisis and the Nagorno-Karabagh Conflict. These developments occurred despite Turkey's NATO membership and firm U.S. opposition to the strengthening of the bonds between Turkey and Russia. Despite this trend's regional and global significance, there is not enough scholarly attention on this specific subject. Aside from occasional articles, books, and book chapters that examine various aspects of these relations, the literature has yet to have an exhaustive account analyzing the Turkey-Russia nexus, together with relevant global, regional, and domestic dynamics. Moreover, the subject is mostly considered from the angle of U.S.-Turkey relations, changes in Turkish and Russian foreign policy, and domestic politics in these two countries. An insightful explanation of their bilateral relations will contribute to understanding the most recent dynamics in the Turkey-Russia nexus, the political dynamics in multiple regions and the emerging global political system in the post–Cold War era. Why did Turkey-Russia relations substantially develop in the twenty-first century?

This book argues that the balance of power between Turkey and Russia has been the primary dynamic that gives direction to different segments of Turkey-Russia relations. Turkey and Russia compete in many regions, especially the Middle East, the Black Sea, and North Africa. In the twenty-first century, the gradual decline of U.S. influence in these regions has had two significant consequences for Turkey-Russia relations: opportunities for Turkey and Russia to expand their influence in these regions and Turkey's weakening hand against Russia. As a result, we have seen more intense engagements between Turkey and Russia in different regions, and sectors. This process does not follow a linear path. Instead, the leaderships in the two countries observe the slowly unfolding developments revolving around the Turkey-Russia nexus, act upon the situation as they perceive it, and this whole process ultimately shapes and reshapes Turkey-Russia relations. Therefore, the domestic politics in both countries, leaderships, and their perception matter as well as the balance of power between Turkey and Russia.

Prominent theoretical frameworks used to understand and explain global politics often fail to account for issues between two countries in different regions and their bilateral relations. Especially in the International Relations discipline, focus is often on more grand issues such as the global balance of power or trends that have direct global significance. I consider the Turkey-Russia nexus as a formation created by two "composite" states. Therefore, although I argue that systemic dynamics are the main reason for the changes in bilateral relations, I also consider dynamics that stem from the domestic level as a factor that affects the course of the relations. Type-3 Neoclassical Realism provides a functional model to explain states' foreign policy choices (as in earlier versions of neoclassical realism) and the international outcomes that these policy choices' interaction produces.[1] I utilize a model based on the Type-3 Neoclassical Realism to account for how the foreign policy choices of Turkey and Russia, under the impact of various dynamics, impact Turkey-Russia relations.

Thus, this research goes beyond the explanations based only on leaders' attitudes, mutual benefits of bilateral trade, or changes in the balance of power. Instead, in this research, I acknowledge that the Turkey-Russia nexus, composed of two countries with "composite" structures, operates within different regional and global political structures. I also recognize that these regional and global structures incorporate political, economic, and normative dynamics.

Such consideration requires analyzing how Turkey and Russia's composite domestic political structures interact in changing regional and global political dynamics. Therefore, the reader will find the analyses of the domestic political systems in the two countries, and the regional and global political dynamics as they relate to the bilateral relations. I also argue that Turkey-Russia relations, or relations between any two countries, could not be confined to the political or strategic dimension because the two countries have intense interactions in normative and economic dimensions. In this book, I show how these countries' interactions in these strategic, economic, and social dimensions interact with the domestic and systemic variables.

This book explains the period between 2001 and 2022, and it is chronologically structured. The first chapter provides historical background. This introduction helps the reader to grasp the following three chapters that chronologically analyze Turkey-Russia relations. The three chapters that follow this historical background starts with a pivotal event that has significant influence on the relations in the following years (Iraq Invasion, Arab Uprisings, and Failed Coup Attempt in Turkey). These events either influence the balance of power between the two countries or the way they perceive the changing dynamics, or both. Every chapter starts with an appraisal of the period, where I discuss the important dynamics that influence Turkey and Russia in each period. Then, I explain how the two countries digested and responded to the changes in the dynamics that affect the Turkey-Russia nexus. Finally, I analyze how their responses shape different segments of the bilateral relations between Turkey and Russia. The book shows how Turkey and Russia respond to the international environment reflects on their bilateral trade, energy cooperation, and engagements in regional issues.

The central argument in this book is that the balance of power between Turkey and Russia is the primary dynamic that impacts the relations. Since Turkey has been the weaker state in this equation for the past two hundred years or so, the Western presence in the regions where Turkey and Russia compete, becomes the main variable. Beyond this main variable, the way Turkey and Russia perceive and respond to the changes in this main variable should be examined as well. Their responses shape and reshape Turkey-Russia relations. Therefore, both systemic and domestic variables matter in the shaping of the Turkey-Russia relations.

LITERATURE

The literature on Turkey-Russia relations could be classified into two groups. The first group analyzes Turkey-Russia relations with a focus on the contrast between the economic cooperation between the two countries and their geopolitical competition. According to this line of thought, the barometer of Turkey-Russia relations depends on the balance between these two dynamics. Accordingly, when economic benefits of developing relations outweigh the cost of strategic competition, the relations improve. The second group comprises many subgroups, which aim to explain Turkey-Russia relations using various theoretical frameworks.

Turkey-Russia relations significantly develop after the Cold War, bringing about economic cooperation and competition for influence in the post-Soviet space and other regions. These developments encouraged many scholars to evaluate the Turkey-Russia nexus by considering the increase in bilateral trade volume and clashes of interest over regional issues. During the 1990s, when the relations between the two countries showed rapid improvement fueled by the rising trade volume, most researchers explained such development by pointing out the balance between the conflicts of interests in multiple regions. For instance, Suat Bilge used the term "cold peace" to describe the bilateral relations.[2] Between the early 2000s and the early 2010s, Turkey-Russia relations continued to develop with no serious regional confrontation. In this period, the analyses of bilateral relations considered this trend to indicate serious improvement. In her 2002 article, Yanık argues that Turkey and Russia took their relations to a higher level by normalizing political ties while developing trade relations.[3] From the beginning of the 2010s until the late 2010s, the deterioration in bilateral relations, which began with the Arab Uprisings, escalated with the Syrian crisis, and culminated in the Jet Crisis, bringing back a cautious approach. Çelikpala indicates that the relations have reached a fragile phase after a honeymoon period where the parties need to put more effort into maintaining and improving them.[4]

The literature on Turkey-Russia relations also contains contributions that choose to approach the topic with a broader theoretical framework in an attempt to bring in a structural approach. These assessments do not ignore the dichotomy between the positive impact of trade relations and the negative impact of geopolitical competition on bilateral relations. They seek to explain how Turkey-Russia relations interact with regional and global dynamics in various dimensions. As described in this subsection, the literature often treats the dichotomy between economic cooperation and regional competition as the central dynamic in Turkey-Russia relations. This dynamic is very significant on the bilateral level in the post–Cold War era. However, relying on this dichotomy often risks missing the bigger picture. In other words, without adopting a framework that explains the relevance of structural, regional, and domestic dynamics, it is hard to discover and analyze the factors that shape Turkey-Russia relations.

Multiple types of frameworks are used in the literature. One of the most prevalent explanations for the positive trends in Turkey-Russia relations is a Western-liberal one, which focuses on the alleged affinity between the leaders of both countries based on their resentment, cynicism, and opposition to the so-called Western political norms. These accounts often link the improvements in Turkey-Russia relations to these countries' moving away from the West under "illiberal leaders." One of the oft-cited examples of this perception is Hill and Taşpınar's 2006 article, which considers the developments in Turkey-Russia relations as a tactical partnership, established out of a shared frustration caused by the aggressive U.S. foreign policy strategy under the Bush administration.[5]

The way Turkey and Russia consider the West does have an indirect impact on their bilateral relations. For instance, as explained in this research, the regional and global changes caused by the U.S. invasion of Iraq in 2003 positively impacted Turkey-Russia relations. However, these changes could be considered to be related to the changing regional and global balance of power and conflict of interest rather than the leadership styles or the non-Western characteristics of the two leaders. Moreover, even if there is a level of convergence in their attitudes towards the West, the explanatory power of a premise that relies on a West-centric understanding of Putin and Erdoğan is dubious. Therefore, I argue these analyses tend to miss several vital dynamics that fundamentally impact Turkey-Russia relations. Moreover, their perspective often promotes and fosters a West-centric bias at the risk of overlooking other dynamics that impact Turkey-Russia relations.

The realist framework is another prevalent scholarly approach some scholars prefer to employ to make sense of Turkey-Russia relations. Şener Aktürk produced multiple works along these lines. In his 2006 article, he argues that the improvements in Turkey-Russia relations occurred due to the diminution of Russian threats toward Turkey after the USSR's demise.[6] In 2014, referring again to the power dynamics, he suggests that Turkey and Russia are "friends in weakness, foes in strength."[7] In his 2019 article, Aktürk argues that the rapprochement after the Jet Crisis resulted from Turkey's attempt to balance internal security threats.[8] Interpreting the developments in Turkey-Russia relations, Oğuzlu also suggests that Turkey's rapprochement with Russia has developed within the framework of the changes in the international system from a unipolar order to a post-unipolar era where Turkey is suited to follow an independent foreign policy approach.[9] The collapse of the Soviet Union precipitated significant changes on global, regional, and bilateral levels. These analyses help reveal the impact of Turkey and Russia's responses to the changes in regional and global structural dynamics on the Turkey-Russia nexus.

This book also considers the impact of a bipolar international system's transition to a more complex one for Turkey-Russia relations. Nevertheless, focusing solely on power dynamics through a Realist framework one runs the risk of missing the relevance of changes in the normative and economic structure or climate and public health issues. Moreover, depending on the type of Realist perspective they employ, this line of scholarship usually does not deal with the way individual states digest and respond to structural changes through their domestic decision-making mechanisms.

The critical geopolitical perspective is a relatively less common but powerful approach utilized in the literature to explain the Turkey-Russia nexus. Scholarly contributions that use this approach often focus on the way that Turkey and Russia imagine their surroundings impact their foreign policies. For example, Aras and Fidan assess how the new political rhetoric under the AK Party government fueled Turkey's activism towards Eurasia in general and toward Russia in particular.[10] Mesbahi argues that Turkey's active foreign policy strategy under Davutoğlu caused the Turkey-Russia partnership to depart from U.S. mentorship. However, this partnership remains limited by Turkey's NATO membership and Russia's suspicions.[11]

THEORETICAL FRAMEWORK

Type-3 Neoclassical Realism

The framework I formulated to examine Turkey-Russia relations is based on Type-3 Neoclassical Realist Theory.[12] In their book, *Neoclassical Realist Theory in International Politics*, Ripsman, Taliaferro, and Lobell provide a sophisticated toolbox for analyzing a wide range of political phenomena, from the decision-making processes during crisis moments to shifts in regional or global political structures. Type-3 Neoclassical Realism[13] borrows insights from the literature of Foreign Policy Analysis, Classical Realism and Strategy. It helps analyze how *systemic stimuli* are translated into foreign policy action after being filtered through domestic decision-making mechanisms and how these foreign policy actions create systemic consequences. I employ Type-3 Neoclassical Realism to investigate how Turkey and Russia interpret and react to different *stimuli* and how their reactions have reshaped the Turkey-Russia nexus (see figure 0.1).

Type-3 Neoclassical Realism attempts to explain the foreign policy actions of states. Ripsman et al. argue that states make foreign policy in response to outside developments, which they call *systemic stimuli*. In explaining how

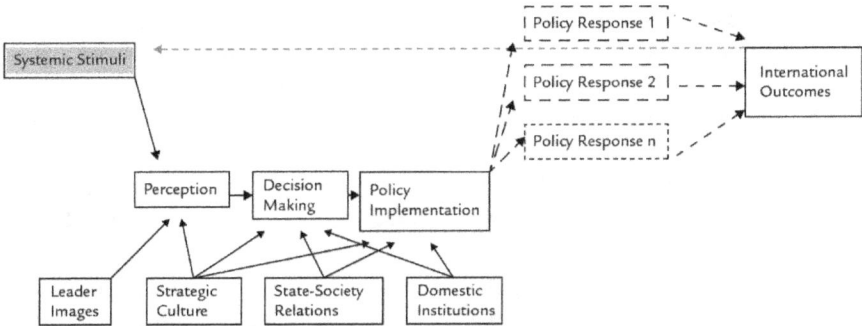

Figure 0.1 Type-3 Neoclassical Realism. Source: Ripsman et al., 34.

systemic stimuli act as a "dependent" variable, Type-3 Neoclassical Realism relies on clarity of systemic signals and whether the strategic environment is restrictive or permissive.[14] In their consideration of the system, Ripsman et al. generally accept the Neorealist view, which suggests that foreign policies of states fit the international political environment.[15] Yet they also imagine a circular causality in the international system by indicating how the grand strategic choices of major powers can also play a role in creating international outcomes that impact other actors.[16] Therefore, Ripsman et al. agree with Waltz on the anarchic nature of the international system and how the system conditions state behavior.[17]

Another important input of Type-3 Neoclassical Realism is that it considers that the *systemic stimuli* are filtered through a domestic transmission belt, which acts as the "intervening" variable. The model offered by Ripsman et al. examines the complex process triggered by the *systemic stimuli* in the decision-making structure of the state. This complex process includes three mini-processes: *perception, decision making,* and *policy implementation.* In the perception phase, the *leader image,* in the form of core beliefs, images, ideologies, personalities, and *strategic culture,* may inform how *systemic stimuli* are perceived in the *perception* phase.[18] Apart from the *strategic culture,* both *state-society relations* and *domestic institutions* may also impact the decision making. This process unfolds in the *decision-making* phase. *Strategic culture* potentially informs the *policy implementation* phase, especially if the state implements a policy in opposition to the dominant *strategic culture.* Depending on the regime type and societal dynamics, the *state-society relations* and *domestic institutions* may also play a significant role in implementing society's degree of economic and moral support and the degree of compliance by *domestic institutions.* These three processes occur under the influence of four variables: leader image, strategic culture, state-society relations, and *domestic institutions.*[19]

In the latest *policy implementation* phase, Ripsman et al. propose that the dynamics inform the state's reaction to the systemic stimuli of the three-mini processes. Yet the dependent variable in Type-3 Neoclassical Realism is not limited to state behavior. Ripsman et al. utilize Jervis's explanation[20] of how the system is formed as the aggregate outcome of several units' strategies to one another.[21] Thus, in Type-3 Neoclassical Realism, the scope of the dependent variable grows in accordance with the time frame. The Neoclassical Realist framework, in its original form, as described by Rose, takes the policy response as the dependent variable, considering domestic factors.[22] Ripsman et al. argue that this scope gets wider with the concepts like strategic culture and grand strategy in what they call Type-2 Neoclassical Realism.[23] When operationalized, these frameworks help explain short-to-medium-term responses by states to *systemic stimuli*. Ripsman et al. argue that the grand strategic adjustments may create international outcomes after the grand strategic adjustments of states begin to interact in the long run (figure 0.2).[24] Therefore, in Type-3 Neoclassical Realism, the *systemic stimuli* are problematized as well since the authors argue that they occur as a result of the accumulation of the policy responses and grand strategic adjustments of individual states.[25]

A Model to Explain Interstate Relations

For this research, I utilize a model based on the model of Type-3 Neoclassical Realism to explain Turkey-Russia relations. Neoclassical Realism is designed to show how states behave under the impact of domestic and systemic variables. Type-3 Neoclassical Realism goes one step beyond this and explains how international outcomes occur as a consequence of interstate relations. On the other hand, this book focuses on the relations between two states. Accordingly, I utilize a modified version of Type 3 Neoclassical Realism. In my version, change occurs in interstate relations—in our case in Turkey-Russia relations—with a simple four-segmented process. These four segments include the emergence of a significant event (*stimulus*), the responses of Turkey and Russia to these events in their domestic decision-making mechanisms (*decision–making*), their responses to the bilateral relations (*feedback*), and the *change* in bilateral relations (see figure 0.2).

I use the original conceptualization of *stimulus* in Type-3 Neoclassical Realism with two important modifications. First, Type-3 Neoclassical Realism considers the changes in the distribution of power as the most important dynamic in international politics that triggers a change in the way states formulate their foreign policies.[26] This view aligns with Neoclassical Realism, which considers economic power as an element of power and does not discuss normative power. Yet, states operate within normative and

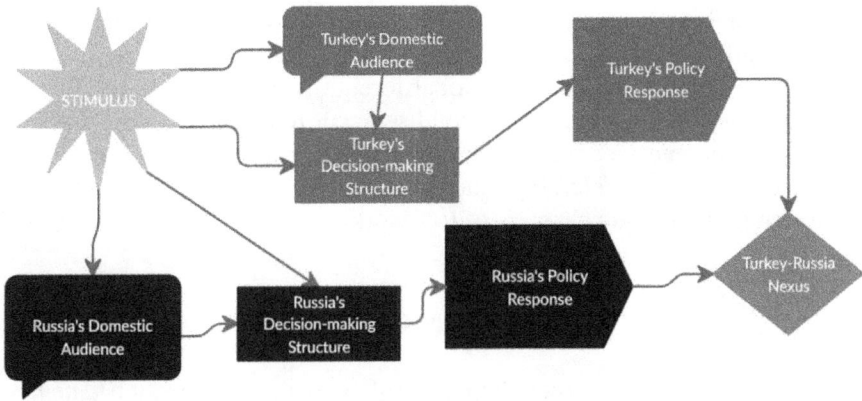

Figure 0.2   The Model Used in This Research. Source: Created by author.

economic structures as well.[27] Therefore, states also respond to *stimuli* of an economic and normative nature as well. I argue that a *stimulus* does not have to be about power distribution in the strategic dimension. It can refer to major events related to changes in normative or economic structures. For example, I consider how the COVID-19 outbreak impacted bilateral trade relations. Second, in Type–3 Neoclassical Realism, Ripsman et al. suggest systemic stimuli occur at a system or regional subsystem level.[28] However, the *stimuli* do not always appear at a system or subsystem level. The significant events I consider as *stimuli* in this work are the Iraq War (2003), Arab Uprisings (2011), and the failed coup attempt in Turkey (2016). These events originated on different levels, but all three influenced the Turkey-Russia nexus.

Covering the second and the third segments, I explain how Turkey and Russia generate a policy response to these events after they digest the stimuli in their respective decision-making mechanisms. By acknowledging the normative and economic structures in this research, I also examine how states interact with these structures. While Type-3 Neoclassical Realism does not explicitly recognize the normative and economic structures, these dynamics can be reflected in the model's intervening variable within the framework of a soft-positivist approach employed in this research. I do not specifically apply the original intervening variable of Type–3 Neoclassical Realism to my study in my model. Instead, I simplify this part in one box, labeled "domestic audience," where I show how policy is produced in each country in response to the major events called *stimuli*.

Lastly, I explain how these policy responses influence and reshape the Turkey-Russia nexus. I specifically look at the impact of policy responses of the two countries on the Turkey-Russia nexus. This is the most extensive part of this research. It demonstrates how the developments in the first and second segments affect Turkey-Russia relations. Since each country has a crucial place in the other's regional and global foreign policy strategy, the *foreign policy response* produced in the second segment influences Turkey's policy towards Russia and vice versa. This influence is felt in various dimensions (trade, conflict, energy, etc.) of bilateral relations. These three segments form the skeleton of the body chapters of this work.

ORGANIZATION OF THE BOOK

This book is composed of four chapters, following this introduction. The first chapter provides a historical background of the relations between Turkey and Russia. The following three chapters can be considered body chapters where I analyze how Turkey-Russia relations developed between 2001 and 2022. In the concluding chapter, I discuss the contribution of this work to the literature, examine its limitations, and provide suggestions for further research.

The subject of chapter 1 is the historical background of bilateral relations. This chapter begins with the first encounters between the two nations in the late fifteenth century and examines their bilateral relations until the contemporary era. Turkey and Russia are the successors of two Eurasian empires. The Ottoman and Russian Empires once dominated the area from Eastern Europe to the Pacific, from the Arctic to Africa. Thus, several important dynamics observed in the Turkey-Russia nexus today have deep historical roots. Examples of these crucial dynamics include the West's role in helping Turkey balance Russia in the Black Sea region, Russia's export of vast raw materials, and the securitization dynamics between the nations stemming from successive wars between them. This chapter is composed of two parts. In the first part, I focus on relations between the Ottoman and Russian Empires. This part investigates the relations until the late nineteenth century. In this part, I also summarize the origins and developments of the two nations. In the second part, I focus on the relations between Turkey and the Soviet Union/Russia during the twentieth century.

In chapters 2, 3, and 4, I examine how Turkey-Russia relations developed between 2001 and 2022. In line with the Type-3 Neoclassical Realism, I start each of these chapters by explaining how Turkey and Russia developed foreign policies concerning the major developments of the period and how their responses remade Turkey-Russia relations. First, I analyze how the two countries interpreted and responded to the vital events (*stimuli*) of each period. Then, I discuss how their responses impact the areas of competition (mostly regional crisis hotspots) and the areas of cooperation (bilateral trade and energy relations) in Turkey-Russia nexus.

The stimulus in chapter 2 is the U.S. invasion of Iraq, which launched a new era in the Middle East and beyond. This chapter examines the period between 2001 and 2009. I argue it had a lasting influence on the balance of power in the Middle East. While initially the war increased the presence of the United States in the region, it tarnished the global prestige of the United States in the social dimension. Most importantly, the consequences of the invasion caused U.S. foreign policy to be more restrained in the following periods. Especially, the diminishing prestige of the United States created the conditions for the two countries to adopt more assertive foreign policies. Since the Iraq War developed within the framework of the foreign policy making of the George W. Bush administration, this chapter's analysis starts in the year 2001 and ends in 2009. This period coincided with the beginning and consolidation of the rules of Erdoğan in Turkey and Putin in Russia. These assertive leaders found a chance to restructure their foreign policy agenda in an environment with a global backlash against U.S. unilateralism. This pursuit of independence promoted cooperation between Turkey and Russia, not only on a bilateral level but also on regional and global levels, in parallel to the alignment in how they considered the role of the United States in global affairs. While the invasion of Iraq is the focal point of this chapter, I also discuss the impact of other events that indirectly influenced the relations between the two countries, such as the Color Revolutions.

The stimulus in chapter 3 is the Syrian Crisis/Arab Uprisings. This chapter examines the period between 2009 and 2016. It deals with the bilateral relations between 2009 and 2016. Though their reactions to the first phase of the Arab Uprisings were similar, there developed a marked divergence between Turkey and Russia over Syria's future. With Turkey and Russia's involvement on opposite sides in the Syrian Civil War, the tensions between the two significantly deteriorated in parallel. Moreover, the adoption of a hands-off approach by Obama toward the Middle East during this period weakened Turkey's leverage in the region. This dynamic's significance is evident in the process that followed the Jet Crisis, which substantially harmed all segments of their bilateral relations.

In chapter 4, I look at the period when the Turkey-Russia partnership reached unprecedented levels after the coup attempt in Turkey in 2016. This chapter examines the period between mid-2016 and 2022. In contrast to the previous two periods, the most crucial development in this era occurred inside Turkey. The failed coup attempt in June 2016 played a significant role in widening the rift between the United States and Turkey and encouraged Turkey to adopt an assertive foreign policy strategy. The continuing U.S. retrenchment away from the Middle East significantly contributed to this trend. This change paved the way for deeper engagement between Turkey and

Russia in their joint resolution of regional issues and brought about broader partnerships in the defense and energy sectors.

In the concluding chapter, I examine the triangulation of the Turkey-Russia nexus with the emerging world order, survey the results of this research and discuss the contributions of my work to the ongoing scholarship on Turkish foreign policy, Russian foreign policy, Turkey-Russia relations, the regional powers, and the emerging global geopolitics.

Chapter 1

Historical Background

The dynamics of the context in which the Turkey-Russia nexus operate are historically rooted. For centuries, Turkey and Russia have competed for influence in the Black Sea, the Caucasus, and the Balkans. Although the two nations originate from distant lands, the Turks and the Russians moved closer to each other. Before their colonization by the Vikings and the Mongols, the Russians were a small community near the Baltics. They would grow and dominate other entities to become the most formidable force in the Black Sea by the eighteenth century. On the other hand, Turks would become the masters of the lands they migrated to (from the East). By the eleventh century, the migrations of the Turks to Asia Minor would make Anatolia a Turkic land. Ottoman Empire would dominate the south and the west of the Black Sea.

By analyzing the historical background of Turkey-Russia relations, this chapter serves three major purposes. First, it supports the main argument by demonstrating how the two countries' reactions to changes in the political context have shaped bilateral relations throughout history. Second, it provides background knowledge to the readers of this book about various perennial issues in bilateral relations that remain relevant in the twenty-first century. Last, despite the prevailing dynamics of competition, Turkey and Russia also had short intervals of cooperation. Hünkar İskelesi agreement and Turkey's rapprochement with Russia in the 1970s could be examples. These intervals explain the dynamics that promote collaboration in bilateral relations in the twenty-first century.

This chapter is composed of two parts. In the first part, I look at the interactions between the Ottoman Empire and the Muscovite Principality/ Russian Empire. This part begins with a brief account of the formation of the two nations. Then, I analyze the relations between the Ottoman and Russian Empires in two subsections. I examine the construction of bilateral ties and then the competition between two empires over multiple regions. In the second part, I look at the twentieth century, when Turkey and the Soviet Union remade Turkey-Russia relations between two post-imperial states. The second part starts with a short analysis of Turkey and the USSR's (Union of Soviet Socialist Republics) phase of establishment and their dominant strategic cultures. Finally, I analyze how the relations between Turkey and the USSR/Russian Federation developed throughout the twentieth century under the influence of a continuing geopolitical clash of interests.

THE RELATIONS BETWEEN THE OTTOMAN EMPIRE AND THE RUSSIAN EMPIRE

Origins of the Ottoman Turks and the Russians

Ottoman Turks

The Ottoman Turks originated from the Altaic nomads located to the north of China. They neighbored other nomadic tribes and China. Starting from the second century BC, changing political, economic, and climatic conditions in this region brought about westward waves of migration of nomadic peoples. Some of the Turkic people who migrated in this period later adopted Islam and founded several significant political entities, including the Karahanids (840–1212) in Central Asia and the Seljuks (1037–1194) in the Middle East.[1] By the late thirteenth century, hundreds of thousands of Turkic people who escaped from Mongol invasions settled in Asia Minor. Most of them became part of the Mongol Empire, which rapidly dominated almost everywhere East of the Adriatic Sea before partitioning into four succeeding states.[2] The decline of the Ilkhanates, one of the successors of the Mongol Empire located in the Middle East, led to the strengthening of Turkic tribes[3] throughout Asia Minor.[4]

One of these tribes, which had settled in Northwestern Anatolia and was led by Osman Bey,[5] was well-positioned to manipulate its advantageous location to expand against the declining Byzantines and Mongols.[6] The conquest of Constantinople in 1453 by the Ottomans[7] destroyed the Byzantium Empire, removing a significant impediment to the Turkic domination of the Balkans. The idea of *ghaza*[8] and the toleration of different faiths in newly acquired territories enabled Ottoman expansion towards the West through the Balkans. The subjugation of other Turkic tribes in Asia Minor through battles or voluntary accessions in Anatolia opened the doors of Eastern Anatolia and then the Middle East to the Ottomans. Under Selim the Grim, in the early sixteenth century, the conquest of Egypt, Syria, and the Hejaz made the Ottoman Empire the preeminent authority within the Islamic world.

Muscovite Russians

The ancestors of today's Russians neighbored the Finnic and Lithuanian people to their north and Turkic peoples located in today's Ukraine.[9] In the ninth century, a Viking (Varangian) tribe named Rus' entered the Baltic, subjugated the local Proto-Slavic population, and formed a political entity around Novgorod. As this Viking tribe named Rus' quickly assimilated into local Slavic culture, the center of its political entity moved to Kyiv in the south. The Russians then adopted Byzantine Christianity as their state religion in 980. In the thirteenth century, the Mongol Empire destroyed Kievan Rus and established political domination over the *knyajestvos* (Slavic principalities) and *khanates* (Turkic political entities) to the north of the Black Sea. The Mongols, later called Tatars by the Russians,[10] established their political center in the Upper Volga Region. Following the disintegration of the Mongol Empire, the political entity that ruled what is today Russia began to be known as the Golden Horde, which later embraced Islam.

From the mid-fifteenth century on, the Muscovite principality began to gain power thanks to Moscow's favorable geoeconomics, its able leaders, and the restoration of an independent church structure in Moscow. Building upon these, the Muscovites' expansion gained impetus under Ivan IV (reign: 1533–1584), crowned in the Cathedral of Dominion in 1547 as the "Tsar of All Russias," indicating authority over all the Slavic principalities in the region. By the late sixteenth century, the Muscovites entered on a path to becoming the most formidable force in the area. They became a force that the Ottoman Empire just could not ignore.

Early Ottoman-Russia Relations (1495–1783)

The first official contact between the Ottomans and the Russians took place in 1495 when a Muscovite envoy visited the Ottoman Sultan in Istanbul to demand economic capitulation to purchase silk and sell fur.[11] At that time, expansion towards the Balkans and preserving the balance of power north of the Black Sea by providing support to the weaker entities against the most powerful ones in that region formed the basis of the foreign policy of the Ottoman Empire towards the region. Aside from supporting their vassal Crimean Tatars, the Ottomans would ally on different occasions with the Poles, and Muscovites as well.[12] While the Muscovites gained strength by capturing the surrounding Turkic Khanates and Slavic Principalities under their domain, the Ottoman Empire did not take a decisive step towards eliminating or curtailing the Russian threat until the seventeenth century.[13] At that point, the Muscovite Principality was not strong enough to worry the Ottomans, the hegemonic power in the Black Sea region. Another reason for this choice had to do with the foreign policy strategy of the Ottoman Empire, which prioritized expansion to the West through the Balkans. Only from the late seventeenth century did the Ottomans begin to provide the Crimeans with active support to balance the Muscovites.[14]

During the eighteenth century, Russia conducted massive administrative reforms and modernized its military under able rulers. In 1695, Peter I (reign: 1696–1725), whose fondness for shipbuilding helped establish the first Russian navy, would surprise the Ottomans with his attempt to take the Azov Fortress on the shores of the Black Sea. With the Russian military beginning to outpower the Ottomans, the change in the balance of power began to influence bilateral relations. Even though Peter's efforts did not immediately lead to Russian supremacy over the Black Sea, his successors continued to push the boundaries of the Empire further. In the second half of the eighteenth century, the Ottoman Empire's stagnation encouraged Catherine II (reign: 1762–1796) to consider extending Russia's influence in the Black Sea and the Mediterranean region.[15] With its victory in the Russo-Ottoman War of 1768–1774, Russia dominated the Black Sea and increased its influence in the Balkans. After the war, Russia gained the protection of the Christian nations in the Balkans and ensured the Crimean Khanate's independence before annexing it in 1783.

Russo-Ottoman Relations amid the Rise of the West

During the period between the French Revolution (1789) and World War I (WWI) (1914–1918), the Ottoman Empire lost further ground to Russia against the backdrop of the rise of the West as a result of the Industrial Revolution and colonialism. Russian influence expanded in the Balkans through Russia's utilizing secessionist movements among the non-Muslim Balkan subjects of the Ottoman Empire during the nineteenth century. The Ottoman Empire aimed to gain the support of the West against Russia. Such partnershion would benefit the West too. The shortest route to Britain's colonies in southern and eastern Asia, the Ottoman Straits was crucial for Russian access to the Mediterranean. Similarly, France would like to protect its influence in the Mediterranean from the Russian expansion. Thus, the West would prefer to have a relatively weaker Ottoman Empire to control this route rather than a formidable and strengthening rival like Russia. Another important consequence of the technical superiority of the West has been the Westernization of the Russian and Turkish elite in this period.

As of the early nineteenth century, the declining Ottoman Empire suffered from nationalist secessionist movements, financial problems, and most importantly, Russian expansionism. In the early 1830s, the Ottoman Sultan asked for help from Britain and France against Egypt's rebellious governor Muhammed Ali Pasha, who sought to secede from the Ottoman Empire. Britain ignored the Ottomans' demand for support, and France sided with Egypt. Deprived with the Western support as Muhammed Ali Pasha's army was fighting its way to the Ottoman capital, the Sultan desperately turned to Russia, which sent its navy to Istanbul.[16] In 1833, the Ottoman Empire and the Russian Empire signed the Hünkar İskelesi Agreement. The treaty included a secret provision where the Ottoman Empire guaranteed to close the straits to the European warships in a war.[17] This was an important occasion in the sense that it was the first occasion when Turkey made peace with Russia at the absence of strong Western support. The agreement and the presence of the Russian army in Constantinople worried the European Great Powers, especially Britain. At that point, Lord Palmerston, who was the British Secretary of State, took the treaty seriously and began to support the Ottoman Empire against Russia to keep the peace in the Levant and prevent the encroachment of Russia.[18] In 1841, after the expiration of the Hünkar İskelesi Agreement, the London Straits Convention met at Britain's request. It closed the Straits to all warships with the agreement of the Russian Empire, the Ottoman Empire, and Britain. Aiming to take advantage of the weakening of the Ottoman Empire, the Russian Empire continued to pressure the Ottoman Empire for concessions over the Orthodox subjects living in Ottoman-ruled Jerusalem. The tensions led to the Crimean War (1853–1856), when the combined forces of the Ottoman Empire, Britain, and France defeated the Russian Empire.

Also in this period, the European economic and social influence significantly increased over the two Empires. With the advancements in military techniques, the European forces began to outperform the Ottoman and Russian armies in a process that started with the Industrial Revolution. Also, Europe's vibrant political and ideological atmosphere deeply impacted the Ottoman and Russian political elites. In the Russian Empire, the growing working class, emerging bourgeoisie, and segments from the bureaucracy and the military had created many political movements that aimed to end the Tsarist autocracy.[19] In 1905, these movements formed the *Duma* (Russian parliamentary assembly with a consultative role) when Tsar Nicholas II (reign: 1894–1917) could not resist political participation demands through strikes and protests that formed the Russian Revolution in 1905.

The Ottoman Empire also experienced a reformation process during the nineteenth century.[20] When Ottoman reformers grew dissatisfied with the pace of reforms, they dethroned Abdulmecid I (reign: 1823–1861), replacing him with Abdulhamid II (reign: 1876–1908), who promised a constitutional monarchy. Yet, Abdulhamid II closed the Parliament two years after its opening and embarked on a crackdown on the reformers. The reformers went underground and abroad, where they formed the Committee of Union and Progress (CUP) in 1895. CUP rapidly gained popularity among the officer corps. In 1908, the Ottoman reformist soldiers restored the Parliament after a coup.[21] Meanwhile, the involvement of military officers in politics led to the defeat of the Ottomans in the Balkan Wars of 1912–1913 and the Ottoman Empire's ill-fated decision to participate in WWI on the side of Germany.

Already a declining force, the Ottoman Empire could not resist the Russian expansion. The consecutive wars fought with Russia devastated the Ottoman economy and undermined modernization attempts. Russia helped secure Balkan nations' independence and invaded the Ottoman territories in the Northern Black Sea coastline. During the nineteenth century, the Ottoman Empire survived thanks to the British policy of keeping an intact Ottoman Empire as a buffer to the southern expansion of the Russian Empire. A similar scenario would come into play during the Cold War. The Soviet Union would follow a similar expansionist policy against Turkey, which would eventually aim to seek the support of the West.

THE RELATIONS BETWEEN TURKEY AND THE SOVIET UNION IN THE TWENTIETH CENTURY

Foundation of Turkey and the Soviet Union

Republic of Turkey

In the Ottoman Empire, following the coup d'état in 1908, the CUP had consolidated their authority over the Ottoman institutions and developed an extensive grassroots network across Anatolia and the Balkans. While the CUP leadership resigned and fled after the defeat in WWI, their network persisted across Asia Minor.[22] With the Moudros Armistice Agreement in October 1918, the Ottoman Empire surrendered all its territories outside Asia Minor to the Allies. In response to the occupation, resistance forces were formed across Anatolia.[23] In May 1919, Mustafa Kemal,[24] an Ottoman general who was sent to Anatolia by the Ottoman Government in Istanbul to alleviate the inter-communal violence there, utilized his authority to supervise the existing resistance against the invading Western forces. Having accumulated support, he resigned from his duties and reformed the Parliament under his leadership in April 1920. The Parliament approved the *Misak-ı Milli* (National Pact), committing to saving Asia Minor and Thrace from occupation.

In August 1920, the Ottoman Government in Istanbul signed the Sevres Agreement, which partitioned the Ottoman Empire's territories among the Allied powers. Rejecting this agreement, the newly formed Turkish army under the command of the Turkish Parliament in Ankara fought the occupying forces (Greeks in the West, French in the South, Armenians in the East, and British troops in several other campaigns across Asia Minor). It saved most of Asia Minor and Thrace from foreign occupation by 1922. In the Lausanne Agreement, signed in July 1923 by Mustafa Kemal's delegation, Turkey achieved independence under the new Parliament, put an end to the economic capitulations, and, with some exceptions, realized the territorial aim outlined in *Misak-ı Milli*. Instead of maintaining and furthering the Ottoman Empire's imperial character and continuing its grievances toward the West, Mustafa Kemal aimed to create a homogeneous, secular Turkish nation with a Westernized lifestyle through widespread top–down reforms.[25] His CHP (Republican People's Party—*Cumhuriyet Halk Partisi*) remained in power for twenty-seven years.

The diplomatic and military struggle to earn independence and sovereignty left a lasting anti-Western strand in Turkish strategic culture and foreign policy. On the other hand, Turkey's new Republican elites continue to see the West as the center of civilization and aimed to make Turkey a respected member of Western international society. This dilemma allowed certain tactical flexibilities, examples of which may be seen in Turkey's cooperation with the Soviet Union while rebuilding relations with Britain and Greece.[26] Aspiration to become a Western nation while carrying suspicions against Western imperialism would remain a Turkish foreign policy dilemma in the following decades. Meanwhile, Turkey adopted the principle of "Peace at Home, Peace in the World" to normalize relations with its neighbors, who were once Ottoman subjects.

The Soviet Union

Despite its revolutionary beginnings, the Soviet Union embraced the fundamental aspects of the Tsarist era political practices. Before WWI, the Bolshevik faction of the Russian Social Democratic Labor Party (RSDLP) was a fringe element on the Russian political spectrum. It relied on the leadership of Vladimir Lenin, who emphasized the workers' need for the leadership of full-time revolutionaries and wanted to transform the RSDLP into a strictly centralized underground organization.[27] As a dedicated, close-knit organization, in October 1917, the Bolsheviks orchestrated a successful coup against the Provisional Government, which was formed after the Tsar's abdication in March 1917.[28] After the coup, the Bolsheviks seized power on behalf of the *soviets*, which were unstructured workers assemblies that mushroomed across

the industrial centers of the Russian Empire and played a significant role in
the 1905 Revolution. Bolsheviks promised land to peasants, peace to soldiers,
and self-determination to the non-Russian nationalities to keep the power.
With the Brest-Litovsk agreement in March 1918, the Bolsheviks hastily
quitted the war, ceding Germany a substantial amount of land in the European
part of Russia. Having fought to consolidate domestic authority with a newly
formed Red army, they seized the entire nation's means of production on
behalf of the workers. Eventually they found the Union of Soviet Socialist
Republics (USSR or Soviet Union) in 1922. When the centralization of economic means caused significant shortages of basic materials, Lenin declared
a New Economic Policy (NEP), which enabled limited private initiative and
foreign investment. Following Lenin's death in 1924, Stalin abandoned the
NEP and emphasized the domestic modernization of the Soviet Union within
the framework of his principle of "Socialism in One Country."

   In the early years of the Soviet Union, Lenin considered a world revolution
to be superior to the national interest of the Soviet Union since the survival
of the regime depended on a global victory over capitalism.[29] In those
years, the Communist International (*Kommunisticheskiy International—
Comintern*), founded in 1919 to supervise foreign communist parties and
conduct propaganda abroad, was the central foreign policy apparatus. This
internationalism gave way to a more adaptive approach by the NEP, which
opened the USSR to enabled the opening of small businesses and allowed
foreign trade.[30] With the foundation of the Commissariat of Foreign Affairs
(*Narodnii Kommissariat Inostrannykh Del—Narkomindel*), the Soviet Union
came to adopt a dual-track foreign policy. Simultaneously, Comintern aimed
to subvert the Western international order and Narkomindel pursued Soviet
interests through normal diplomatic channels. Under Stalin, the USSR
readopted the essential features of the Tsarist strategic culture, recentralizing
political and economic power. In effect, fear and suspicion of the outside
world and the constant drive for expansion to achieve status and security
made a strong comeback.[31] These changes would have a significant impact
on Turkey-Soviet relations, with the Soviet suspicion of the Turkish political
elite and the reemergence of the Turkish Straits as a strategic point for the
defense of the Soviet motherland.

The Interwar Years

Both established as post-imperial nations, Turkey and the Soviet Union
inherited reduced territories and the imperial legacy of the Ottoman and the
Russian Empires. In the initial phase of their foundation, during the Turkish
War of Independence and the Russian Civil War, their shared opposition
toward the West enabled the Treaty of Friendship and Brotherhood in 1921

between them during the Turkish War of Independence. They resolved border disputes within this framework, and the Soviet Union promised military and financial aid to Mustafa Kemal's army.[32] Such relations continued even after the war. In 1925, the two countries signed the Soviet-Turkish Treaty of Friendship and Neutrality. Both sides promised not to enter into alliances against each other. Trade relations also developed. The Soviet Union aimed to influence Turkey politically through trade; Turkish officials aimed to learn about the Soviet economic model for rapid development.[33] In 1932, the Soviet Union provided Turkey with a loan of $8 million for twenty years. The credit was for military equipment and textile mills in Nazilli and Kayseri in Turkey.[34] As a result, Turkey became the first foreign state to adopt a Soviet-advised development plan voluntarily.[35] As Turkey built bridges of partnership with the Soviet Union, it also mended ties with Britain.[36]

From the mid-1930s on, however, Turkey's desire to be a part of the Western international order and the two states' responses to the turbulent atmosphere in Europe prevented further rapprochement. In response to Italian aggression in the Mediterranean, Turkey aimed to maintain its territorial integrity through building alliances and amending the status of disputed territories in favor of Turkey. Turkey's strategy drew an adverse reaction from the Soviet Union. For example, Turkey's diplomatic maneuvers between Britain and the Soviets during the Montreux conference in 1936, when Turkey regained control of the Straits, frustrated Moscow.[37] To maintain the solidarity of its neighbors within the framework of the emerging German and especially Italian revisionism, Turkey also led the foundation of two regional security orders: the Saadabad Pact (composed of Turkey, Iran, and Iraq) and the Balkan Pact (composed of Greece, Turkey, Yugoslavia, and Romania). These steps further antagonized Moscow, which considered the formation of these pacts as moves to contain Soviet influence.[38]

The bitterness in relations continued during World War II (WWII). Before the beginning of the war, in 1939, Turkey signed a defense treaty with Britain and then a Trilateral Agreement with France and Britain, while the Soviet Union signed the Molotov-Ribbentrop Pact with Nazi Germany. Following the beginning of the Nazi invasion of the Soviet Union, the tensions between Turkey and the Soviet Union increased due to the revelations of Nazi plans to attack Soviet military targets from Turkish soil.[39] Subsequently, Turkey's wartime neutrality antagonized the Soviet Union as Turkey maintained trade relations with Nazi Germany until 1944. Meanwhile, after recapturing invaded territories, the Soviet leadership accused all the Muslim populations across the Black Sea of treason and in 1944 ordered their deportation *en masse* to Siberia and Central Asia. Even though this act did not directly impact bilateral relations, it demonstrated Soviet antagonism and suspicion toward Turkic peoples. It also influenced the balance of power in the Black Sea region by Russifying the north of the Black Sea.

During the interwar years, the continuing instability in the international system prevented Turkey, the Soviet Union, and the West from establishing consistent foreign policy strategies against one another. Turkey and the Soviet Union, both were born after a struggle against Western imperialism, remained isolated from the Western international society. For example, the two countries were included in the League of Nations in the 1930s after several years of resistance. The global economic instability caused by the 1929 Crisis and the rise of fascism in Europe further prevented the efforts to establish a working international order and paved the way for World War II (WWII).

Cold War

During the Cold War, the instability of the interwar years ended with the firm victory of the Allied Forces against Nazi Germany during WWII. The United States and the Soviet Union appeared as two superpowers and a bipolar international system was born. In the decades following WWII, the impact of the global balance of power on Turkey–Soviet Union relations increased as Turkey began to play a vital role in containing the Soviet Union as a member of NATO. Such a role was similar to the one played by the Ottoman Empire from the mid-nineteenth century on. During the Cold War, the literature on Turkey-Russia relations remained weak. Turkey's ties with Russia/the Soviet Union, and vice versa, could be assessed with the help of studies on Turkey's foreign policy during WWII and later.[40]

A significant turning point in bilateral relations occurred as early as 1945 when the Soviet foreign minister conveyed Stalin's demand to the Turkish ambassador to have Soviet bases on the Straits and redraw their shared border.[41] Bewildered by the Soviet demands, the Turkish elite turned to the West just like their grandfathers did in the nineteenth century. After diplomatic initiatives from Turkey, the U.S. Congress approved a plan to provide financial and military support to Turkey and Greece to prevent Russian control over the Near East.[42] According to this strategy, Turkey was supposed to slow down a potential Soviet offensive toward the Mediterranean.[43] The region was crucial for U.S. foreign policy as a conduit for Middle Eastern oil.[44] Turkey's strategic position as a bridge between the East and West provided a strategic advantage similar to the nineteenth century when the Ottoman Empire used its strategic advantage in the eyes of the British.

The U.S. strategy, known as the Truman Doctrine,[45] generated a significant breakthrough in Turkey's domestic and foreign policy in decades to come. In 1952, Turkey joined NATO after sending troops to the Korean War. NATO membership was in line with one of Turkey's strategic culture's core elements: the Westernization of Turkey.[46] It is important to note that the United States and the European countries initially resisted Turkey's membership because Turkey would not fit into the "civilizational" aspects of the NATO Alliance.[47] This point is important because the continuing hesitation of the West for considering Turkey as part of the "West" would serve as an impediment to Turkey's membership in the European Union (EU). Turkey's NATO membership increased the U.S. military's presence on Turkish soil, which had begun as early as WWII.[48] Turkey's signaling to the United States that it might end its military partnership and return to neutrality also played a role in Turkey's joining the alliance.[49] U.S. military equipment and Turkish officers' training by the United States cast a vast influence on the Turkish Armed Forces.[50]

Following Stalin's death in 1953, the *Détente*[51] and the deterioration of U.S.-Turkey relations positively impacted Turkey-Soviet relations. The new Soviet leadership sent a note to Turkey demanding good-neighborly relations and stating that it harbored no territorial claims.[52] Turkey initially disregarded this notice and participated in two anti–Soviet regional pacts: the Balkan Pact (with Yugoslavia and Greece) in 1953 and the Baghdad Pact (with Iran, Iraq, Pakistan, and the UK) in 1955.[53] In the late 1950s, however, Turkey faced an economic crisis after the United States stopped funding its ambitious development with credits and put pressure on Turkey to stop opium cultivation. U.S. president Johnson's strongly worded letter in 1964[54] to discourage Turkey from undertaking a military intervention into Cyprus rekindled Turkey's suspicion of the "imperialist" West, which was a dormant dynamic in Turkey's strategic culture. This dynamic was one of the main drivers behind Turkey's War of Independence.

Meanwhile, starting in the late 1960s, the easing of Cold War tensions between the United States and the Soviet Union harmed U.S.-Turkey relations. Turkey faced a U.S. embargo following its intervention in Cyprus.[55] In response, Turkey attempted to balance U.S. influence by developing relations with the Soviet Union, which, in turn, provided support to Turkey through developmental assistance.[56] The improvements in bilateral relations were crowned with the Principles of Good-Neighborly Relations in 1978 when the Turkish prime minister Ecevit declared that Turkey no longer saw the Soviet Union as a threat.[57] It was no coincidence that the limited rapprochement between Turkey and the Soviet Union coincided with an era when Turkey's strategic importance in the eyes of the United States diminished during *Détente*.

From the early 1980s, globalization of the world economy brought about a structural change to the world political system. This change had a positive impact on the bilateral relations between Turkey and the Soviet Union through unleashing the economic potential in their bilateral trade relations.

After the 1980 coup in Turkey, the political stability enabled Turkey's new prime minister, Turgut Özal, to undertake Turkey's transition to a market economy. In the Soviet Union, Gorbachev, who came to power in 1985, attempted to rescue the Soviet Union from its highly bureaucratized and stagnant economy through economic and administrative reforms. These changes in both countries paved the way for an increased bilateral trade volume and a gas agreement. As a result, Turkey's exports to the USSR increased by 260 percent, and USSR's exports to Turkey increased by 506 percent in the 1980s.[58] In this period, Turkey paid Soviet natural gas with export material. The increase in the volume of bilateral trade relations brought regional cooperation. Throughout the 1980s, the two governments signed treaties arranging their shared border, cultural exchange, and the Black Sea flight information zone.[59] The steps taken in this period laid the ground for a broader and more intense rapprochement in the 1990s.

During the Cold War, the Cold War dynamics almost determined the course of the relations between Turkey and the Soviet Union. Turkey utilized its strategic advantage as the buffer against a possible Soviet expansion to the Middle East to secure the U.S. support. Thanks to its membership in NATO, Turkey modernized and transformed its army and received U.S. economic aid. However, such economic and military assistance increased Turkey's dependence on the West. The Turkish elites would realize this, during the 1960s, when Turkey received the Johnson letter upon its plans to intervene in Cyprus. The Soviet Union considered Turkey as the pawn of the West but also aimed to develop and maintain good relations with Turkey through various channels. The economic ties between the two countries would gain further importance in the post–Cold War era.

The 1990s: The First Decade after the Dissolution of the USSR

The demise of the USSR enabled an improvement in Turkey-Russia bilateral relations, especially in trade, with the disappearance of the Cold War–era securitization dynamics but paved the way for regional competition. Gorbachev's reforms, which were supposed to strengthen the Soviet system, instead brought it to its end. In less than ten years, Soviet satellite republics in Eastern Europe cut their ties with Moscow, and the foundation of the Commonwealth of Independent States (CIS) ended the USSR in 1991. In the absence of the Soviet threat, Turkey attempted to regain its strategic significance in the eyes of the Western Alliance and take advantage of the decrease in Moscow's influence over Central Asia and Caucasus regions to develop relations with Russia.

Meanwhile, after the dissolution of the USSR, the decrease in Moscow's hegemonic influence over its periphery enabled Turkey and the West to compete with Russia for influence in the post-Soviet region. At this point, the new Russian president, Boris Yeltsin, and his foreign minister, Andrei Kozyrev, deprioritized the post-Soviet region and followed a Western-friendly foreign policy to attract financial and political support from the United States. Taking the opportunity, Turkey attempted to exert economic and strategic influence on Central Asia and the Caucasus, emphasizing their shared Turkic and Muslim identity. TIKA (*Türkiye İşbirliği ve Kalkınma Ajansı*—Turkish Cooperation Coordination Agency) was founded in 1992 to coordinate the Turkish developmental assistance in the region. With the active encouragement of Özal, the first Summit of the Heads of Turkic Speaking States convened in Ankara in 1992.[60] In 1993, the International Organization of Turkic Culture (TÜRKSOY) was founded to foster their common Turkic culture. Turkey's trade volume with the post-Soviet region substantially increased in the same period.

From the mid-1990s, however, the restoration of the Russian strategic culture, Turkey's inability to assert itself in the post-Soviet region, and the inadequacy of Western support for Turkey brought back Moscow's hegemonic influence in the post-Soviet region. In Russia, due to resistance to Kozyrev from the security establishment, the foreign minister was replaced by Yevgeny Primakov, who emphasized Russia's great power role in the post-Soviet space and proposed that Russia should foster global multipolarity. In 1997, these two aims became essential parts of Russia's official strategic and foreign policy doctrines.[61] The enlargement of NATO and Russia's failure to amalgamate with the U.S.-led Western international system played a significant role in this turnaround. In Turkey, the death of Özal in 1993 paved the way for the heightening of PKK terror,[62] weak coalition governments, and economic crises. As a result of these factors, Russia maintained its hegemonic influence in the post-Soviet space while Turkey and the West could enjoy only limited economic influence in the region.

The mutual effort to increase bilateral trade between the Soviet Union and Turkey began as early as the mid-1980s and continued during the 1990s between Turkey and the Russian Federation. During Turkish president Süleyman Demirel's visit to Moscow in 1992, the two countries signed the Principles of Relations between the Republic of Turkey and the Russian Federation.[63] This agreement followed the general principles put forward in the 1925 Turkey–Soviet Union Friendship and Neutrality Treaty. In 1994, the Black Sea Economic Cooperation (BSEC) was established as an umbrella institution to enhance multilateral political and economic cooperation in the Black Sea area with other states' participation in the region.

The most significant achievement was in trade relations. Until 1998, when both countries went into economic recession, bilateral trade increased several-fold, reaching $8–10 billion annually.[64] A significant portion of this commerce took place as shuttle trade in the absence of a relevant institutional framework. In the same period, Turkey also bought armored vehicles, machine guns, and helicopters from Russia, making it the first NATO country to purchase Russian arms.[65] At this point, however, Turkey-Russia relations were still lacking bilateral platforms to ensure the improvements and maintenance of the positive trend.[66] Moreover, despite the strengthening of trade relations, the economic potential in trade and tourism was still under-explored.[67] In 1997, Turkey and Russia signed the Blue Stream agreement that enabled the transportation of natural gas by Russia to Turkey through a direct pipeline under the Black Sea. The Blue Stream Agreement significantly expanded bilateral trade relations. However, due to the rising number of confrontations in the Caucasus and Central Asia, the researchers hesitated to consider expanding trade relations to indicate substantial improvement in bilateral relations. Trenin would use the word "schizophrenic" to describe the relations at the time.[68]

The competition between Turkey and Russia for influence in multiple regions manifested itself during the crises in those regions. In the course of the Nagorno-Karabakh conflict,[69] Russia supported Armenia with mercenaries and weaponry.[70] Turkey's attempts to intervene were met with the threat of a "third world war" from the then commander in chief of the CIS.[71] The toppling of pro-Turkey Azerbaijani president Elchibey further limited Turkey's influence over Azerbaijan and the South Caucasus region. Meanwhile, following Armenia's occupation of Azerbaijani lands beyond the Nagorno-Karabakh region, Turkey suspended its relations with Armenia.

In contrast, Russia's influence in the region—as a power broker, protector of Armenia, and mediator of the conflict through the Minsk Group—grew.[72] Turkey's sympathy for the Chechens' bid for independence[73] has not turned into outright support after Russia threatened Turkey with supporting PKK[74] and the hijacking and bombing activities of Chechen guerillas in Turkey. In such an environment, the Baku-Tbilisi-Ceyhan pipeline project (BTC), projected to transport Azerbaijani oil to the Mediterranean coast through Georgia and Turkey, threatened Russia's monopoly in the region's energy geopolitics. Russia considered BTC to be against its interests but did not take serious measures to prevent the agreement due to a deep U.S. commitment to BTC and the existing Blue Stream agreement.[75]

During the 1990s, in the absence of firm Western support to Turkey against Russian expansionism, the bilateral relations between Turkey and the Soviet Union significantly improved. At the same time, the absence of Cold War dynamics and the dissolution of the Soviet Union made the Black Sea, South Caucasus, and to a limited extent Central Asia open to competition. Turkey aimed to influence these areas, where millions of Turkic-Muslim people lived. However, the comeback of Russia, Turkey's lack of expertise and capacity, and limited Western support to Turkey, preventing Turkey from establishing meaningful influence in these regions.

HOW DOES HISTORY MATTER IN
TURKEY-RUSSIA RELATIONS?

Turkey and Russia have engaged in intense competition in the Black Sea, the Caucasus, and the Balkans while also developing and maintaining economic and social relations. Someone could typically observe this dynamic in bilateral relations between any two neighbors. In the case of Turkey and Russia, the Imperial past, Great Power politics, Western overlay, and peculiar securitization dynamics have also played crucial roles. In particular, the changes in the regional and global balances of power, through regime changes, major events, and policy changes, played the primary role in shaping bilateral relations.

An examination of the historical background shows that the position of the West vis-à-vis Turkey and Russia has been the most important dynamic that has set the trend in their bilateral relations since the mid–nineteenth century. In that period, the Ottomans began to need Western assistance to resist the Russian expansion. In an attempt to prevent Russia from dominating the Ottoman Empire and expanding to the Mediterranean and the Middle East, the European Empires became involved in the region. From the early nineteenth century, Western interests in the Mediterranean region (pursued first by Britain and France, then predominantly by the U.S.-led NATO alliance) have played a significant role in shaping Turkey-Russia relations. During the 1830s, the 1920s, and the *Détente,* for instance, Turkey-Russia relations improved, as Turkey did not confront Russia in the absence of proper backing. Similarly, when Turkish and Western interests were aligned—as in the second half of the nineteenth century and the early Cold War period—Turkey was better positioned to confront Russia's expansionist agenda. The 1990s may be considered a unique period when—due to the sudden collapse of the Soviet Union—Russia also surrendered to the West normatively, and Turkey-Russia relations progressed under the mentorship of the West.

However, it is hard to argue that changes in the West's interest in the region have determined the course of relations. As the investigation of Turkey-Russia relations in this book shows, these systemic changes have been filtered through domestic determinants of both countries before reflecting on their bilateral relations. For instance, Lenin, Stalin, and Khrushchev had differences in their interpretation of the Cold War dynamics and had different goals for Turkey in their foreign policy vision. Similarly, the obsession with political independence and Westernism in the Turkish strategic culture has made a crucial impact on Turkey-Russia relations.

In line with how this book analyzes bilateral relations, critical junctures have often played pivotal roles in how the political elites perceive and act upon the systemic dynamics and changes in the system. For example, following the Cuban Missile Crisis, both the United States and the Soviet Union calculated that the end of humanity could result if they did not decrease tensions. This juncture brought about the process of *Détente* during the 1960s. The relieving of tensions between the United States and the Soviet Union paved the way for improving relations between Turkey and the Soviet Union, especially in trade. Similarly, the end of the Cold War and the dissolution of the USSR brought drastic changes to bilateral relations by paving the way for intense cooperation.

In the next three chapters, I examine Turkey-Russia relations between 2001 and 2022, considering pivotal events and domestic decision-making mechanisms.

Chapter 2

Turkey-Russia Relations in 2001–2009

This chapter examines Turkey-Russia relations in the period between 2001 and 2009. In this chapter, the invasion of Iraq by the United States is the *stimulus* that gave direction to the relations between the two countries in this period. To consider the impact of the invasion of Iraq with its underlying dynamics, I also look at the beginning of the Bush administration, the 9/11 attacks, and the emergence of the leadership of Erdoğan in Turkey and Putin in Russia. Therefore, although the invasion of Iraq began in 2003, this chapter focuses on the period between 2001 and 2009.

In this period, the reactions of Putin and Erdoğan to the regional and global context emerged after the invasion of Iraq played the most significant role in shaping the bilateral relations between Turkey and Russia. Unlike during the Cold War, where the bipolarity could limit middle powers, the post–Cold War era provided more maneuvering space. The failure of the United States to maintain unipolarity with the invasion of Iraq enabled the Turkey-Russia nexus to escape U.S. control and helped Ankara and Moscow to strengthen bilateral and regional platforms and break records in bilateral trade throughout the 2000s.

This chapter starts with an appraisal of the period. In that part, I summarize the formation of the AK Party (Justice and Development Party—*Adalet ve Kalkınma Partisi*) government in Turkey under Recep Tayyip Erdoğan and the emergence of Vladimir Putin's leadership in Russia. Then, I analyze how the changes in Russia and Turkey's foreign policy strategies influenced their bilateral trade relations, energy relations, and the dynamics of cooperation/competition between the two countries in the Middle East, the Black Sea, and the post-Soviet regions (see figure 0.2).

APPRAISAL OF THE ERA

Regional and Global Context

During the 2000s, U.S. unilateralism indirectly strengthened the dynamics of cooperation in the Turkey-Russia nexus. Following the 9/11 attacks, the United States invaded Taliban-led Afghanistan, which refused to extradite Bin Laden. Turkey and Russia came forward among those who provided firm support to the United States in its "Global War on Terror." When the idea of invading Iraq came to the table, however, the Bush administration could not find support from most of its allies and regional actors.[1] This time, Turkey and Russia opposed what they saw as U.S. imperial expansion. Moreover, despite the minimal impact of the invasion on the functioning of NATO, and WTO, how the United States conducted the intervention created a rift between the United States and its European allies.[2] For example, in late 2002, France, China, and Russia as three members of the UNSC released a joint statement underlining that Resolution 1441, which indicated the breach of Iraq of its disarmament obligations, excluded automaticity in the use of force.[3] These developments also had systemic reverberations by fostering multipolarity.

Despite the international opposition, the United States went forward with the intervention. In a mere five weeks, U.S. forces would capture Baghdad. However, winning the war was easier than keeping the peace. The dismantling of the Iraqi state brought instability to Iraq, which became a hotbed for various terrorist organizations the United States had originally sought to eliminate. The military interventions to Iraq and Afghanistan harmed the invulnerability of the United States, as the U.S. troops were bogged down in guerilla warfare in both Afghanistan and Iraq. Moreover, the human rights violations, which were revealed in the gruesome photos from the Abu-Gharib prison, fueled global anti-Americanism.[4] In the economic dimension, the United States could prevent Iraq[5] from selling oil with euros but the burden of these wars to the U.S. budget reached over $8 trillion as of 2021.[6]

In this period, Turkey-Russia relations began to strengthen from the point Putin came into power in Russia. During Turkish prime minister Ecevit's visit to Moscow in November 2000, Turkey and Russia signed a number of agreements ranging from media cooperation to diplomatic passports, visa exemption, veterinary issues, and cooperation in the fight against terrorism.[7] Subsequently, during Russian foreign minister Sergey Ivanov's visit to Turkey in June 2001, two parties agreed to develop bilateral cooperation and projects to contribute to the security and welfare in the region. Then, foreign ministers of Turkey and Russia signed the "Action Plan between the Republic of Turkey and the Russian Federation on Cooperation in Eurasia" in November 2001 in New York. The plan called for developing regional cooperation and strengthening bilateral cooperation in political, security, and economic issues.[8] In an interview he has given, Russia's ambassador to Turkey, Alexander Lebedev, noted that the document marked the transition from competition to cooperation on regional issues in Turkey-Russia bilateral relations. He also pointed out that the days of the Cold War were over and there should be unity against international terrorism.[9]

Within the framework of the international backlash to the invasion of Iraq, Turkey and Russia revised their foreign policy strategies. Strong leaderships established in both countries amplified this process. Under the AK Party, Turkey refused to join the invasion of Iraq and began to promote relations with regional actors and the EU. Under Putin, the Russian foreign policy strategy gave more emphasis on promoting multipolarity in the global order and increasing Russia's hegemonic influence over the post-Soviet space compared to previous administrations.

These revisions had positive reflections on Turkey-Russia relations. During the 2000s, the two countries not only developed mutual relations in trade and energy but also deepened their partnerships in multiple regions. The continuation of the U.S. unilateralism through the so-called Color Revolutions, which threatened Russia's self-designated sphere of influence, and the U.S. decision to plant missiles in Eastern Europe further provoked Russia. Turkey developed its economic and political relations with Iran, Syria, and Russia, while also preserving ties with the NATO alliance and making progress in the EU accession process.

The emergence of Turkey and Russia as two independent actors in Eurasia paved the way for bilateral and regional cooperation outside of the mentorship of the United States.[10] In his 2002 article, Trenin argues that the "schizophrenia" was cured, and Russia and Turkey had "buried the hatchet" as the competition over various regional fault lines cooled off.[11] Such a trend was observed in bilateral visits, regional agreements, and trade relations between Turkey and Russia in this period. One of the first countries Erdoğan visited in 2002 after his election victory was Russia, where the two leaders agreed to develop bilateral cooperation and deepen economic relations.[12] In 2004, Turkey's foreign minister, Abdullah Gül, brought 150 Turkish businessmen with him to Moscow and took part in a business forum of Turkish and Russian entrepreneurs.[13] During Putin's visit to Turkey in December 2004, the two leaders signed the "Joint Declaration between the Republic of Turkey and the Russian Federation on Deepening Friendship and Multi-Dimensional Partnership."[14] During this visit, Putin underlined that the two countries had similar attitudes towards many regional issues, including post-war Iraq and Afghanistan.[15] In 2005, during the opening ceremony of the Blue Stream Pipeline Project in Samsun, Putin noted the significance of the city where Mustafa Kemal arrived to initiate the War of Independence in 1919, a time when the Soviet Union provided substantial military and economic support to Turkey.[16] These efforts brought about a steady increase in the volume of bilateral trade between them until the 2008 global financial crisis (see figure 2.1) and ensured the continuation of the positive trend in bilateral relations.

Domestic Context and the Foreign Policy Strategy of Turkey

Conservative Democrats

A new chapter opened in Turkey's political history with the AK Party's election victory in 2002. The party was founded in November 2001 by a dissident group from the members of Necmettin Erbakan's[17] Islamist Felicity Party. In the 2002 general elections AK Party gathered enough votes to form a one-party government. This was a major development because throughout the 1990s Turkey's politics was dominated by weak coalition governments and the *laicist* pressure of the judiciary and army on Turkey's conservative Muslims.[18] Such pressure made it hard for the conservative Muslims to fully participate in economic and political life in Turkey. Moreover, Turkey's successive coalition governments' inability to deal with the country's economic crises, political instability, and the PKK terror throughout the 1990s contributed to the AK Party's election victory. Tayyip Erdoğan's[19] charisma and his

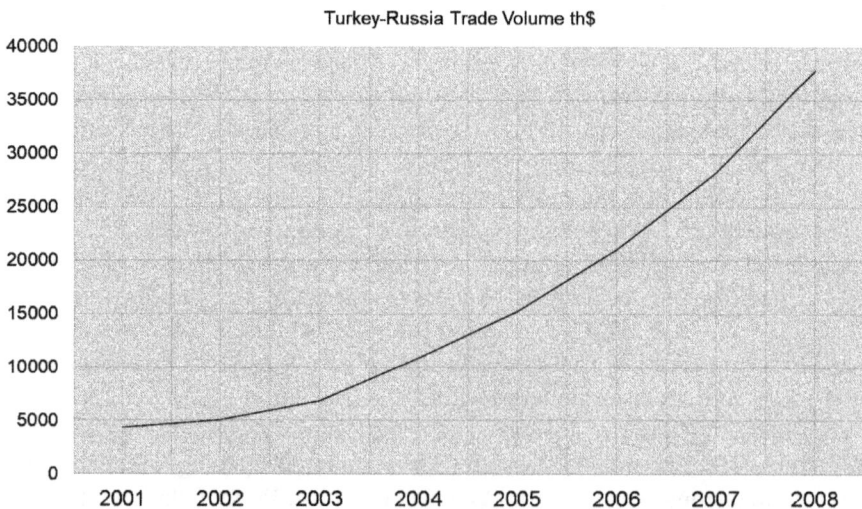

Figure 2.1   Turkey-Russia Trade Volume, 2001–2008. Source: "Dış Ticaret İstatistikleri" [Foreign Trade Statistics], Turkish Ministry of Trade, accessed April 10, 2022, https://ticaret .gov.tr/istatistikler/dis-ticaret-istatistikleri.

success during his tenure as the mayor of Istanbul were also major factors in the AK Party's electoral success.

During its first term (2002–2007), the AK Party aimed to establish itself as a legitimate political actor at home and abroad by seeking to increase the power of its elected government vis-à-vis the army and the judiciary through EU reforms. In order not to face any immediate closure case and to develop a partnership with the West against Turkey's secular order, AK Party promoted an image close to the Christian Democrats of Europe by framing itself in a non-threatening manner as a "conservative democrat" party.[20] AK Party pursued liberal, center-right policies while having Turkey's Muslim conservatives at its core base. Through EU reforms, the AK Party government sought to diminish the power of the army and judiciary within Turkey's state machinery and increase the power of the elected government. Its EU-friendly policies, positive image, and economic success enabled the AK Party to maintain and expand its voter base in the subsequent elections. The party's self-identification and constructive foreign policy contributed to its international image. Nevertheless, Turkey's bureaucratic elites in the judiciary and military continued to problematize the political background of leading AK Party members.[21]

As the AK Party established itself, it took multiple steps to neutralize the guardians of regime. In 2007, the election of leading AK Party figure Abdullah Gül as the president sidelined the former president Ahmet Necdet Sezer, who acted as the balancer on behalf of Turkey's secular establishment by vetoing hundreds of bills between 2002 and 2007.[22] Between 2007 and 2010, many prominent secular figures including military officers, intellectuals, and lawmakers, were indicted on charges of attempting to overthrow the elected government through undemocratic means. By and large, these trials removed the guardians of the regime from critical positions in the Turkish bureaucracy. However, the support of the Gülen Movement[23] to these prosecutions would create an important problem for the AK Party and Turkey in the following decade.

Turkey's Multidimensional Foreign Policy

Within the framework of Ahmet Davutoğlu's roadmap,[24] the AK Party ushered in a significant change in Turkey's foreign policy strategy. Adopting the "zero problems with neighbors" initiative, the AK Party government aimed to actively resolve bilateral issues and develop economic and political relations with its neighbors. AK Party's foreign policy was a drastic shift from Turkey's original strategic culture, which advises avoiding exerting influence in the Middle East and the Balkans, adopting pro-Western and strong anti-adventurist nature. This change in foreign policy was partially a consequence of the AK Party's pious base in the decision-making process. AK Party's base was sensitive towards the Muslim countries in the Balkans and the Middle East.[25] Meanwhile, under the AK Party, Turkey preserved its Western orientation by attempting to join the EU and secure U.S. support in its new endeavors. These diverse elements of the AK Party's multidimensional foreign policy could find supporters across a broad range of the political spectrum in Turkey. For instance, a portion of Turkey's secular establishment, which continued to be suspicious of the West, supported Turkey's new aspirations for independent foreign policy, even suggesting that Turkey leave NATO and seek closer relations with Russia instead.[26] CHP, the only opposition party in the Parliament until 2007, supported the AK Party's EU policy due to the Westernizing impact of the EU accession process.[27]

Under the AK Party, Turkey generated flexible responses towards its regional problems and improved its relations with the non-Western world. It strengthened its ties with the EU and developed its relations with Russia and its neighbors. According to the observations of Abdullah Gül,[28] the international actors started to consider Turkey as an independent country capable of making decisions based on its own security needs, thanks to Turkey's stance toward the invasion of Iraq.[29] After a series of reforms, the AK Party government started the accession talks with the EU in 2005. Turkey supported the UN-sponsored resolution in Cyprus known as the Annan Plan, which proposed to unite two Cypriot republics under a federal state. Despite Turkey's ambitious reform attempts and bold steps in Cyprus, the categorical opposition of some EU members to Turkey's membership hindered Turkey's prospects.[30] The EU also accepted Cyprus as a member state despite the refusal of the Annan Plan by the Greek Cypriot administration in Southern Cyprus. This feedback that Turkey received from the EU accession process curbed Turkey's enthusiasm for the EU while also feeding suspicions of the West's double standards. In the Middle East, Turkey signed trade agreements with Syria and Israel and developed relations with Iran. Despite the deterioration of U.S.-Turkey relations the AK Party government continued to work with the United States within the framework of the AK Party's multidimensional foreign policy. For instance, Turkey considered the U.S.-led Greater Middle East Project[31] as an opportunity to amplify its own status and influence in the Middle East.[32] Turkey contributed to Iraq's reconstruction and became one of the most important trade partners for post-Saddam Iraq.[33] In trade and energy, the AK Party aimed to bolster Turkey's trade ties with its neighbors and to make it a regional hub.

The shift in Turkey's foreign policy positively impacted Turkey-Russia relations for multiple reasons. First, The AK Party government's attempts to establish mutually beneficial trade relations with Turkey's neighbors and its "zero problems with neighbors" motto helped intensify economic ties with

Russia. Within the framework of its foreign policy, the AK Party Government attempted to defuse tensions with Russia in the South Caucasus and the Black Sea regions. Finally, Turkey's refusal to participate in the invasion of Iraq, which was in convergence with Russia's stance, promoted Turkey's image as an independent actor in the eyes of Moscow.

Domestic Context and the Foreign Policy Strategy of Russia

The Recentralization of Power in Russia

Unable to cope with the Chechen Insurgency, the economic crisis, and his falling approval rates, Russia's president Boris Yeltsin appointed Vladimir Putin, a former KGB officer who entered politics after the dissolution of the USSR, as his prime minister in August 1999, before the Russian legislative and the subsequent presidential elections. In December 2000, Yeltsin resigned and left his seat to Putin. The decision came days after Yeltsin's favored political party *Yedinstvo* (Unity)[34] came in behind the Communist Party in the Russian legislative elections. Thanks to Yeltsin's backing and the support of the media, Putin achieved a landslide victory in the 2000 presidential elections.[35]

Putin's primary aim concerning domestic politics was restoring the state authority. He committed to a Russian concept of "sovereign democracy" in an attempt to prevent external pressure on Russia's domestic politics. To realize this aim, Putin aimed to establish a "power vertical" as a representation of Russia's historical tendency to adopt centralization as a solution for administering vast lands.[36] In bureaucratic administration, the Russian Federation was divided into seven administrative divisions, headed by governors directly appointed by the Kremlin.[37] In economy, Putin summoned the new Russian oligarchs to the Kremlin and declared that he would tolerate their unjustly accumulated wealth as long as they did not meddle in politics.[38] Putin also replaced several Yeltsin-era bureaucrats with his former co-workers in the Saint Petersburg Municipality and the KGB. In party politics, he oversaw the creation of *Edinaya Rossiya* [ER, United Russia] by merging the competing *Yedinstvo* (Unity) and *Oteshestvo-Vsya Rossiya* [Fatherland-All Russia] alliances to ensure a legislature in compliance to the presidential office.[39] With a strong emphasis on economic recovery, political stability, and security, Putin secured the support of the majority in Russia.

Russia's economic recovery under Putin, which occurred thanks to political stability and rising gas prices, brought easy victories to the ER in the 2003 legislative elections and Putin in the 2004 presidential elections. Further steps followed these victories in the direction of centralization. In 2004, Putin reorganized the presidential administration, making the institution more effective and dependent on the president.[40] The electoral threshold was increased to 7 percent, and regional parties were banned from running in general elections.[41] The procedure of the election of governors was changed so that candidates were nominated by the president and then confirmed by the legislature.[42] These measures would enable the president to utilize and manipulate state structure for Russia's foreign policy more effectively.

The Return of the Anti-Western Attitude in Russian Foreign Policy

Putin gave impetus to the trend of change in Russian foreign policy strategy. He took multiple steps to return to Russia's original strategic culture, which considers relations with the West from a zero-sum perspective.[43] Accordingly, in Putin's first year as the president, Russia officially identified NATO's enlargement and domination of the West as the primary threats to the national security of Russia.[44] Under his leadership, Russia also aimed to increase its hegemonic influence in the post-Soviet region.[45] These steps strengthened the trend of moving away from the Kozyrev-era Westernization of the early 1990s, while Primakov's aim of balancing the United States remained an important goal. Yet Putin differentiated himself from Primakov by designating Russia as a European state and aimed at "pragmatic" cooperation with the United States.[46] Putin also gave particular emphasis to Russia's economic recovery and economic power.

Such change manifested itself in Russia's relations with the West and Russia's foreign policy towards multiple regions. Before the invasion of Iraq, Putin attempted to establish Russia's hegemonic influence in the post-Soviet space and increase its global influence in close engagement with the West. Putin's attempt developed despite the growing suspicion towards the West during the 1990s. Despite its support for the U.S. War on Terror after the 9/11 attack,[47] Russia considered the Iraq invasion an assertion of a U.S.-led unipolar world[48] and adopted an independent stance. In the following years, Moscow considered the Color Revolutions, a wave of popular protests aimed at regime change in post-Soviet space, as an expansion of the Western sphere of influence through Western-funded NGOs.[49] Similarly, Russia considered a possible NATO enlargement that would include Ukraine and Georgia, and the United States plans to install missile shields in Poland and the Czech Republic as threats to Russia's security.[50] As a result of these, Russia's ruling elite under Putin decided that the West was ignoring Russia's security interests and that it should protect those interests by reasserting its influence and challenging the U.S. attempt at global dominance.[51] *The Foreign Policy Concept of Russia*, which came into effect in 2008, clearly underlined this consideration.[52]

Russia put special emphasis on its relations with Turkey under Putin. Turkey was a significant market for Russian gas and one of the multiple emerging powers with whom Russia sought "extraordinary" ties in its attempt to counter U.S. hegemonic influence and foster a multipolar world order.[53] Turkey was also an actor that could not be ignored in Moscow's attempts to regain its regional and global influence. In return, Russia expected Turkey to respect its sphere of influence in the post-Soviet space and hoped to create a rift between Turkey and the West. Thus, as emphasized by Putin during his visit to Turkey in 2004, Turkey's independent foreign policy approach and the rejection of participation in the Iraq War were positive developments for Russia.[54]

TURKEY-RUSSIA RELATIONS

Regional Cooperation and Competition

The Middle East in the Context of the Invasion of Iraq

The most significant development in the Middle East in this period was the invasion of Iraq. Following the quick victory of U.S. forces, the sudden disappearance of the Iraqi state structure created political instability that reached beyond the borders of Iraq and caused civil strife, sectarian violence, and political instability in the Middle East. The indifference of the United States to the sensitivities of regional and global actors before, during, and after the military invasion encouraged Turkey and Russia to ensure their security through independent foreign policies.[55] In that sense, the invasion of Iraq helped Turkey and Russia to discover their shared opposition to the U.S. unilateralism. This discovery would play a significant role in their foreign policy strategy and consideration towards one another.

When Russia was fighting Chechen rebels, Putin considered the post-9/11 period as a process where human rights violations could be tolerated when fighting "radical Islamic terrorism." However, Putin viewed terrorism as a stateless phenomenon and a challenge to the system of states. In contrast to the United States, Putin decided that eliminating a functioning state would not remedy the fight against international terrorism.[56] As a result of the wave of global anti-Americanism caused by the invasion of Iraq, Putin's stance found significant domestic support. Moreover, by opposing the invasion, Putin saw a chance to improve Russia's relations with European partners to foster a counter-bloc to the U.S. unilateralism.[57]

Turkey's reaction to the series of U.S. invasions was similar to Russia's. Turkey actively participated in the Afghan War as part of the NATO mission. However, when the United States demanded to use Turkish territory for an incursion into Iraq from the north, it could not secure Turkey's cooperation.[58] The bill that would authorize U.S. troops to use Turkish soil was rejected by a narrow margin in Parliament. Erdoğan was among those who supported Turkey's participation in the war since that would help Turkey better protect its security and economic interests and gain U.S. support.[59] But he did not force the AK Party members to vote favorably, enabling enough AK Party members to prevent the passing of the bill along with the opposition MPs. At that point, the government and bureaucracy in Turkey were concerned that support to the U.S. invasion without proper legality could deteriorate Turkey's relations with the regional actor and with the EU. Public opinion was also against the war. The invasion of Iraq enabled Turkey to benefit from the anti–American critical discourse in the region.[60] As a result, Turkey's "no" vote facilitated a rather multidimensional foreign policy.

Following the invasion of Iraq, Turkey and Russia recognized the fundamental policy differences regarding regional politics between them and the United States. In contrast to the U.S. ambition to bring democracy to Middle Eastern autocracies, the two countries considered the protection of the territorial integrity and state structures of regional powers to be more important for regional security. This difference would facilitate partnerships between them beyond the region. For instance, one of the reasons Turkey did not fully cooperate with the United States in the Black Sea region was that Turkish foreign policy decision makers began to see U.S. activities there through the prism of the invasion of Iraq.[61]

The Black Sea Region in the Context of the Georgian War

The period of the early 2000s was a tumultuous era for the Black Sea region. In this period, the United States and the EU carried on the penetration of the West to the Black Sea through institutional ties. Bulgaria and Romania joined NATO in 2004, and the EU in 2007. The so-called Color Revolutions, the waves of protests and civil resistance activities against the incumbent regimes loyal to Russia in various former Soviet countries, resulted in the overthrow of the governments in Georgia and Ukraine. These steps significantly antagonized Russia, which considered the Black Sea as its primary sphere of influence.[62] Turkey, in its turn, did not show interest in U.S. designs in the Black Sea region. Instead, it adopted a strategy seeking to further its regional interests through protecting regional organizations like BSEC and continuing to develop bilateral relations with the countries in the region.[63]

Within the framework of these dynamics, the cooperation in the Black Sea region between Turkey and Russia strengthened. In 1999, when the BSEC Charter was confirmed, almost all countries in the Balkans and the Caucasus had become members of the organization, which aimed to perpetuate cooperation in various areas, including economic development, combatting international terrorism, and environmental protection.[64] BSEC's focus on soft security areas created an occasion for Turkey to oppose the extension of NATO's Operation Active Endeavor, which was tasked with fighting international crime, to the Black Sea region.[65] BSEC enabled the adaptation of former Soviet countries to market economies by way of transferring know-how from Turkey and Greece. BSEC also promoted cooperation among members whose interests did not necessarily align on other issues.[66] The Black Sea Naval Cooperation Task Group (BLACKSEAFOR), which was established in April 2001, aimed to strengthen good–neighborly relations between littoral states and promote confidence among their navies through a multinational on-call task force. The responsibilities of the Force included search and rescue operations, humanitarian assistance operations, and environmental protection.[67] While these initiatives demonstrated a common will to strengthen the regionalization of the Black Sea, serious political and security issues remained under the control of bilateral mechanisms in this period.[68]

The Russia-Georgia War in 2008[69] seriously tested the emerging harmony in the region with Russia's violation of Georgia's territorial integrity. During the conflict, Turkey intended to preserve the relatively peaceful situation by pursuing active diplomacy and staying in contact with all the parties. In line with Turkey's dedication to solving regional issues with its regional partners, Erdoğan proposed "The Caucasus Stability and Cooperation Platform" to resolve the conflict.[70] The platform would be composed of Turkey, Russia, Georgia, Azerbaijan, and Armenia and exclude the United States.[71] During the conflict, Turkey also barred the entry of two U.S. relief vessels to the Black Sea, citing the Montreux Agreement's tonnage limitations to foreign warships in the Black Sea.[72] In line with its neutral stance and good relations with Georgia, Turkey also supplied electricity to Georgia during the war.[73] Russia appreciated Turkey's neutral stance during the conflict and did not resent Turkey for not fully recognizing two de facto states created within Georgia with Russian support after the war.

The Caucasus and Central Asia

Due to Turkey's recognition of Russia's privileged interests in the post-Soviet region, the two countries avoided a standoff over the differences between their regional projections. Within the framework of its strategy towards the post-Soviet region, Russia took additional steps towards strengthening its control over the Caucasus and Central Asia. In its turn, Turkey strengthened bilateral relations with the countries of the region and regional organizations.

During this period, one of the most significant regional developments in the South Caucasus related to the Turkey-Russia nexus was Turkey's pursuit of normalization with Armenia. At the initiative of the president of Armenia, Serzh Sargsyan, and Turkey's newly elected president, Abdullah Gül, Turkey and Armenia took the first step towards normalization in 2008. In this atmosphere, both countries signed the Zurich Protocols, where foreign ministers of both countries agreed on opening the borders and establishing normal diplomatic relations.[74] Yet they could not honor the agreement due to the opposition of nationalist circles in Turkey and Armenia, as well as that of the Azerbaijani government. In order to salvage the normalization process, Erdoğan called on Russia to put pressure on Armenia to resolve the Nagorno-Karabakh problem. However, Putin dismissed Erdoğan's appeal, noting the difficulties in reconciling Turkey, Armenia, and Azerbaijan.[75] Meanwhile, the Nagorno-Karabakh issue remained frozen as Turkey continued to stay out of the conflict. In short, the generally positive trend in relations between Turkey and Russia prevented these disagreements from becoming a significant problem in bilateral relations.

In the North Caucasus, aside from the impact of the positive trend in bilateral relations, the radicalization of the Chechen insurgency and Russia's restoration of control in Chechnya enabled the defusing of tensions between Turkey and Russia. During the 2000s, the radicalization of the Chechen insurgency, the hostage-taking acts in Turkey, and the events of 9/11,[76] the UN Convention for the Suppression of the Financing of Terrorism (ratified in January 2002), and the Protocol Amending the European Convention on the Suppression of Terrorism (ratified in January 2005)—all played a role in Turkey's stance.[77] Putin's promise not to support the PKK in exchange for Turkey's ceasing its support to the Chechens also discouraged Turkey from supporting Chechen separatism.[78] Yet the disagreements between Russia and Turkey over Chechnya persisted. For example, Turkish government and state institutions avoided relations and contact with the Chechen Autonomous Republic, while Turkish construction firms continued to receive lucrative contracts from the Kremlin-backed authority. The Chechen diaspora in Turkey continued to provide funds to families who had fled the conflict and organized protests against the extradition of Chechens to Russia. During Gül's visit to Russia in 2004, the Russian side expressed its concern over some Turkish non-governmental organizations' actions.[79] However, these differences did not create a significant problem in bilateral relations in this period.

In Central Asia, Russia took further steps towards restoring a hegemonic power in the region, and Turkey focused on projecting soft power towards the region and developing trade relations with the post-Soviet states without antagonizing Russia. In line with Putin's foreign policy vision, Russia strengthened the regional structures intended to restore Moscow's hierarchical relations with the Central Asian countries. The Collective Security Treaty Organization (CSTO)[80] was founded in 2002, and joined by Russia, Tajikistan, Kazakhstan, Armenia, Belarus, and Kyrgyzstan. While initially, the CSTO was open to cooperating with the United States for the security of the region, the organization later began to adopt a rather independent presence in the region with its armed forces. The Eurasian Economic Community was founded in 2000, establishing a common market among its member states. As opposed to the rising Russian influence, the Turkish influence in the region continued to be limited to developmental aid and trade. During the 1990s, the independence of Turkic nations excited Turkey, which dreamed of connecting the Turkic world stretching from the Adriatic to the Wall of China. However, the unwillingness of the Turkic countries to consider Turkey as a big brother and the growing competition for influence in the region limited Turkey's influence in the region.[81]

Trade Relations

The most significant indication of the independent course in the development of Turkey-Russia relations was the improving volume of trade between the two countries. The bilateral trade volume between Turkey and Russia/Soviet Union had steadily increased since the late 1980s. During the 2000s, this increase accelerated due to the Blue Stream agreement, the strengthening of institutional ties, and joint efforts by Putin and Erdoğan (see figure 2.1). Warhola and Mitchell draw attention to how mutually beneficial economic relations prevail over the geopolitical competition in bilateral relations.[82] The mutually beneficial nature of the rising trade levels promoted and complemented cooperation in other segments of their bilateral relations. The only downside of Turkey's increasing bilateral trade volume was its increasing trade deficit with Russia (see figure 2.2). The high volume of natural gas Turkey purchased annually from Russia increased its reliance on the country and enabled Russia to maintain the upper hand in their relations. However, Russia did not utilize its advantage in this period because there was no need for such a move.

Russia's gas exports to Turkey constituted the bulk of the bilateral trade volume between the two countries. This trend resulted from Russia's continuing diplomatic and lobbying efforts to increase the share of Russian gas in Turkey's energy imports in the 1990s. Russia's volume of exports to Turkey showed a steady increase from the start of the 2000s until the 2008 global financial crisis (see figure 2.2). Besides exporting natural resources, in 2009 Turkey also bought anti-tank weapon systems that included eight hundred missiles and eighty units from Russia, instead of buying an Israeli option.[83]

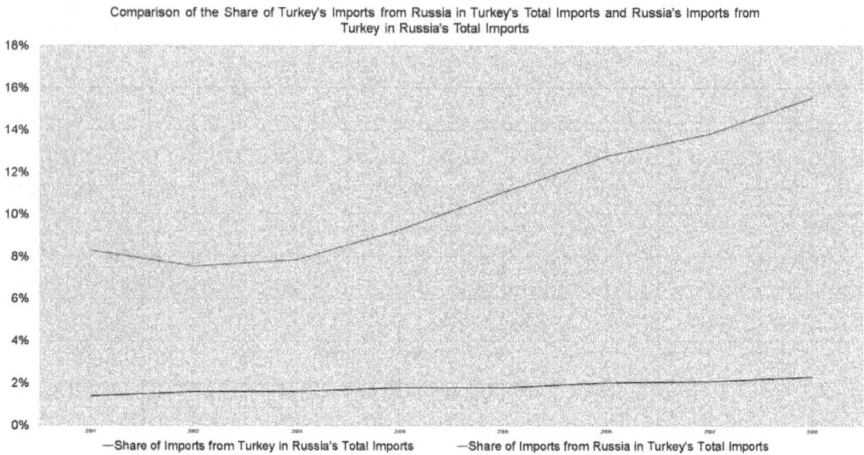

Comparison of the Share of Turkey's Imports from Russia in Turkey's Total Imports and Russia's Imports from Turkey in Russia's Total Imports

—Share of Imports from Turkey in Russia's Total Imports   —Share of Imports from Russia in Turkey's Total Imports

Figure 2.2   Import-Export Balance in Turkey-Russia Bilateral Trade, 2001–2008. Source: "Dış Ticaret İstatistikleri" [Foreign Trade Statistics], Turkish Ministry of Trade, accessed April 10, 2022, https://ticaret.gov.tr/istatistikler/dis-ticaret-istatistikleri.

To close the trade deficit with Russia, the AK Party government encouraged Turkish businessmen to export to Russia and encouraged the tourism sector to bring more Russian tourists to Turkey. While the 1984 agreement allowed Turkey to pay for natural gas through its exports, it is important to note that the Blue Stream agreement did not provide such an opportunity.[84] Focusing on the guarantee of supply, Turkey ignored the problem of reliance upon Russia. Natural gas constituted the bulk of Turkey's imports but Russian imports from Turkey were diversified. Also, Turkish exporters had to compete for the Russian market with several other countries in the automobile, textile, and food sectors. The activities of Turkish business people in Russia increased with the proliferation of Turkish factories and the activities of construction firms. Yet, Turkey's trade deficit with Russia showed a steady increase until 2008 (see figure 2.2), despite the increasing flow of Russian tourists to Turkey (see figure 2.3). The rising price of natural gas, and the fact that the volume of Turkey's imports from Russia increased at a pace much higher than the volume of Russia's imports from Turkey, preserved Turkey's trade deficit.

Energy Relations

Turkey's Energy Demand and Blue Stream

One of the most important elements of Turkey-Russia relations in the post–Cold War period is the Blue Stream pipeline agreement. Turkey's increasing

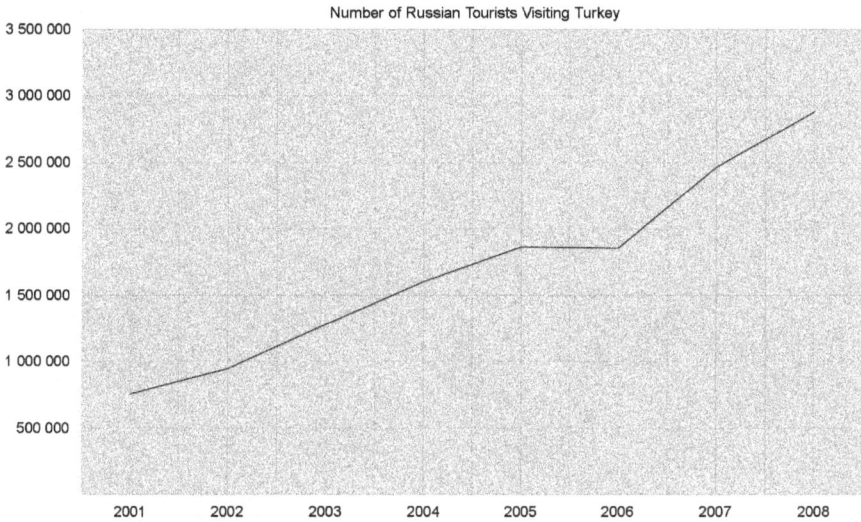

Figure 2.3 **Number of Russian Tourists Visiting Turkey, 2001–2008.** Source: "Sınır Giriş Çıkış İstatistikleri" [Border Crossing Statistics], Turkish Ministry of Culture and Tourism, accessed March 30, 2022, https://yigm.ktb.gov.tr/TR-9854/sinir-giris-cikis-istatistikleri .html.

need for energy resources and Russia's pursuit of marketing its oil and natural gas on favorable terms brought about the signing of an intergovernmental natural gas agreement in December 1997. The route of the pipeline would go directly through the Black Sea without passing through any other third country. Thus, Blue Stream would provide cheaper gas and carry less political risk compared to the formerly used Trans-Balkan pipeline, which was costly and often caused shortages of gas in Turkey (see figure 2.4). The construction of the pipeline was completed in February 2003 and became operational in 2005.

The Blue Stream created controversies in Turkey. The Blue Stream Pipeline was constructed to meet Turkey's peak demands during winter seasons or in case of a problem in the transportation of Iranian gas to Turkey.[85] However, in return for this, Turkey guaranteed Russia the continuous purchase of natural gas for twenty-five years.[86] The high price of Russian natural gas determined in the agreement brought about multiple lawsuits in Turkey against the ministers and bureaucrats involved in realizing the deal with Russia.[87] The agreement was labeled "Blue Treason" by Şükrü Elekdağ, an influential former diplomat and politician, who argued that the government ignored the more favorable Turkmen option and increased Turkey's energy dependency on Russia.[88] The protests of the United States, which aimed to

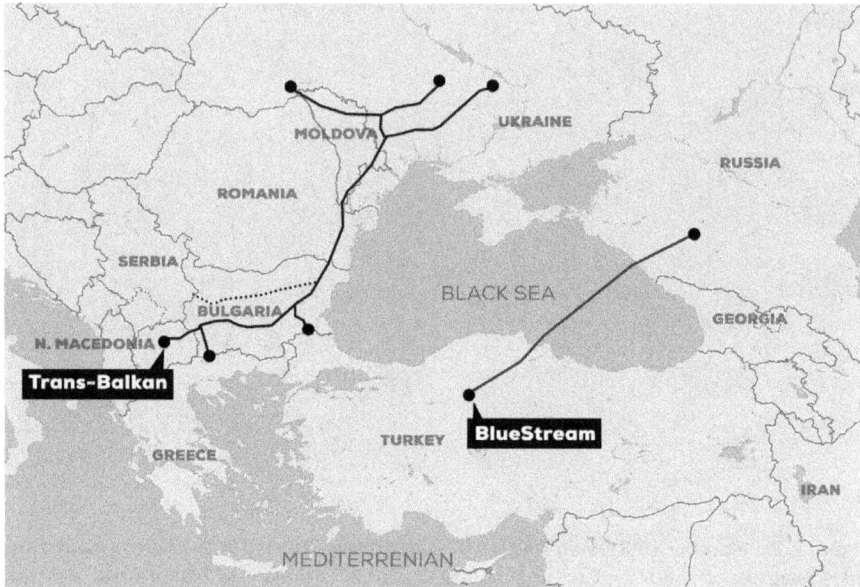

Figure 2.4 Comparison of Trans-Balkan and the Blue Stream. Source: Mapbox, accessed March 30, 2022, www.mapbox.com/about/maps.

bypass Russia in the transportation of energy resources to the West, also fell on deaf ears.[89]

The Blue Stream has been a lucrative and strategically beneficial deal for Russia. By partially eliminating the Balkan route, which would be completely defunct in 2020, Russia could cut costs and minimize the risks in transporting its natural gas to Turkey. Russia also secured a substantial share of the Turkish energy market through the deal. In addition, Russia gained a strategic advantage against Turkey by holding an important share of Turkey's natural gas imports. Despite these advantages, not everything went according to Russia's plan. Following the economic crisis in Turkey, Ankara found itself unable to purchase the amount of natural gas previously guaranteed and approached to Russia to renegotiate the deal. Having already started the project, Russia accepted Turkey's request for a decrease in the amount and gas price.[90]

Transportation of Caspian Oil to Europe

The changes in the regional geopolitics with the demise of the USSR brought about a change in the web of pipelines in the region that took its shape in line with the differing interests of Turkey, Russia, former Soviet countries, the European countries, and the United States. In competition with Russia's aims to increase its hegemonic influence over the post-Soviet region through agreements like the Blue Stream, the United States and the energy-importing countries of Europe aimed to secure the continuous flow of Caspian oil, while diminishing Russian and Iranian power and influence in the regional energy geopolitics. Their allies in this quest were the newly independent countries having access to the Caspian energy resources. Azerbaijan (similar to Turkmenistan and Kazakhstan) aimed to utilize its access to Caspian oil to bolster its economic and political independence from Moscow.

The Baku-Tbilisi-Ceyhan (BTC) oil pipeline project resulted from this set of dynamics. Within the framework of the BTC agreement, the oil from Azerbaijan's Azeri–Çırak-Güneşli field would be transported to Ceyhan in Turkey's southeast, opening up to the Mediterranean through Georgian land (see figure 2.5). Bypassing the existing Russian–controlled pipeline system (Druzhba), BTC complemented the Caspian Pipeline Consortium (CPC), which transports Kazakh oil to the Black Sea through Russia, and Baku-Supsa (BS), which transports Azeri oil from the Sanqaçal field to the Black Sea through Georgia. After signing the agreement in 1999 and a ground-breaking ceremony in 2002, the pipeline came into operation in 2006. By linking South Caucasus to Europe through BTC, Turkey gained a strategic advantage in the region against Russia. Through the increased independence of Georgia and Azerbaijan, and with the commitments of the EU and the United States, BTC considerably increased Turkey's maneuvering area in the South Caucasus.

Against the backdrop of the emergence of tensions in Ukraine during the Orange Revolution, Europe's energy security issue gained further significance due to the decreasing reliability of the Russian gas supply. The EU aimed to construct the Southern Gas Corridor (SGC), a project intended to secure sufficient gas supply to Europe through pipeline projects controlled by European firms operating under EU jurisdiction within the framework of the cooperation between the EU and the countries in the region.[91] A parallel pipeline from the Azeri Shah Deniz field to Erzurum (Baku-Tbilisi-Erzurum, BTE) was also completed in 2006. BTC supplied Turkey and Georgia with Azeri gas.

The Nabucco project, which was promoted within the framework of SGC, also heightened the dynamics of competition in the energy geopolitics of the region. The agreement was to enable the transfer of Azeri gas to Europe through the Trans-Anatolian Pipeline and deliver gas to the Baumgarten an der March gas hub in Austria through Bulgaria, Romania, and Hungary.[92] Through another pipeline project that would connect Iranian gas to Nabucco, Turkey also attempted to include Iran in the project, despite U.S. opposition.[93] Russia counter-proposed South Stream as a rival pipeline route (see figure 2.6).[94]

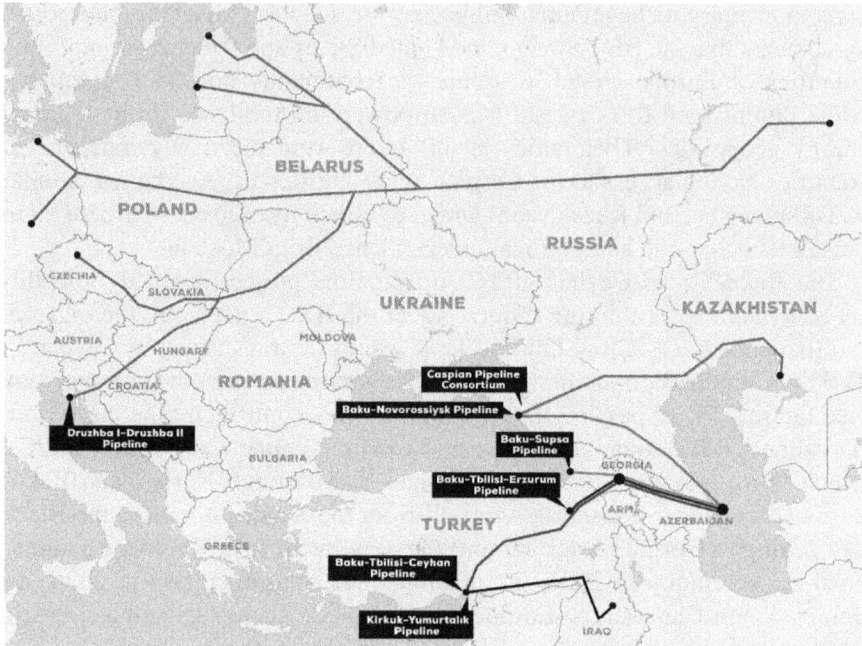

Figure 2.5   The Outflow of Caspian Oil to Europe and Turkey. Source: Mapbox, accessed March 30, 2022, www.mapbox.com/about/maps.

It is noteworthy that Turkey participated in the Russian-sponsored South Stream project since the pipeline was passing through Turkey's exclusive economic zone in the Black Sea. This move was demonstrative of Turkey's emerging independent foreign policy strategy and Turkey's desire to become an energy hub. However, the Nabucco project, another important part of Turkey's pursuit of becoming an energy hub, could not be realized due to the financial issues stemming from the 2008 crisis, disagreements between Turkey and its European partners, and Russia's opposition to the project. In the end, Azerbaijan preferred to transfer its gas TANAP and TAP to Europe (see figure 2.6).

COOPERATION AT GLOBAL LEVEL

The impact of the Iraq invasion went beyond the region by provoking a global reaction towards U.S. unilateralism. This process was complemented with economic trends such as the rise of China, the emergence of the networks between rising powers like BRICS (Brazil, Russia, India, China, and

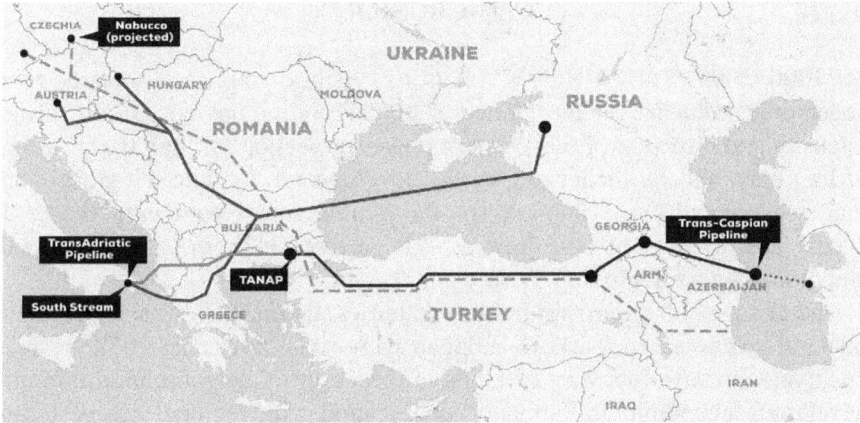

Figure 2.6 Nabucco and South Stream Pipelines. Source: Mapbox, accessed March 30, 2022, www.mapbox.com/about/maps.

South Africa) and MIKTA (Mexico, Indonesia, South Korea, Turkey, and Australia), and the recession in the United States during the 2008 crisis. The positive developments in regional affairs between Turkey and Russia as well as their bilateral economic relations strongly reflected on the stances of both countries towards each other in international organizations and multilateral platforms.

During the 2000s, Turkey's multidimensional foreign policy strategy included taking part in mediation efforts and improving Turkey's standing in global and regional platforms. Russia approached Turkey's efforts favorably, but with reservations regarding Turkey's possible stronger alignment with the West. For example, within the framework of fostering multipolarity in the global system, Russia took a discouraging stance towards Turkey's EU membership but encouraged Turkey's efforts to increase its global influence. Thus, Turkey could count on Russia's support in its candidacy for nonpermanent membership in the UN Security Council for the 2009–2010 term. In turn, Turkey placed no reservation on Russia's effort to achieve a more influential status in the international system after the massive multilateral Cold War–era network disappeared with the demise of the USSR.[95] For example, Turkey played a significant role in Russia's membership in the Organization of Islamic Cooperation in 2005.[96] Turkey and Russia's support for one another was the consequence of the overlap in their global vision. While they did not see eye to eye on every regional matter, Turkey and Russia were on the same page regarding the idea that a global system could increase their independent influence at the global level.

CONCLUSION

In 2000–2009 Turkey-Russia relations visibly improved outside the hegemonic influence of the United States. Their mutual opposition to the intensity and direction of the Western power projection through the invasion of Iraq played a significant role in this development. Despite the global and regional sympathy and support for the United States following the 9/11 events, the invasion of Iraq drew a negative reaction from several regional and global actors, including Turkey and Russia.

The changes of leadership in both countries also positively affected their bilateral relations. In Turkey, Erdoğan came into power in 2002, with a positive agenda to increase Turkey's influence in its neighborhood through developing economic and strategic cooperation with regional actors. Putin also intended to bolster Russia's economic power and increase its regional and global influence. While Putin considered Turkey a vital trade partner and welcomed its relative independence from the West, Turkey, under the AK Party, focused on developing mutually beneficial relations with Russia.

Multiple regions where Russia and Turkey compete were subjected to increased activism by the West, the reassertion of Russia's influence, and Turkey's pragmatic cooperation attempts. Aside from this, Turkey realized that it could not compete with Russia in the post-Soviet space. U.S. support for such a project had already dissipated and post-Soviet Turkic-Muslim nations did not consider Turkey a source of inspiration. These dynamics paved the way for the coexistence and even cooperation between Turkey and Russia in multiple regions. The positions of the two countries vis-à-vis the Middle East began to converge after the Iraq invasion. In the Black Sea, the Caucasus, and Central Asia, Turkey's economic influence and Russia's hegemonic influence achieved a modus vivendi. This improvement occurred through both countries' compartmentalizing bilateral relations by ignoring differences in problematic areas and focusing on cooperation.

The differing interests of Turkey, Russia, former Soviet countries, European countries, and the United States—as well their ability to pursue these interests in a politically less confined regional and global environment—ushered in a transformation in the energy geopolitics of the region in the 2000s through the Blue Stream Agreement and the EU's SGC project. The dynamics of cooperation and competition in the region's energy geopolitics reflected the increasing assertiveness of the West, Russia's attempts to restore its hegemonic influence over the post-Soviet space, and Turkey's attempt to increase its regional influence through a multidimensional foreign policy. Russia aimed to maintain the relevance of the Soviet-era web of pipelines, Turkey aimed to diversify its energy supplies and to become a hub for new pipelines, the EU and the United States aimed to decrease Russia's hegemony over the region's energy geopolitics, and the newly independent resource-rich post-Soviet countries aimed to bolster their economic independence. While the BTC increased Turkey's influence in the South Caucasus, the Blue Stream secured natural gas flow to Turkey while increasing Russia's influence over Turkey through energy dependence.

Chapter 3

Turkey-Russia Relations in 2009–2016

This chapter examines Turkey-Russia relations in the years between 2009 and 2016. This chapter considers the Arab Uprisings, particularly the Syrian Civil War, as the *stimulus* that had an immediate impact on the dynamics of the Turkey-Russia nexus in this period. The conflict of interest between Turkey and Russia over the Syrian Civil War, which began as part of the Arab Uprisings,[1] played the most significant role in shaping Turkey-Russia relations in this period. The Arab Uprisings created an opportunity to shape the region's future for both countries. Both Turkey and Russia got involved in the crisis by supporting their proxies. However, the conflict between Turkey and Russia's vision for the future of the Middle East spilled over to other segments of the bilateral relations within the framework of the escalation of the Syrian crisis. The U.S. attitude toward the conflict also played a significant role in this period. The false expectation of U.S. intervention caused the escalation of the conflict by encouraging the regional powers to either bandwagon or balance the U.S. presence.

This chapter starts with an appraisal of the period, where I analyze the regional and global context, the changes of the domestic dynamics in the two countries, and the emergence of the Syrian Civil War as an essential dynamic that influenced Turkey-Russia relations. Then, I analyze how their reactions to the regional turbulence influenced the dynamics of cooperation/conflict between Turkey and Russia in different regions, bilateral trade relations, bilateral energy relations, and cooperation between them at a multilateral level (see figure 0.2 in the introduction).

APPRAISAL OF THE ERA

Regional and Global Context

In this period, Turkey-Russia relations deteriorated as a result of the differences in their policies over the Arab Uprisings/Syrian Civil War. The change in the U.S. foreign policy toward the region played a significant role in shaping the regional dynamics within the framework of the Syrian crisis. The U.S. foreign policy in this period, which developed in reaction to the Iraq war, aimed to decrease the military commitments of the United States and is widely known as the retrenchment strategy.[2] Although the Obama administration's foreign policy strategy included "appealing to people's aspirations for justice" in the Middle East,[3] he also promised to decrease the U.S. military commitments and pivot toward Asia.[4] This strategy was intended to prevent further decline of the U.S. economic and military power through internal balancing by investing U.S. power in revitalizing the U.S. economy instead of unnecessary military conflicts.[5] Within the framework of this strategy, the United States would stay away from sending boots on the ground while aiming to preserve its global influence through multilateral institutions without incurring a high economic cost. To put it bluntly, the United States would expect middle powers to follow its lead without providing economic or military support.

The Obama administration's strategy had important reverberations for the Middle East, where Turkey and Russia competed to exert influence during the time of turbulence caused by the Arab Uprisings. In the absence of substantial U.S. involvement, Russia appeared as a deal-breaking actor in Syria, which eventually became the main arena for the competition of influence between many regional and global actors including Turkey and Russia. Turkey's failure to convince neither the United States nor the EU to realize a political transition in Syria or ensure the removal of Bashar al-Assad compromised Turkey's security and economy and deteriorated Turkey's relations with Russia and the West. Obama's retrenchment had visible implications in the Black Sea region as well. The United States failed to prevent the Russian annexation of Crimea and pave the way for future expansion of Russia. Russia considered this an opportunity and attempted to further its regional interests through decisive steps. On the other hand, Turkey continued to seek U.S. support in regional issues. This process most visibly played out within the framework of the Syrian Civil War, where the initially conflicting interests in the Middle East between Turkey and Russia turned into a confrontation.

In the initial phase of this period, the continuing synergy between Putin and Erdoğan and their habit of overlooking regional competition between the two countries enabled a positive trend in trade and energy relations between

Turkey and Russia. The strengthening of the bilateral ties facilitated projects that required deeper long-term trust. In 2011, Turkey and Russia established the High-Level Cooperation Council, which enabled the two countries to coordinate their bilateral trade relations better. In 2014, Russia canceled the South Stream via Ukraine, a pipeline project favoring the TurkStream via Turkey. It also began the construction of the Akkuyu Nuclear Power Plant (NPP) started in 2015 in Turkey. Until Russia's military intervention to Syria, Turkey and Russia could contain their clash of interests in Syria. However, the tensions over Syria significantly escalated due to Turkey's shooting down of a Russian fighter jet over the Turkey-Syria border on November 24, 2015. The tensions in the following period, known as the Jet Crisis, temporarily affected other segments of the bilateral relations.

Domestic Context and the Foreign Policy Strategy of Turkey

Erdoğan's Consolidation of Power and Domestic Opposition

In this period, the AK Party's continuing electoral successes provided the government with self-confidence and motivation to realize significant reforms. The 2010 referendum, which substantially increased the power of elected officials against the judiciary and military, was a severe blow to the long-running secular tutelage over the Turkish state. In the 2011 parliamentary elections, thanks to notable reforms tripling of Turkey's GDP per capita, the AK Party won a comfortable victory with almost 50 percent of the vote. With the confidence gained from this success, the AK Party initiated the Reconciliation Process to resolve the Kurdish issue.[6]

It was also in this period that Turkey faced severe economic, political, and security challenges. In the summer of 2013, the tensions between Erdoğan and the secular urban class peaked with the Gezi Park protests.[7] Moreover, the relations between the Gülen movement and the AK Party deteriorated when various organs of the Gülen Movement began to target the AK Party through judicial processes, police operations, leaks, and media manipulations.[8] The PKK effectively ended the Reconciliation Process by resuming terrorist activities on civilian targets in 2014.[9] Yet, these challenges did not obstruct AK Party's electoral success. They gained another victory in the 2014 local elections, which had turned out to be a confidence vote against the backdrop of a fierce Gülenist anti-governmental campaign. In 2014, Erdoğan ran for president as a first step to establishing a presidential system. He left the party leadership and the office of prime minister to Davutoğlu only to sack him two years later.[10] Although the AK Party failed to achieve a majority in the Parliament in June 2015 to form a one-party government, the failure to bring about a coalition in the upcoming process brought about another election in November of the same year where the AK Party once more received nearly 50 percent of the vote. By 2016, Turkish society was polarized between Erdoğan's supporters and several opposing groups.

The Implementation of the AK Party's Foreign Policy Vision

In this period, Turkey developed a more assertive foreign policy while remaining in close tandem with the West. Having consolidated power over the state institutions, Turkey aimed to play a leadership role in the Middle East, which was undergoing a political and economic transformation. Ahmet Davutoğlu, who became foreign minister in 2009 and prime minister in 2014, played a central role in forming Turkey's foreign policy making in this period. The initial U.S. encouragement was also an essential factor. Obama chose Turkey for his first trip abroad, and during his visit Obama praised Turkey as a model nation, providing substantial encouragement to Turkey's bid for regional leadership.[11] Therefore, the decision makers of Turkey considered the regional and global conditions as ripe for implementing Davutoğlu's strategic vision.

Turkey's foreign policy endeavor in the Middle East eventually created various major security issues for Turkey. The United States had no intention to get more involved in the Middle East despite signaling the opposite. From the initial phase of this period until 2013, Turkey's foreign policy strategy seemed to be a success. It enjoyed splendid economic and political relations, not only with post-Revolution regimes but also with Iraq's Kurdistan Regional Government (KRG).[12] Aside from its popularity in the Arab streets, Turkey also had good relations with Iran.[13] It was also well-positioned to develop ties with the post-Revolution regimes established after the Arab Uprisings in the Middle East.[14] However, the direction of the political developments in the Middle East upset Turkey's bid for regional leadership. The conflict in Syria turned into a civil war in 2012, Egypt's elected pro-Turkey government was toppled by a coup in 2013, and Turkey's Resolution Process began to crumble in 2014. Such a turnaround decreased Turkey's newfound influence in the Middle East and North Africa, where counter-revolutionary forces curtailed Turkey's endeavors.

In this period, Turkey considered Russia as an essential partner in trade and energy. Turkey welcomed Russia's initiative of the Turkish Stream and cooperated with Russia in building a nuclear reactor. Turkey continued to avoid confrontation with Russia in the post-Soviet space, even during the Ukrainian Crisis. However, the conflict of interest over Syria negatively impacted other segments of the bilateral relations, testing the limits of compartmentalization. Russia obstructed multiple UNSC resolutions against the

Syrian regime and continued to support Assad economically and militarily. When directly involved in the conflict in early 2015, Russian airplanes indiscriminately bombed the opposition forces, targeting the groups supported by Turkey. Russia's military involvement in Syria significantly decreased Turkey's influence in Syria. When Turkey shot down a Russian fighter jet violating the Turkish-Syrian border in late 2015, killing two Russian pilots, Turkey-Russia relations saw its nadir.

Domestic Context and the Foreign Policy Strategy of Russia

Further Centralization of Power Under Putin

Between 2008 and 2012, Putin left his seat to Dmitry Medvedev, a law professor with limited political experience, in compliance with the Russian Constitution, which did not allow him to run for three consecutive terms. Medvedev prioritized economic reform against the backdrop of the negative impact of the 2008 crisis on the Russian economy.[15] There was a relative calm in U.S.-Russia relations under Medvedev.[16] Despite the Georgian War of 2008, the Obama administration dropped the Bush-era plan to set up a nuclear defense shield in Eastern Europe and have a "reset" in U.S.-Russia relations, which made the "New START" treaty and Russia's accession to WTO possible. The centralization trend in Russia's domestic politics continued under Medvedev, who extended the length of the term for the presidency to six years.[17]

After the end of Medvedev's term, Putin returned to the presidency. He achieved a landslide victory in the 2012 presidential elections, despite ER's losing its constitution-changing majority in the 2011 Duma elections. Medvedev went back to his post and became the prime minister of Russia. Under his third term, Putin took other steps toward strengthening Russia's "power vertical." Control over public gatherings was tightened through higher fines for participation in unauthorized protests. A new law required NGOs that receive funding from abroad to register as foreign agents. Manipulation of nomination processes, changes in the electoral procedures, and restrictions on emerging parties enabled the ER to preserve its dominance over Russia's party politics.[18] The annexation of Crimea in 2014 and the economic sanctions helped Putin further consolidate his power by relying upon an anti-Western nationalist narrative.[19]

Increasing Assertiveness in Russian Foreign Policy

During this period, promoting multi-polarity and restoring Moscow's influence over the post-Soviet space remained among Russia's essential strategic goals, as emphasized in the national security documents.[20] The consolidation of Putin's power and Obama's retrenchment strategy decreased the domestic and international checks on Russia's international power projection. Compared with the previous period, Russia adopted a more assertive stance in protecting and furthering its strategic interests, especially in the post-Soviet region.

The revision of the U.S. foreign policy strategy under Obama enabled Russia to increase its influence primarily in the post-Soviet region and the Middle East. In Eastern Europe and post-Soviet space, the United States aimed to preserve and expand its influence without committing resources and taking risks. Following the war with Georgia, Obama's support for expanding NATO and the EU toward the post-Soviet space met with Russia's harsh response, increasing tensions in the Black Sea region.[21] Russia's assertiveness continued with the annexation of Ukraine's Crimea in 2014 and its military intervention in Syria in 2015. In both instances, Russia minimized the risk by using private military contractors, airstrikes, and the local militia, along with conducting hybrid wars. Moreover, the Eurasian Economic Union, modeled after the EU for the post-Soviet region, became effective in 2015.

In this period, despite Russia's continued willingness to develop trade relations, its decisive steps negatively affected its relations with Turkey. Russia continued to expand its partnership with Turkey on energy and trade despite conflicts of interest on several regional issues. When the South Stream was no longer viable due to the Ukrainian Crisis, Russia relied on Turkey and initiated the Turkish Stream. Furthermore, Turkey's objections to Russia's actions in Syria and the Black Sea regions did not deter Putin, who expected Turkey to adjust its strategy to the new regional balance of power. Turkey's non-recognition of the Crimean annexation as well as Turkey's continuing support to the Crimean Tatars in the peninsula did not make a game-changer impact on Russia's policies in the region. However, Turkey's downing of the Russian fighter jet was a turning point for Russia's consideration of Turkey. Following the incident, Russia embarked on an anti-Turkey campaign including economic sanctions and anti-Turkey propaganda at home and abroad.

TURKEY-RUSSIA RELATIONS

Regional Cooperation and Competition

The Middle East in the Context of the Syrian Crisis

The limited level of convergence in Turkey and Russia's perception of Arab Uprisings disappeared after the uprisings' flames reached Syria. Both countries adopted a positive stance toward the emergence of the Arab Uprisings in Tunisia and Egypt[22] and protested against NATO intervention in Libya.[23]

During the initial phase of the unrest in Syria, Turkey and Russia hoped that the Assad regime could mollify the domestic discontents.[24] Yet, the situation in Syria deteriorated rapidly with indiscriminate shelling of protesters, the polarization of Syrian society, and the defections from the Syrian Army, and the strengthening of radical terrorist groups.[25] In mid-2011, the Free Syrian Army,[26] an umbrella organization claiming to represent the opposition, was formed. However, it lost ground to more radical groups such as ISIS[27] and the YPG[28] from the early phases of the conflict.

Meanwhile, the Iran-backed militia and the Lebanese Hezbollah further negated the fighting force of the disunited opposition. In this period, the escalation of U.S. diplomatic pressure on the regime and strong signals from the Obama administration for a U.S. military involvement[29] created a false expectation that the Assad regime was about to fall, following the example of the Ghaddafi regime in Libya.[30] This expectation increased the diplomatic and military support toward the regime and the opposition. However, Syria was different from Libya, where the Ghaddafi regime faced larger defections and stronger international pressure. In effect, the expanded military conflict in Syria became a violent platform for several regional and global securitization dynamics (U.S.-Russia, Iran-Saudi Arabia, Shia-Sunni-Salafi/Jihadist, PKK-Turkey, etc.). As the conflict escalated, the conflict of interest between Turkey and Russia over the fate of Syria came to the surface.

Turkey's Syria policy changed in line with the course of the Syrian Civil War. Before the conflict, Turkey's relations with Syria had developed positively due to Turkey's initiatives per Turkey's "zero problems with neighbors" approach.[31] By April 2011, however, Turkey was frustrated with futile diplomatic efforts to convince Assad into a more serious process for dialogue and began to back the opposition by hosting the Syrian National Council (SNC) in İstanbul in August 2011.[32] However, Turkey's initiatives to foster a competent army of opposition failed. As a result of the unwillingness of the West to share the cost of the Syrian crisis with Turkey, the relations between Turkey and the EU and Turkey's relations with the United States substantially deteriorated since the year 2014. The EU did not honor its responsibilities in the Readmission Agreement, where Turkey guaranteed to accept back illegal immigrants who had passed through Turkish soil into Europe.[33] The emergence of the PYD/YPG and the ISIS along the Turkey-Syria border threatened Turkey's security with frequent terrorist attacks in its major cities.[34] The Patriot missiles placed on Turkey's border by Germany, the Netherlands, and the United States were pulled back in the year 2015 while Turkey was receiving almost daily missile attacks from across the border.[35] The United States tacitly approved the 2013 coup in Egypt against the elected pro-Turkey government. The United States also provided significant military support to the PYD to fight ISIS,[36] making the presence of the

United States in Syria a liability for Turkey, which saw in PYD an imminent security threat.

Before the Syrian Civil War, Russia had negligible economic relations with Syria, which hosted two small Russian military bases on Syria's Mediterranean coast.[37] But the escalation of the crisis created the conditions in the region where Russia could enforce its position in countering the U.S. global hegemony and promoting a multipolar world system by supporting the Assad regime. Moreover, with the legitimate Assad government on one side and Islamist rebels on the other, it was not hard for Russia to justify its allegiance. The opposition in Syria could be heavily securitized by Russia, which could draw similarities between the Syrian conflict, the Color Revolutions,[38] and the Chechen insurgency.[39] In line with this, having blocked several UNSC Resolution efforts against the Assad regime,[40] the Russian military directly intervened in the Syrian conflict in September 2015, effectively turning the tide in favor of the Assad Regime.

Until late 2015, incidents that raised the tensions in the Turkey-Russia nexus did not dramatically impact the general course of Turkey-Russia relations. In this period, the political authority of Turkey and Russia could handle several crises. The first prominent confrontation occurred when Syria shot down a Turkish reconnaissance jet in international waters in June 2012. In response to Assad and Putin's conciliatory statements,[41] Erdoğan accused Putin of using the language of the illegitimate Syrian regime.[42] In October 2012, Turkey forced a Damascus-bound commercial plane from Moscow to land in Ankara on suspicion that the plane was carrying illicit material to Syria.[43] Russia protested to Turkey for hindering the safety of Russians on the plane.[44] Russia also expressed discomfort toward the placement of Patriot missiles on the Turkey-Syria border, even though Putin also stated that Russia understands Turkey's security concerns.[45] Russia's military intervention in Syria would drastically change this trend.

Following significant losses suffered by the overstretched Syrian Army against the opposition in the summer of 2015, the Russian military intervened in Syria in September 2015. Although it was portrayed as a war against terrorism and ISIS by Russia, most Russian airstrikes targeted the northwest of Syria, where other rebel groups operate.[46] Russia's bombing of Turkmen villages, which had an ethnic affinity to Turks, created outrage in Turkey, which expressed its concerns to Russia.[47] To add insult to injury, in his speech at the seventieth session of UNGA in late September, Putin voiced his support for the PYD, noting that the Syrian regime and the YPG are the only forces fighting terrorists in Syria.[48] Such a discursive stance prompted a harsher response by Erdoğan.[49] Turkey also warned Russia multiple times about the border violations by the Russian fighter jets operating over the sinuous border between Turkey and Syria.[50]

The tensions between Turkey and Russia quickly escalated on November 24, 2015, when a Turkish F-16 shot down a Russian fighter jet flying over the Turkey-Syria border for violating Turkey's airspace.[51] In his first reaction to the incident, Erdoğan underlined that the plane was in breach of Turkey's border and was warned multiple times.[52] Putin described the incident as a "stab in the back by terrorist accomplices."[53] In its last attempt to use its alliance as leverage, Turkey called for a NATO meeting and sought support from the West. However, Turkey's pleas for help met with calls for calming down the tension by NATO.[54] Turkey's attempts to involve its NATO partners further aggravated Putin, who expected to resolve the matter on a bilateral basis.[55] Such stance from Russia developed as an extension of their strategy since the development of Turkey-Russia nexus on a bilateral basis would weaken Turkey's ties with the West. On Putin's invitation, the PYD opened a representative office in Moscow in the following process.[56] Russia activated the S-400 missile system at the Hmeymim airbase, closing Syrian airspace to Turkey, which was planning for a military operation in Northern Syria.[57] This process was posthumously called the Jet Crisis. The impact of the Jet Crisis was not confined to the confrontation between the two countries on the Turkish-Syrian border. Russia also placed economic sanctions on Turkey and initiated international propaganda against Turkey's Syria policy. The Jet Crisis made a significant negative impact on the dynamics of cooperation in Turkey-Russia relations.

The Black Sea Region and the Annexation of Crimea

Russia's annexation of Crimea and the course of the Syrian Civil War primarily affected Turkey-Russia relations over the Black Sea region in this period. Russia's actions in the Black Sea region substantially narrowed Turkey's maneuvering area. However, Turkey expected the issue in the Black Sea to be resolved between Russia and the West and did not show a strong reaction toward Russia's aggression. As with every segment of the bilateral relations, the tensions of the Jet Crisis briefly spilled over into the Black Sea region as well.

In late 2013, widespread protests erupted in Ukraine against the pro-Russian president Viktor Yanukovich, who had decided not to sign the Association Agreement with the EU in favor of a customs union agreement with Russia. Within the framework of its "sovereign democracy" concept, the Putin administration considered the protests as the meddling of the United States into Ukraine.[58] After Yanukovich fled to Russia, his coalition government was replaced by a pro-Western coalition. This transformation increased tensions and led to pro-Russian protests in the east of Ukraine and Crimea, home to over two hundred thousand Crimean Tatars and about 1.5 million Russians.[59]

In Eastern Ukraine, the violent clashes between the Ukrainian security forces and separatist militias persisted for months. Russia's activities in Eastern Ukraine and Crimea represented Russia's new approach toward war-making. In Crimea, Russian soldiers in unmarked green uniforms paved the way for the annexation without creating accountability and plausible deniability for the Russian government.[60] In Eastern Ukraine, Russia supported the local militia that eventually formed two separatist governments named Donetsk (DPR) and Luhansk People's Republics (LPR).[61]

In response to Russia's annexation of Crimea, the United States[62] and the EU[63] applied a series of economic sanctions, but the measures failed to deter Russia.[64] The economic sanctions and falling oil prices had a profound impact on the Russian economy. However, while Russia considered Ukraine as an area within its core security interests, it was not an issue that was worth going to war over with Russia for the Obama administration.[65] Therefore, the sanctions could not create a reversal in Russia's Ukraine policy. Meanwhile, through countersanctions on certain European products, Russia even boosted economic independence in its agriculture and defense sectors, especially in the agricultural sector.[66]

The events had profound implications on the Turkey-Russia nexus. Having established full control over the Crimean Peninsula, Russia deployed S-400 missiles and anti-ship cruise missiles there, establishing a formidable A2/AD (anti-access/area denial) in the Black Sea.[67] The military buildup in the peninsula also supported Russia's naval deployment through the Mediterranean in Syria as well.[68] Following the annexation, the Crimean Tatars' representative body was abolished, and the community faced immense persecution by the new Russian authorities of the peninsula.[69]

Despite the dramatic impact of the annexation of Crimea on its strategic interests in the Black Sea region, Turkey did not exhibit a strong reaction against Russia. Turkey's limited capability, its preoccupation with Syria, and Russia's determination also prevented a strong reaction from Turkey toward Russia's aggression. Therefore, Turkey expected the tensions to be resolved between the United States, EU, and Russia.[70] Turkey did not recognize the annexation but neither did it join the economic sanctions on Russia during the crisis.[71] In compliance with the Montreaux Convention, Turkey continued to limit the passage of military vessels from non-littoral countries to the Black Sea through the Straits.[72]

During the Jet Crisis, Turkey briefly sought to use the Black Sea as leverage against Russia. With a U-turn from Turkey's neutral stance, Erdoğan expressed his desire to see an increased role of NATO in the Black Sea region to prevent the Black Sea from becoming a Russian lake.[73] However, as with Turkey's pleas to NATO for support in Syria, Turkey's call for greater NATO involvement in the Black Sea fell on deaf ears. Turkey also sowed the seeds of stronger cooperation with Ukraine in this period. In May 2016, Turkey and Ukraine signed a military cooperation plan as a clear indication of collaboration against Russia.[74]

The Post-Soviet Region

The volatilities in their bilateral relations also reflected on how Turkey and Russia reacted to the developments in other parts of the post-Soviet region. In Central Asia and South Caucasus, Turkey continued to pursue its influence by developing economic, cultural, and political ties with the regional actors through bilateral and institutional ties. However, even though Russia continued to consider the post-Soviet region as its sphere of influence and took steps toward strengthening its hegemonic influence. It also did not consider Turkey's pursuit of economic and cultural influence as threatening its national interests.

In this period, the issue of Chechnya continued to be one of the hot issues between Turkey and Russia. Russia's dissatisfaction with Turkey's position regarding the Chechen issue increased as Chechen fighters began to use Turkey as a passage to Syria and Turkey's Chechen Diaspora continued to harbor Chechen refugees.[75] The activities of Chechen fighters within multiple radical organizations[76] and the subsuming of the Chechen insurgency by ISIS[77] influenced the elevation of the importance of the issue for Russia. Meanwhile, a series of assassinations of important personalities in the Chechen Diaspora in Turkey drew the reaction of Turkey's deputy prime minister, who stated that the Russian hand in the assassinations is a well-known secret.[78] During the Jet Crisis, Prime Minister Davutoğlu drew attention to Russia's Chechen issue by arguing that Russia's Syria vision is similar to the political arrangement in Chechnya.[79]

During the Jet Crisis, the renewed conflicts between Azerbaijan and Armenia in April 2016 created an occasion for Turkey and Russia to reassert their contrasting positions on Nagorno-Karabakh. The Azerbaijani military offensive, which was a long coming development due to the changing economic and demographic balance of power in the region, began on April 2, 2016, and ended after a few days with a unilateral cease-fire declared by Azerbaijan. Following these developments, Erdoğan blamed Russia and the Minsk Group's unjust and indecisive attitude and showed open support to the Azerbaijani forces.[80] In response, Russia's foreign minister Lavrov pointed out Turkey's one-sided approach and said Turkey should stop meddling in other states' affairs.[81] Russia, which had already increased support to Armenia before the conflict,[82] intervened as a peacemaker.

The modus vivendi between Turkey and Russia prevailed in Central Asia with Turkey's continuing recognition of Russia's primacy in the region.

Russia trumped up its efforts to increase its influence over the region through the Eurasian Economic Union, which entered into effect in 2015. Efforts to summon Turkic nations around a table provided a modest result with the foundation of the Turkic Council [Cooperation Council of Turkish Speaking Countries or Turkic Council] in 2009. With the Turkic Council gaining official status in 2011, a multilateral platform for intensified cultural ties between Central Asia and Turkey was established. The Jet Crisis negatively affected Turkey's trade relations with Central Asia after Russia blocked the passage of Turkish trucks. Considering the damage this tension did to the Central Asian economies, it was not surprising that Kazakh president Nazarbayev played an active role in the writing and delivering of Erdoğan's letter of regret to Putin.[83]

Trade Relations

As a result of their mutual commitment to compartmentalizing relations, bilateral trade continued to be the locomotive of Turkey-Russia relations despite tensions over the Syrian crisis. The further consolidation of Erdoğan and Putin's power and the establishment of the High-Level Cooperation Council contributed to the positive momentum in developing trade relations. Turkey's continuing dependence on gas imports from Russia and the trade deficit with Russia remained in place. Russia's upper hand in bilateral trade relations gained relevance during the Jet Crisis when Russia's economic sanctions played a significant role in changing Turkey's attitude.

Despite the disagreements over the Syrian crisis, Turkey and Russia expanded trade ties and preserved the bilateral trade volume until the Jet Crisis (see figure 3.1). Russian tourists visiting Turkey, Russia's agricultural imports from Turkey, and Turkey's gas imports from Russia made up the bulk of the bilateral trade volume. Three factors contributed to the resilience of trade relations. First, at this point, Turkey's imports from Russia reached the $20–25 billion range, and Russia's imports from Turkey reached the $5–7 billion range. The total trade volume reached to $25–30 billion range (see figure 3.1). These figures made it harder for both countries to ignore the existing trade ties despite the escalations of tensions over Syria. Second, the synergy between the two leaders and the shared commitment to increase bilateral trade volume to $100 billion also provided an impetus to the positive trend.[84] Third, the establishment of the High-Level Cooperation Council between Turkey and Russia in 2011 helped the coordination of bilateral trade relations with efforts from both governments.[85] Thus, Turkey and Russia carried on with the compartmentalization and maintained good economic relations until the Jet Crisis.

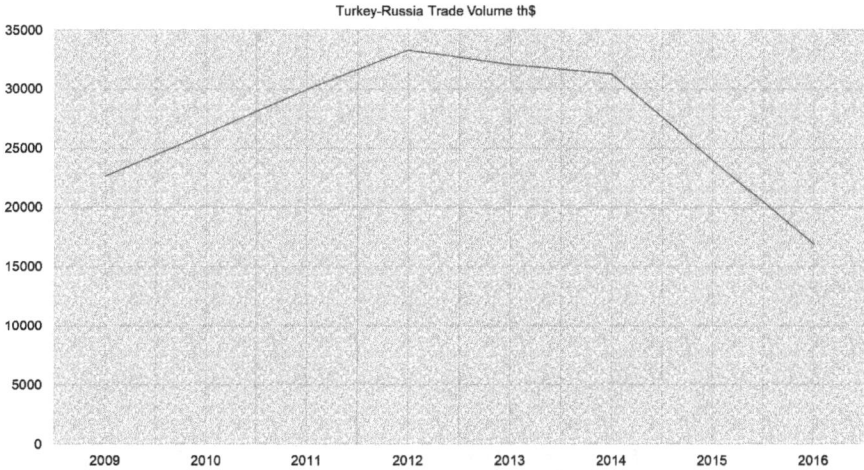

Figure 3.1   Turkey-Russia Trade Volume, 2009–2016. Source: "Dış Ticaret İstatistikleri" [Foreign Trade Statistics], Turkish Ministry of Trade, accessed April 10, 2022, https://ticaret .gov.tr/istatistikler/dis-ticaret-istatistikleri.

The Jet Crisis had a serious negative impact on the bilateral trade as Russia used its advantage in trade ties as leverage against Turkey on an unprecedented scale. Immediately after Turkey's shooting down of the Russian jet on November 24, 2015, Putin signed an executive order announcing an extensive economic sanctions package that included a ban or restriction of charter flights, suspension of package tours to, and imports from Turkey.[86] Subsequently, the package was expanded to include restrictions on Russian firms controlled by Turkish citizens.[87] The sanctions caused a significant drop in Russia's imports from Turkey and Russian tourists visiting Turkey (see figures 3.2 and 3.3). The existence of many hotels and firms whose business was based on their ability to serve Russians weakened Turkey's hand.[88] Moreover, Turkey could not threaten Russia with cutting gas exports. In fact, at this point, Turkey's concern was planning to cope with a scenario where Russia cut the natural gas supply.[89]

Energy Relations

Turkey as a Hub? TANAP and Turk Stream

Within the framework of its aim to become an energy hub and bolster its regional influence, Turkey continued to strengthen its energy cooperation both with the West and Russia. In this period, the deterioration of Russia's relations with Ukraine created opportunities for Turkey. Meanwhile, the SGC gained a significant addition to Azerbaijan's TANAP (Trans-Anatolian Pipeline) initiative.

Turkey - Russia Trade Deficit

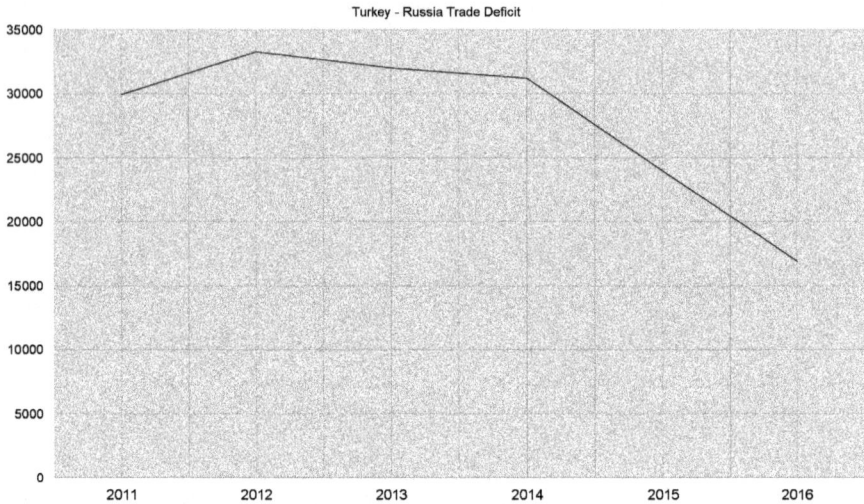

Figure 3.2 Turkey's Trade Deficit with Russia, 2009–2016. Source: "Dış Ticaret İstatistikleri" [Foreign Trade Statistics], Turkish Ministry of Trade, accessed April 10, 2022, https://ticaret.gov.tr/istatistikler/dis-ticaret-istatistikleri.

Number of Russian Tourists Visiting Turkey

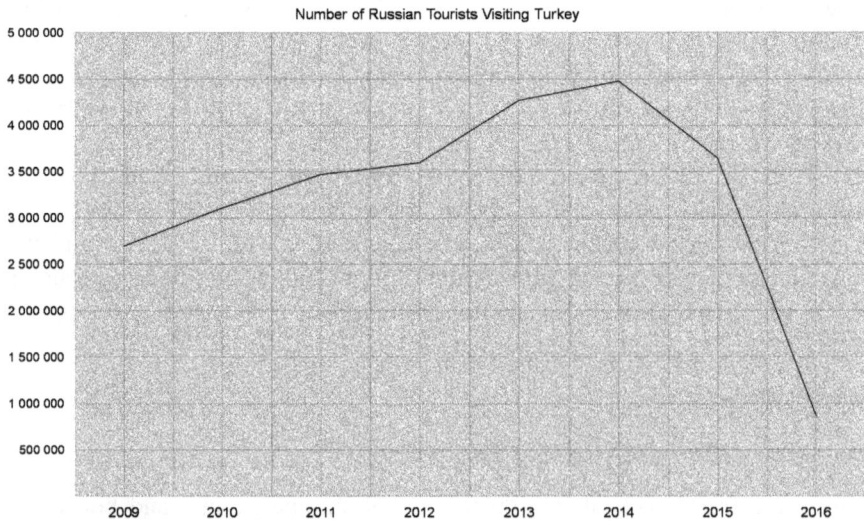

Figure 3.3 Number of Russian Tourists Visiting Turkey, 2009–2016. Source: "Sınır Giriş Çıkış İstatistikleri" [Border Crossing Statistics], Turkish Ministry of Culture and Tourism, accessed March 30, 2022, https://yigm.ktb.gov.tr/TR-9854/sinir-giris-cikis-istatistikleri .html.

Russia considered Turkey as an alternative route for the South Stream to avoid harsh EU regulations, making it harder for the EU countries to host Russian pipelines even through intergovernmental agreements and circumvent Ukraine after the crisis.[90] During his visit to Turkey in 2014, Putin announced Russia's Turkish Stream Pipeline Project, which was welcomed in Turkey. Following this announcement, however, the project ran into some problems with an escalation of disagreements over the price of gas between BOTAŞ and Gazprom, which led to the suspension of talks in July 2015.[91] In contrast to most issues in bilateral relations, the tension caused by the Jet Crisis did not have a decisive impact on the negotiation process for the Turkish Stream. The disruption in the agreement over the price was settled in April 2016.[92]

In 2011, Azerbaijan initiated the Trans-Anatolian Pipeline Project (TANAP) to transport Azerbaijani oil to Europe across Turkish land. In 2012, Turkey and Azerbaijan signed the Intergovernmental Agreement for TANAP, and the project effectively ended Nabucco. Following the approval of TANAP by the Turkish Parliament in 2013, the groundbreaking ceremony was held in March 2015. TANAP created a rival pipeline network for EU's gas imports and decreased Turkey's dependence on Russia. (See figure 3.4.)

Figure 3.4 TurkStream and TANAP Pipelines. Source: Mapbox, accessed March 30, 2022, www.mapbox.com/about/maps.

Akkuyu Nuclear Power Plant

Another important segment of the energy cooperation between Russia and Turkey that formed in this period was the cooperation for the construction of the Akkuyu NPP in Turkey.[93] Akkuyu NPP emerged due to Turkey's long-running desire to launch its nuclear capacity. After decades of efforts to realize the construction of a nuclear power plant, Turkey declared its intention to build one and invited foreign companies for investment proposals. Upon Russia's demonstration of interest in Turkey's need, intergovernmental talks started and then finalized with an agreement between Russia and Turkey in 2010. In the following process, the Russian company that was founded to carry out the project obtained relevant construction permits from Turkish authorities and the project started. Within the framework of the agreement, dozens of Turkish students were sent to Russia to gain an engineering education, which would enable them to work at Akkuyu.

This project has added yet another dimension to the cooperation between Turkey and Russia. Given the strategic nature of nuclear energy, the project could be considered as one more indication of how far Turkey-Russia relations have progressed. The construction of Akkuyu NPP was not affected by the Jet Crisis with Putin referring to the project as strictly commercial.[94]

COOPERATION AT GLOBAL LEVEL

In this period, the souring of relations between Turkey and the West caused Turkey to reconsider its place in global politics. The most visible symptom of this trend was Turkey's membership bid to the Shanghai Cooperation Organization (SCO). Having emerged as a regional organization focusing on border security issues in 1996, the SCO transformed into a multilateral organization with the economic rise of China and the deterioration of relations between Russia and the West. In 2012, Turkey's became a dialogue partner in the SCO. Even though this development did not give Turkey any substantial responsibility, the way Turkey perceived the SCO demonstrated its potential impact on the Turkey-Russia-West triangle. During his visit to Moscow in 2013, Erdoğan shared his exchange with Putin about this issue. He stated: "I said to Russian President Vladimir Putin, 'You tease us, saying, "What [is Turkey] doing in the EU?" Now I tease you: Include us in the Shanghai Five, and we will forget about the EU.'"[95] Even though Erdoğan's overtures did not lead to Turkey's membership in SCO, his remarks were significant by showing the discursive turn in Turkish foreign policy.

CONCLUSION

The period from 2009 to 2016 was one of the few occasions in history when Turkey had unfavorable relations with both Russia and the West. This situation arose as a result of the change in U.S. foreign policy toward a diminished involvement in the Middle East and the Black Sea, the conflict of interest between Turkey and the United States within the framework of regional turbulence caused by the Syrian Civil War, and Russia's increasing assertiveness. Most importantly, Turkey's maladaptation to these regional and global changes and insisting upon its foreign policy strategy brought about a situation where Turkey had to deal with multiple challenges in isolation.[96]

The stiffening of tensions in Syria, the involvement of non-state actors in the conflict, and the increasing political and military investments to the opposing sides, from both parties, created a profound challenge to Turkey-Russia relations. The escalation of conflict made it harder for Turkey and Russia to ignore their differences in Syria and carry on with partnership in energy and trade. In this process, the mixed signals coming from the United States about an intervention, as well as the widespread expectation that Assad's fall was near, played very significant roles in the process by encouraging all sides of the conflict to increase their efforts to ensure their regional, political, and security interests. The developments in the post-Soviet space remained under the shadow of more prominent developments in Syria. While Russia strengthened its impact in the region, Turkey, Central Asia, and the Caucasus remained regions of secondary importance compared to the Middle East.

In this period, Russia's upper hand in bilateral trade between Turkey and Russia gained relevance as a result of Russia's manipulation of its advantageous position in trade relations to force concessions on other issues. During the Jet Crisis, Russia's using sanctions as leverage for political ends showed that the compartmentalization of relations between Turkey and Russia had its limits.

The continuing mutual trust, intensifying trade ties, and strengthening of the synergy between the two leaders led to two important energy projects. The Akkuyu NPP was initiated as a result of Russia's interest in Turkey's decades-long plan to have its own nuclear energy source, while the Turkish Stream emerged as a result of Russia's desire to circumvent Ukraine and rely on Turkey as a transit country for transfer of its natural gas.

Chapter 4

Turkey-Russia Relations in 2016–2022

This chapter examines Turkey-Russia relations in the years 2016 through 2022. In this period, the *stimulus* that played the most significant role in shaping the bilateral relations stemmed from Turkey's domestic politics. The July 2016 coup attempt brought about a substantial change in Turkey's foreign policy strategy by encouraging the Turkish leadership to pursue a comparatively more independent foreign policy strategy from Turkey's Western allies. In this period, the continuing U.S. support to the YPG in Syria and its providing haven to the Gülen Movement caused Turkey to reconsider the place of the United States in its security calculations. Such a process significantly strengthened the strategic cooperation between Turkey and Russia. Despite the continuing conflicts of interest between the two countries on several regional issues, Turkey took drastic steps to improve its cooperation with Russia. The trilateral mechanism between Turkey, Russia, and Iran on Syria and Turkey's purchase of the S-400 missile defense system from Russia developed due to this trend.

The change in Turkey's foreign policy in this period enabled Turkey and Russia to deepen their partnerships in bilateral trade and their cooperation in restoring peace in Syria. On the other hand, the change in Turkey's foreign policy also encouraged Turkey to pursue its interests more assertively in the regions where the interests of Turkey and Russia conflicted. For Russia, deepening cooperation with Turkey was a positive development for its own attempts to diminish the U.S. global hegemonic influence. Yet, in the absence of a solid Western involvement, Russia appeared as a hegemonic player to check Turkey's ambitions by limiting Turkey's influence in the Middle East, the Black Sea, and the post-Soviet regions.

This chapter starts with an appraisal of the era where I summarize the main dynamics that influenced Turkey-Russia relations. I then analyze the changes in cooperation/competition dynamics between Turkey and Russia in multiple selected regions. Finally, I examine the developments in trade and energy relations and the narrowing of differences in Turkey and Russia's global projections (see figure 0.2, in the introduction).

APPRAISAL OF THE ERA

Regional and Global Context

In this period, the continuing turbulence in the Middle East, the Black Sea, and the South Caucasus provided Turkey and Russia opportunities to further their regional influence. The continuation of the decrease in U.S. security commitments in the region complemented this trend. In this period, the new U.S. president, Donald Trump, continued Obama's foreign policy toward the Middle East and the Black Sea. He called for reducing global U.S. military and economic spending. President Biden did not change course. At the same time, the U.S. foreign policy establishment tended to retain the leadership role of the United States in Western international institutions.[1] Friction and disharmony in the U.S. foreign policy decision-making mechanism paved the way for Turkey and Russia to deepen their partnership further and increase their regional influence outside of the West's control.

The resolution of the Jet Crisis and the synergy between the two leaders enabled Turkey and Russia to repair trade relations while intensifying their bilateral partnership. In July 2016, Turkey averted a bloody coup attempt masterminded by the members of the Gülen Movement. After the coup attempt, Erdoğan made his first diplomatic visit to Russia and met with Putin in Moscow, where the two leaders pledged themselves to a complete recovery of the bilateral relations from the impact of the Jet Crisis.[2] In the following months, Russia began to lift the economic sanctions on Turkey and enabled the High-Level Cooperation Council meetings to restart. The bilateral trade volume also grew. The assassination of Russia's ambassador to Turkey, Andrey Karlov, by a Turkish police officer in December 2016, and Russia's killing of three Turkish soldiers in Syria in February 2017 did not drastically negatively impact on Turkey-Russia relations. The Astana Process, in which Turkey, Russia, and Iran participated, became a main venue for Syria's restructuring. The ties in the defense sector significantly deepened with Turkey's purchase of the S-400 missile defense system from Russia, despite strong U.S. opposition. Despite the competition over the Caspian energy sources and influence in the Black Sea and the Middle East, Turkey and Russia sustained intense diplomatic communication. When Russia started the invasion of Ukraine in February 2022, and faced sanctions from the West, Turkey came forward to facilitate the negotiations between Ukraine and Russia.

Following the emergence of COVID-19 as a "pandemic" in March 2020,[3] nations across the globe took steps toward preventing the further spread of the disease in their own countries by closing down borders. The precautions impacted Turkey-Russia relations by decreasing bilateral trade and preventing diplomatic visits for several months. The conflict in Syria was frozen for several months while the Second Nagorno-Karabakh War occurred during the pandemic. The global restrictions began to ease in 2021 after a peak in 2020.

Domestic Context and the Foreign Policy Strategy of Turkey

The Establishment of Executive Presidency under Erdoğan

On July 15, 2016, a faction within the Turkish army led by the members of the Gülen Movement attempted to take over the government by killing or capturing Erdoğan, control state institutions, and intimidating the public.[4] On the night of July 16, the coup plotters killed dozens of resisting civilians, bombed the Turkish parliament, and kidnapped the Turkish chief of staff to convince him to lead the coup. By the morning, however, the coup was suppressed with the active involvement of Turkish citizens who went out to protest the coup plotters. Erdoğan, who was the primary target of the coup plotters, narrowly escaped assassination and played the most significant role in suppressing the coup by inviting everyone onto the streets to show opposition to the attempted coup.[5] The night of the coup attempt had a strong psychological impact on the Turkish citizens and decision makers. Having survived the coup, Erdoğan declared a state of emergency, which enabled the government to shut down Gülenist schools, companies, and endowments. The state also fired thousands of government employees accused of being members of the Gülen Movement.[6]

In the context of Erdoğan's increasing popularity and power within the framework of the post-coup political atmosphere, Turkey officially adopted a presidential system following a referendum in April 2017.[7] The system came into force after the early elections in June 2018. Erdoğan became the first president with the support of the MHP (Nationalist Movement Party— *Milliyetçi Hareket Partisi*).[8] The transition empowered the president within Turkey's political system. The alliance with the nationalist MHP facilitated Erdoğan to pursue his agenda of creating a strong and effective state. Although Erdoğan's power over Turkish politics and bureaucracy considerably grew in the post-coup political atmosphere, Turkey's economic preferences and political quarrels with the United States deteriorated the Turkish economy. Under these conditions, AK Party lost the municipalities of Ankara and Istanbul to the opposition in the 2019 local elections. Meanwhile, as a result of the global rise of commodity prices during the pandemic, Turkey's insistence of low interest policy, frequent changes of economy minister and Central Bank governors, Turkey's economy deteriorated. As a result of this process, Turkish Lira lost 75 percent of its value between 2018 and 2022.

The "Independent" Turn in Turkish Foreign Policy

In this period, Turkey adopted a far more independent foreign policy strategy to resolve its immediate security concerns stemming from Syria. The first step toward the beginning of such a turn was Erdoğan's letter of regret[9] to Putin. The Western attitude toward the coup attempt[10] and the residence of Fetullah Gülen in the United States strengthened the belief in Turkey's necessity to fend for itself,[11] a major dormant dynamic of the Turkish strategic culture.[12] Regarding this, in October 2016, Erdoğan stated, "Turkey has left behind an incorrect notion of security. From now on, we will not wait for the problems to come and knock on our door. Instead, we face our own problems."[13] Within the framework of this change, Turkey would feel far less constrained by the Western preferences when forming alliances, conducting cross-border military operations, developing its independent defense industry, and fighting with the Gülen Movement, ISIS, and the PKK at home and abroad. As a representation of its revisionist approach toward the global system, Turkey also adopted "The World Is Bigger Than Five" as a motto and drew attention to the failure of the UNSC in promoting global peace and justice and a rather pluralist world system.[14]

The shift in the foreign policy strategy brought significant changes in Turkey's foreign policy conduct. Between 2016 and 2022, Turkey conducted four major military operations in Syria, provided substantial military and political support to the UN–recognized Libyan government, and assisted Azerbaijan in the Second Nagorno-Karabakh War. Turkey also deepened relations with Georgia and Ukraine to balance Russia in the Black Sea, and remained adamant in protecting its offshore exploration rights in the Eastern Mediterranean. Despite the convergence of interest between the West and Turkey in several issues and regions, the level of cooperation between the West and Turkey remained low. At the earlier phase of the COVID-19 outbreak, Turkey delivered aid to 138 countries to boost its soft power and international status as an independent power.[15] Turkey also managed the production of various weaponry,[16] which enabled the Turkish Armed Forces to intervene in regional crises through its army and armaments directly.[17] Turkish UAVs and UACVs played a significant role in Turkey's military operations in Syria. Turkey also exported its UAVs to Libya, Azerbaijan, and Ukraine, directly influencing the conflicts in these areas.

These steps substantially harmed Turkey's relations with the United States, which opposed Turkey's newfound activism. Moreover, the arrest and imprisonment of an American evangelical pastor in Turkey,[18] the continuing residence of Fetullah Gülen in Pennsylvania, a trial against *Halkbank* in the United States,[19] and Turkey's decision to purchase the S-400 missile defense system from Russia further worsened the U.S.-Turkey bilateral relations in this period.

Turkey deepened its partnership with Russia in the context of its deteriorating relations with the West and the regional dynamics stemming from the Syrian crisis. Putin did not see eye–to–eye with Erdoğan on multiple regional issues. Yet, he did not contest Turkey's "independent" foreign policy strategy. He was also one of the first leaders to call Erdoğan to offer his support and advance the idea that there was U.S. involvement in the coup attempt.[20] Most importantly, the rising influence of Russia in Syria compelled Turkey to work with Russia. Turkey also did not follow the lead of the United States by joining economic sanctions against Russia following Russia's invasion of Ukraine. Turkey continued to challenge Russia in multiple regions, and Russia did not always give the green light to Turkey in its efforts to expand its regional influence.

Domestic Context and the Foreign Policy Strategy of Russia

Putin's Presidency Continues

In this period, Putin's domestic power further strengthened. In the 2016 Legislative Elections, the ER, headed by Prime Minister Medvedev, increased its seats by 105, reaching a comfortable majority in the Duma. In the 2018 presidential elections, Putin was elected the president of Russia once again with the support of 76 percent of the votes. Meanwhile, Russia's economy considerably worsened in this period. Aside from the sanctions, the falling oil rates resulting from conflict with Saudi Arabia followed by the COVID-19 outbreak also damaged Russia's flow of revenue.[21] As a result of the worsening economy and the controversial pension reform, which raised the retirement age, multiple country-wide protests emerged, joined by millions of people across Russia between 2017 and 2019.[22] The protests did not produce a concrete challenge to Putin's rule, but they represented the growing discontent in a portion of the population.

In January 2020, Putin unveiled his plans to make a series of changes[23] to the Russian Constitution.[24] The proposed constitution reiterated the president's role as the ruler of the country by lowering the authority of the prime minister over his or her own cabinet while strengthening the Parliament.[25] Following the declaration of the changes, Medvedev resigned along with his cabinet, and Putin replaced him with the little-known head of the Russian Federal Tax Service, Sergey Mishutin. Aside from facilitating a smooth transition to the new system, with this move, Putin also eliminated Medvedev as a potential future alternative to him.[26] Meanwhile, a new amendment reset Putin's served presidential terms to zero, paving the way for him to serve as president until 2036.[27] Although this amendment did not clearly respond to the question of whether Putin will run for president in 2024, it guaranteed Putin's control over Russia's political elites until 2024.

Maturing of Russian Foreign Policy Strategy

In this period, Russia maintained its core foreign policy principles and continued to aim for dominance in the post-Soviet region and multipolarity in the world political system. In this period, the further erosion of the U.S. foreign policy influence enabled Russia to increase its regional influence from the Caucasus to North Africa. Despite Trump's favorable comments about Putin,[28] and his (later retracted) comments on the irrelevance of NATO,[29] the poisoning of the U.S. foreign policy decision-making mechanism on issues regarding Russia,[30] due to the allegations of Russian interference in the U.S. elections to help Trump win the elections,[31] harmed the U.S.-Russia relations. On the other hand, the U.S. foreign policy strategy provided an advantage to Russia in multiple regions. As the United States prioritized China at the expense of the Middle East and Eastern Europe, Russia gladly filled the power vacuum by becoming an effective player in a wide region spanning from Africa to the Baltics. In those regions, Russia competed with Turkey, which mostly faced more pressure from the West, particularly from France and the United States, than from Russia.

In this period, Russia continued to protect its interests and expand its influence in multiple regions. Until the invasion of Ukraine in 2022, Russia preferred flexible responses toward the developments in the Middle East and the post-Soviet regions instead of direct, assertive, and unilateral military interventions. In this period, Russia pursued its interests in Syria through the Astana Process, supported Khalifa Haftar in Libya albeit through mercenaries, and intervened in the Second Nagorno-Karabakh War only as a power broker after the Azerbaijani army recaptured most of the occupied region. Despite being relatively less aggressive, Russia continued to protect its redlines in Ukraine and Georgia by objecting to their closer ties with NATO and not retreating in Abkhazia, South Ossetia, or Crimea.[32] In such an environment, Trump's scrapping START, and INF nuclear agreements caused Russia to adopt more aggressive naval[33] and nuclear[34] doctrines. In 2022, Russia's aggressive turn gained another dimension with the invasion of Ukraine.

Russia continued to consider Turkey an important regional power to construct arrangements to deter Western hegemonic control at the global and regional levels. Within the framework of its flexible regional foreign policy,

Russia cooperated with Turkey in Syria and did not take dramatic steps to deter Turkey from increasing its influence in the Black Sea. Turkey also became one of the few countries to which Russia agreed to sell the S-400 missile system, indicating the strategic partnership between the two countries. Russia also enabled Turkey to play an important role as "good offices provider" during Russia's negotiations with Ukraine. Despite the deepening of regional partnership, Russia did not grant Turkey excessive regional influence by putting limitations to Turkey's political and strategic regional influence.

TURKEY-RUSSIA RELATIONS

Regional Cooperation and Competition

The Middle East in the Context of the Astana Process and Turkey's Cross–Border Operations

The Syrian Civil War remained the most crucial segment of bilateral relations in this period. But Turkey's attitude toward the conflict changed. With the further diminishing of U.S. influence on the ground in Syria, the relevance of the dynamics of the Turkey-Russia nexus gained additional significance. Despite their contrasting interests, Turkey cooperated with Russia in resolving the crisis through the Astana Process, a trilateral platform also joined by Iran. Meanwhile, within the framework of its assertive foreign policy strategy and with the help of its more robust defense industry, Turkey conducted four major military operations in Syria.

Following the Jet Crisis's resolution and the July 15 coup attempt, Operation Euphrates Shield (*Fırat Kalkanı*) became the first of Turkey's operations in Northern Syria. The Euphrates Shield operation targeted the ISIS-controlled territories in the towns of Jarabulus and Al-Bab (see figure 4.1). During the operation, which ran from August 24, 2016, until February 2017, the normalization process with Russia was still ongoing, so Turkey could not take full benefit of its air power resources.[35] The United States also gave the green light to the operation and also agreed to Turkey's red line regarding the YPG forces' staying east of the Euphrates River.[36] The Turkish Armed Forces conducted the operation with local opposition forces and limited support from U.S. and Russian airstrikes.[37] In February 2017, a Russian airstrike in Al-Bab killed three Turkish soldiers. The incident paved the way for deepening military cooperation in Syria to prevent similar occurrences.[38] By the end of the operation, the Euphrates Shield forces had captured the strategic cities of Jarablus and Al-Bab from ISIS. However, there were limits to how much control the United States and Russia would allow Turkey to have

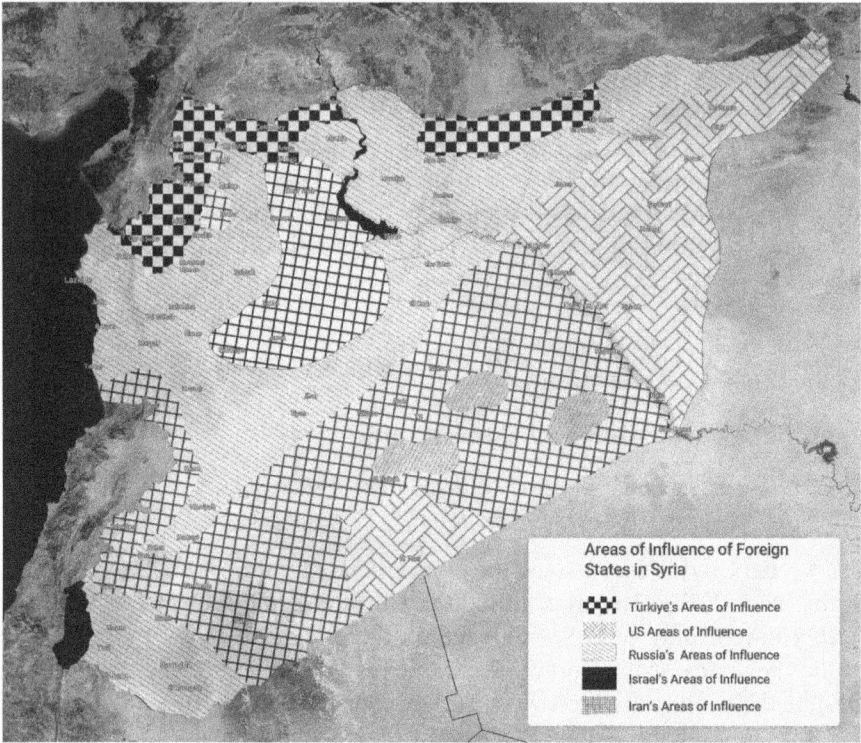

Figure 4.1   Areas of Influence in Syria. Source: Mapbox, accessed on August 30, 2021, www.mapbox.com/about/maps.

in Syria. Regime forces and the PYD prevented the Euphrates Shield forces from advancing further into the south beyond Al-Bab (see figure 4.1 for the operation's borders).

The Astana Process offered a platform for Turkey, Russia, and Iran to work together to deescalate the conflict in Syria and ensure their security interests in proportion to their influence. In December 2016, the intense diplomatic contacts and negotiations between Turkey and Iran enabled opposition fighters and civilians from Eastern Aleppo to move to Idlib.[39] One week after this agreement, the foreign ministers of Russia, Turkey, and Iran met in Moscow and signed the Moscow Declaration, committing to support a new negotiation process between the opposition and the Assad Regime. This declaration laid the Astana Process's groundwork, which commenced with the first meeting on January 23, 2017, in Astana, Kazakhstan's capital. In the fourth meeting, the parties agreed to create four deescalation zones within the rebel-held areas in Syria. By reassuring Russia and Iran, Turkey could eliminate PYD and ISIS from Northern Syria. Increasing Turkish control in Northern Syria would augment its border security by weakening the PYD. By engaging in partnership with Turkey in Syria, Russia could consolidate its political and military influence in the Middle East and contain the U.S. hegemonic influence by acting as a power broker and alienating Turkey from the United States. The United States considered the Astana Process as a Russian attempt to steer the peace process away from Geneva.[40] Nevertheless, the Astana Process acted as the main forum for the negotiations between Turkey, Russia, Iran, the Assad Regime, and the Syrian rebels.

The PYD-controlled Afrin province in Northwestern Syria was Turkey's next target for a military operation. In addition to the security threat posed by the PYD, the Afrin province had geoeconomic significance as the Northwesternmost corner of Syria near the Mediterranean Sea, well-positioned to act as a transit location for energy pipelines in the future (see figure 4.1). The Olive Branch (*Zeytin Dalı*) operation began in January 2018. In contrast to the situation during the Euphrates Shield operation, Turkey used a better organized and more professional local militia as well as extensive air power, which would not have been possible without Russia's tacit approval. Turkish UAVs and UACVs also played a crucial role in collecting intelligence and neutralizing targets. For Russia, which began to consider the increasing U.S. support toward the PYD in Afrin as a provocation,[41] the best-case scenario was restoring regime control over the area. For this purpose, Russia approached the PYD to hand over the area to the Assad Regime.[42] When the PYD insisted on defending the area from the Olive Branch forces, Russia attempted to mediate between Turkey and the Assad Regime to establish regime control over Afrin, but Erdoğan immediately rebuked this proposal, moving forward with the operation.[43] The Olive Branch forces completed the combat phase of the operation in March 2018 with the capture of Afrin province.

In 2018, the regime forces captured three of the four rebel-held territories, despite their designation as deescalation areas in Astana. In April 2018, due to the rapid advancement of the regime forces in the Eastern Ghouta suburb of Damascus, the rebel forces surrendered and evacuated to Idlib and Al-Bab.[44] A similar scenario played out in Homs in May[45] and Deraa in July.[46] This process turned Idlib into an overburdened massive refugee camp with around 3.3 million people, who had already migrated multiple times. To maintain the situation in Idlib, Turkey built twelve, Russia built ten, and Iran built seven military observation posts around the province.[47] The situation posed a danger for Turkey since the coming regime offensive would create another wave of refugees toward the country. To alleviate the situation, in October 2018, Erdoğan and Putin signed the Sochi Memorandum, whereby Turkey promised to remove terrorist groups from Idlib and the opening of the M4 and M5 highways[48] in exchange for the preservation of the status quo via

Russia's prevention of the Syrian regime's military offensive.[49] The emphasis on the Adana Agreement[50] in the Sochi Memorandum indicated the Russian desire to push Turkey to resolve the matter with the Syrian regime.

Meanwhile, as of late 2018, in Manbij, the PYD-held territory between Al-Bab and the Euphrates River, Turkey and the United States could not agree on a solution. Having failed to enable the removal of the YPG forces from the region, the United States proposed to maintain the security of the province together with Turkey through independent and coordinated patrols. Within the framework of an agreement, Turkish and U.S. armed forces conducted patrols in late 2018.[51] In the meantime, Turkey continued its preparations for a new operation in Northern Syria toward the east of the Euphrates River. At this juncture, in December 2018, with a surprising declaration, Trump declared that the U.S. troops would "return home" after the "historic victory" against ISIS.[52] Following this decision, the U.S. secretary of defense, Jim Mattis, and the U.S. envoy to the Coalition Against ISIS, Brett McGurk, resigned, an indication of the disorder in the U.S. foreign policy-making administration.[53] After months of diplomacy, the execution of Trump's earlier decision came with another surprising declaration stating that Turkey's next military operation would begin on October 6, 2019.[54] Turkey initiated the Peace Spring (*Barış Pınarı*) operation three days later and began to capture the area between Tal-Abyad and Rasulayn. Left without the protection of the U.S. forces, YPG abandoned the control of Manbij province to the Syrian regime forces to prevent the area from being Turkey's next target.[55] Finally, on October 22, with an agreement reached between Turkey and Russia, the Assad forces moved to the border area between Turkey and Syria outside the Tal-Abyad-Rasualyn line (see figure 4.1).[56]

Despite the Sochi Memorandum, Turkey and Russia's Idlib issue remained unresolved. In April 2019, the Syrian regime forces initiated a military operation to capture the highways of Idlib. The operation started with Russian and Syrian airstrikes on rebel positions.[57] The Syrian regime forces captured several villages and hilltops during the offensive, encircled one Turkish observation post, and conducted an airstrike on a Turkish convoy.[58] After multiple attempts for a cease-fire, through meetings between Turkish and Russian officials, the Syrian regime declared a unilateral cease-fire on August 30, 2019.[59] But the offensive resumed in December 2019. By February 2020, the Syrian forces had killed eight Turkish soldiers and encircled multiple other Turkish observation posts.[60] Moreover, the advance of the Syrian regime forces created a flow of refugees to the rebel-controlled part of Idlib, further deteriorating the humanitarian situation in the province. The Turkish army did not actively fight to push back the offensive until this point.

On February 27, 2020, an airstrike on a military post that hosted more than a hundred Turkish soldiers killed at least thirty-three Turkish soldiers, injuring several others. Upon allegations over the Russian forces' culpability, the Russian defense ministry stated that the Syrian regime conducted the airstrikes and that Turkey had not revealed Turkish soldiers' presence in the area to Russia.[61] Contesting Russia's claim, Turkish defense minister Hulusi Akar claimed that Russia was well informed about the Turkish soldiers' location. Regardless, Turkey avoided openly accusing Russia of targeting Turkish soldiers. Operation Spring Shield (*Bahar Kalkanı*) began on the same day to push back the Syrian regime forces from the recently captured areas in Idlib province. The Spring Shield forces recaptured the strategic Saraqib town at the intersection of the M4 and M5 highways during the operation. They reportedly killed hundreds of Syrian regime forces.[62] On March 5, 2020, after a meeting between Erdoğan and Putin, a cease-fire agreement was announced. Within the framework of the agreement, the regime forces kept the captured areas plus the strategic Saraqib town, ensuring control of the M5 highway. The M5 highway also opened under Russia and Turkey's supervision through joint patrols (see figure 4.1).

The agreement left a small territory with 3.3 million refugees, stripped from access to strategic highways to the rebel forces in Idlib. The presence of radical groups in the area also remained a potential occasion for an operation by the regime forces. The Syrian regime offensive on Idlib did not resume in the following months, partially due to the COVID–19 outbreak. Turkey, Russia, and Iran also prioritized dealing with the pandemic. They did not push for a change in the status quo. During the height of the pandemic, the Astana Summit was held virtually through videoconference on July 1, 2020.[63] The next Astana Summit would convene one year later. As a result of these series of conflicts, Syria became a contested space among a number of regional powers plus Russia and the United States (see figure 4.1).

Eastern Mediterranean in the Context of the Libyan Civil War

The overthrow of Ghaddafi in 2011 did not bring stability to Libya. In 2014, the UN-recognized Government of National Accord (GNA) led by President Fayez Al-Serraj was formed in Libya's capital Tripoli. However, this government was challenged by former Libyan general Khalifa Haftar. Having failed to take over the government with two coup attempts in 2014, Haftar moved to Eastern Libya and established control in the oil-rich regions of Northeastern Libya through his self-designated Libyan National Army (LNA). The Libyan conflict was internationalized, with Turkey, Italy, and to some extent Qatar backing the GNA and France, Russia, Egypt, and UAE backing the LNA.

Turkey and Russia picked their sides in the Libya conflict as per their securitization dynamics and foreign policy strategies. The GNA formed as a government after Ghaddafi's deposition and signified the last stronghold of Turkey's competition for regional influence with the United Arab Emirates (UAE) Saudi Arabia, since the beginning of the so-called Arab Uprisings process.[64] The exclusive economic zone agreement between Turkey and Libya, which will be analyzed under the relevant section below, gave another reason for Turkey to back the GNA. Haftar's visit to Russia in 2015, where he offered them access to Libya's natural resources, reportedly shaped Russia's Libya policy.[65] Within the framework of its global strategy, increasing its political influence over Libya would serve Russia's aim to foster global multipolarity by confronting Western hegemony. Haftar also appealed to Russia's securitization dynamics by promising to "drive out Islamists" when he first emerged as a renegade general in 2014.[66] From 2015 onward, Russia supported Haftar by printing money for his self-declared government, blocking UNSC resolutions to condemn Haftar's army's atrocities, and sending mercenaries to support him (through Wagner, a Russian private military contractor, whose members in Libya were paid by the UAE).[67] Following the advance of Haftar's forces on Tripoli in April 2019, with the help of the Wagner forces and UAE drones,[68] Turkey began to increase its political and military support to GNA.[69]

The escalation of the conflict opened another front in the map of regional competition between Turkey and Russia. Meanwhile, under the Trump administration, the United States further diminished its involvement in Libya; a step criticized for paving the way for Russia's increased influence through Haftar.[70] Trump also called Haftar and supported his effort to "ensure stability in Libya" during the offensive against GNA forces toward Tripoli in April 2019.[71] Against the backdrop of the intense clashes in Libya, Turkey and Russia attempted to broker a cease-fire deal between the legitimate Libyan government and Haftar. The parties met in Moscow in January 2020 and worked on a potential agreement, yet, the sudden departure of Haftar from Moscow, amid the negotiations, ended the initiative.[72] This was a significant representation of Turkey and Russia's concerted effort to form alternative platforms for the resolution of international conflicts. Haftar would sign a cease-fire agreement in the Berlin Conference, under the auspices of the UN, a few days later. Meanwhile, the EU propped up its efforts to impose an arms embargo through Operation IRINI's military mission with France, Italy, Greece, and Germany.[73] Turkey vehemently criticized this step and blamed Operation IRINI for enabling the arms *en route* to Haftar to pass while blocking those for the legitimate Libyan government.[74]

South Caucasus in the Context of Nagorno-Karabakh War

The conflict in Nagorno-Karabakh was a long-expected development due to Azerbaijan's military and economic superiority and the failure of light diplomatic pressure on Armenia to secure Armenia's departure from the occupied territories.[75] The tensions between the two countries evolved into a full-scale military conflict in September 2020 and ended with a Russian brokered cease-fire after a decisive Azerbaijani victory. Turkey actively supported Azerbaijan during the battle, Russia preferred to play the role of power broker.

Following the beginning of the war, the Azerbaijani forces quickly recaptured several villages and strategic hilltops with a quick land offensive, supported by UAVs and UACVs, purchased from Israel and Turkey. The Armenian prime minister Nikol Pashinyan attempted to turn the tide with diplomatic maneuvers in a series of phone calls to European leaders and Putin.[76] Pashinyan also tried to attract attention by magnifying Turkey's involvement in the war, claiming that Turkey was working toward re-creating the Turkish Empire.[77] Following Shusha's capture, the second biggest city in Nagorno–Karabakh, a Russian-brokered cease-fire was declared on November 10, 2020. Armenia left the territories yet to be captured by the Azerbaijani army, and five thousand Russian peacekeepers settled in the Nagorno-Karabakh proper to keep the peace.

Within the framework of its new foreign policy strategy, Turkey provided significant military, political, and moral support to Azerbaijan from the beginning of the conflict.[78] Following the skirmishes in July, the Turkish Armed Forces conducted joint military drills with the Azerbaijani army. Turkey's capable UAVs and UACVs played a significant role in the quick defeat of the Armenian forces through reconnaissance flights and precise strikes on Armenian targets.[79] In contrast to its stance in the Nagorno–Karabakh War in 1992–1995, Russia was neutral. Russia's relations with Armenia had deteriorated due to the arrest of pro-Russian political figures by the Armenian prime minister Pashinyan, who was elected after a wave of popular protests.[80] When asked whether Russia would assist Armenia, Putin responded that it could do so only if Azerbaijan attacks the Armenian territory,[81] concerning the status of Nagorno-Karabakh in international law.[82] From the beginning of the conflict, Russia never objected to Turkey's support toward Azerbaijan, and Putin stated that the country's support is within the framework of international law.[83] Yet, in South Caucasus, too, there were limits to how much Turkish influence Russia could tolerate. Despite Turkey's willingness to participate in the peacekeeping mission, Russia prevented the Turkish military from accessing newly recaptured territories allowing their access only in the joint peacekeeping center with no troops on the ground.[84] The synergy in Nagorno-Karabagh had positively impacted Turkey's relations with other Turkic nations in Central Asia.

The Black Sea Region

The Black Sea region, particularly Ukraine, became the most important issue for Russian foreign policy in this period. Aside from its deepening cooperation with Azerbaijan, Turkey also took multiple steps toward strengthening collaboration with Ukraine and Georgia to balance the increasing Russian military superiority in the Black Sea region. Russia preserved the status quo following the annexation of Crimea while not opposing Turkey's moves with tough measures.

In this period, Turkey's partnership with Ukraine in the military and defense industry sector significantly strengthened through agreements[85] that paved the way for cooperation between the defense sectors of the two countries and Ukraine's purchase of Turkish drones.[86] Turkey's partnership with Georgia deepened as well with a donation of $17 million to Georgia for reforms in military logistics[87] and a declaration of its support for Georgia's membership of NATO.[88] Moreover, in this period, the Baku-Tbilisi-Kars railway project and the TANAP pipeline project became operative, strengthening economic cooperation between Turkey, Azerbaijan, and Georgia.

In 2021, tensions began to rise in the region after Russia amassed as many as two hundred thousand soldiers along its border with Ukraine and medics, engineers, and other units that indicated preparations for a large-scale invasion.[89] Western intelligence services repeatedly warned that such movements were in preparation for an invasion throughout the crisis,[90] while some analysts argued that Russia was merely bluffing.[91] On February 22, 2022, in a televised address, Putin declared Russia's recognition of the independence of DPR and LPR. Two days later, he then declared the beginning of a "special operation" in Ukraine. Putin's stated aims were to achieve Ukraine's demilitarization, "denazification" to end the victimization of the Russian-speaking people in Ukraine.[92]

The advance of Russian troops in Ukraine caused significant destruction to civilian infrastructure though the speed of advance has been disappointing. In less than two months, close to 2 million people left their homes for neighboring countries in Europe.[93] Thousands of people were killed or wounded by shelling or bombing from the Russian troops. Meanwhile, the Russian troops lost over ten thousand soldiers, dozens of helicopters and jets, and hundreds of tanks and armored vehicles, according to figures published by the Ukrainian government.[94]

Upon beginning the invasion, Russia faced unprecedented economic sanctions while Ukraine began to receive arms and ammunition from the West, at an unprecedented scale. Among the weapons provided by the United States and North Atlantic Treaty Organization (NATO) allies, manpads and anti-tank missiles are making a significant difference on the ground.[95] Russian banks were removed from the SWIFT financial transaction system, most Western companies stopped their operations in Russia, European airspace was closed to Russia's flights, and the assets of Russian politicians and oligarchs were frozen.[96]

Throughout the crisis, Turkey pursued an active foreign policy to help resolve the conflict. The prolongation of war would inflict a significant damage not only to Turkey's security but also to Turkey's economy. Together with the rest of the international community, Turkey condemned Russia's actions and voted for Russia's removal from the UN Human Rights Council. Yet, Turkey managed not to antagonize Russia by closing the Straits to all warships and not joining sanctions. Its success in hosting negotiations contributed to Turkey's claim to be a stabilizing power.[97] In addition, Turkey consolidated its position as an independent power within the Western alliance. The U.S. president Biden expressed appreciation of Turkey's attempts to bring about a diplomatic resolution to the crisis.[98] Russia, which had criticized Turkey's defense cooperation with Ukraine, also appreciated Turkey's position.[99]

Central Asia

In this period, Central Asia continued to be a region where conflicts of interests between Russia and Turkey did not negatively influence their bilateral relations. Russia continued to strengthen its hegemonic influence in the region and Turkey strengthened its cultural and economic ties without antagonizing Russia. China's economic influence continued to increase as the Belt and Road Initiative expanded, but China's careful diplomacy kept the project strictly to the economic dimension so as not to antagonize Russia.[100] The commencement of the Baku-Tbilisi-Kars railway linked Turkey to the Chinese-led economic network. The establishment of such a connection formed an alternative to the economic transportation network that passed through Russia.[101]

Trade Relations

Following the resolution of the Jet Crisis, Turkey and Russia reactivated their commitment to increase their bilateral trade volume. Most economic sanctions placed by Russia on Turkey were lifted, re-enabling Turkey's agricultural exports to Russia and Russian tourists' visits to Turkey but the suspension of the visa-free regime on Turkish citizens remained in effect.[102] The High-Level Cooperation Council meetings took place as scheduled, while the ninth meeting was canceled due to the COVID-19 outbreak. The leaders reiterated the target of $100 billion volume in bilateral trade.[103] As a result, the bilateral trade relations experienced a significant recovery in 2017–2019 (see figure 4.2).

However, in 2020, the COVID–19 outbreak damaged the bilateral trade between the two countries due to the global economic stagnation (see figure 4.2). Meanwhile, Turkey's deficit in its trade with Russia diminished due to Turkey's diversification of its natural gas supply until 2020 (see figure 4.3). In 2021, however, Turkey relied upon Russia for guarantee of supply (see figures 4.3. and 4.4). To reduce the dollarization in their bilateral trade, the two countries signed an agreement to use the Lira and Ruble in 2019. However, the usage of Ruble and Lira is yet to have substantial shares in bilateral trade.[104]

In this period, the arms sales between Turkey and Russia, more specifically Turkey's purchase of the S-400 missile defense system from Russia, added a strategic edge to the Turkey-Russia trade. Until this period, the United States and Turkey's other NATO allies had been Turkey's most significant partners in its arms purchases. As a result of the "independent" turn in Turkish foreign policy, deterioration in relations with the West, Turkey's pursuit of reaching independence in the defense industry, and Turkey's need for a missile shield system, Turkey's interest in the Russian-made S-400 missile defense system emerged. Following Russia's offer, Turkey and Russia finalized negotiations for the sale in December 2017. Turkey faced significant diplomatic, political, and economic pressure from the United States. Emphasizing the interoperability problems and risk to the security of the data in the NATO defense systems, the United States canceled the delivery of F-35 fighter jets[105] and threatened Turkey with sanctions within the framework of Countering America's

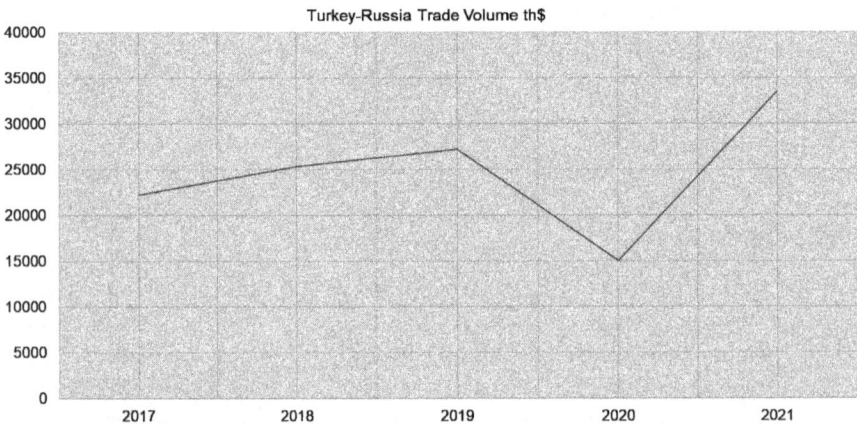

Figure 4.2   Turkey-Russia Trade Volume, 2017–2021. Source: "Dış Ticaret İstatistikleri" [Foreign Trade Statistics], Turkish Ministry of Trade, accessed April 10, 2022, https://ticaret .gov.tr/istatistikler/dis-ticaret-istatistikleri.

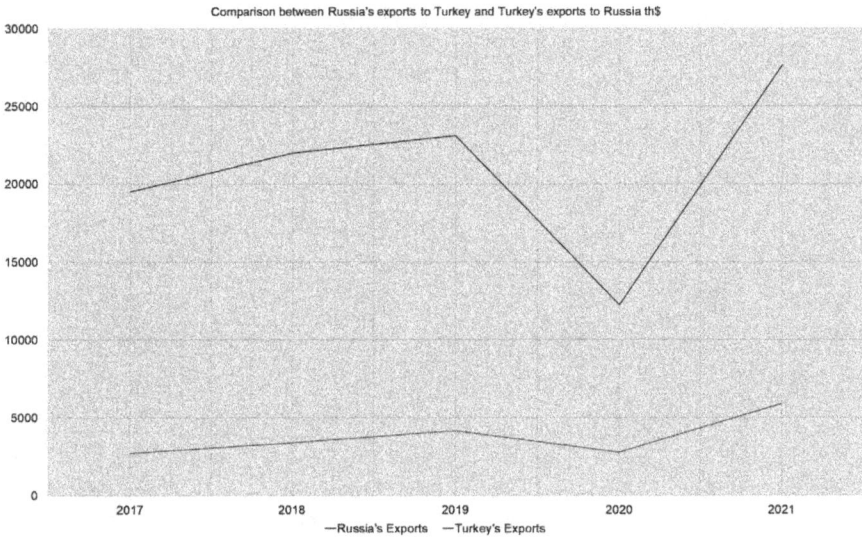

Figure 4.3 **Import-Export Balance in Turkey-Russia Bilateral Trade, 2017–2021.** Source: "Dış Ticaret İstatistikleri" [Foreign Trade Statistics], Turkish Ministry of Trade, accessed April 10, 2022, https://ticaret.gov.tr/istatistikler/dis-ticaret-istatistikleri.

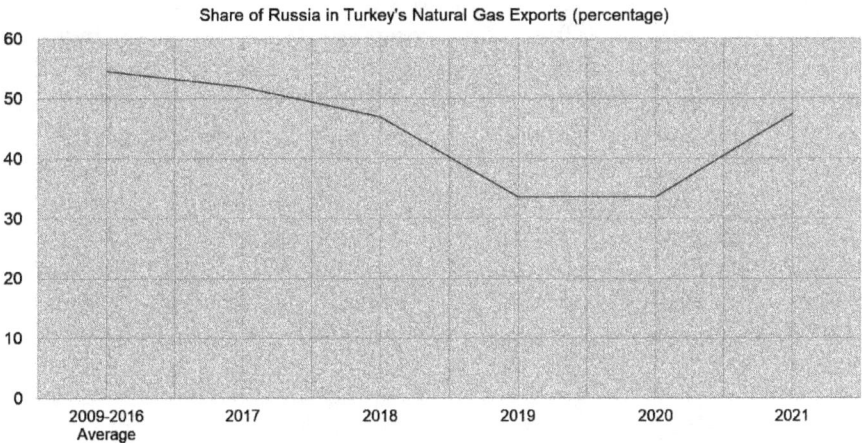

Figure 4.4 **Share of Russia's Gas Exports in Turkish Market, 2009–2021.** Source: "Doğal Gaz Piyasası Yıllık Sektör Raporu Listesi" [Natural Gas Market Yearly Sector Report List], Republic of Turkey Energy Market Regulatory Authority, accessed April 29, 2022, www .epdk.gov.tr/Detay/Icerik/3-0-94/yillik-sektor-raporu.

Adversaries Through Sanctions Act (CAATSA).[106] Meanwhile, the U.S. Congress secretly blocked any kind of defense cooperation with Turkey starting from 2018.[107] U.S. president Trump initially used his political influence to delay

Number of Russian Tourists Visiting Turkey

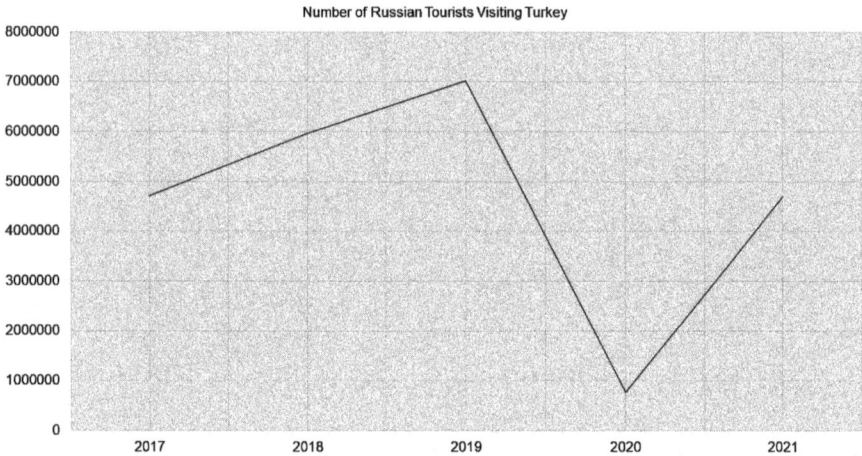

Figure 4.5   Number of Russian Tourists Visiting Turkey, 2017–2021. Source: "Sınır Giriş Çıkış İstatistikleri" [Border Crossing Statistics], Turkish Ministry of Culture and Tourism, accessed March 30, 2022, https://yigm.ktb.gov.tr/TR-9854/sinir-giris-cikis-istatistikleri .html.

the application of CAATSA, while Turkey tested the S-400s multiple times.[108] In December 2020, the CAATSA sanctions eventually came into force.[109]

Meanwhile, with the lifting of sanctions on Turkey's tourism industry, its southern coasts became a top tourism destination for Russian tourists again and the number of Russian tourists visiting the country continued to rise steadily. Moreover, Turkey's currency crisis in 2018, which led to the Turkish Lira's losing value, contributed to this process. To add to the developing relations, Turkey and Russia declared 2019 as "Turkey-Russia Cross-Cultural Year of Culture and Tourism."[110] However, due to the COVID-19 outbreak's decisively negative impact, the number of Russian tourists visiting Turkey substantially dropped in 2020. In 2021, this number increased but could not reach near the numbers caught in pre-COVID years (see figure 4.5).

Energy Relations

Competition over the Energy Resources in Eastern Mediterranean

The geological studies on potential energy resources, conducted since the early 2000s, demonstrated that the Eastern Mediterranean is home to one of the world's richest natural gas reserves.[111] The contested maritime jurisdiction areas among the countries with a coastline to the Mediterranean Sea complicated the geoeconomics in the Eastern Mediterranean region. Diminishing, or at least diversifying, its reliance on foreign sources for its natural gas demand became a significant part of Turkey's foreign policy strategy following the coup in 2016. In line with this, Turkey closely monitored the developments and took steps toward securing its commercial interests in the region. In turn, Russia was also actively involved in the region through military and diplomatic efforts.

The disputes between Turkey and Greece on their claims to maritime jurisdiction and the island of Cyprus's legal status caused a conflict over the resources in its Eastern Mediterranean coasts. Turkey also had problematic relations with Israel, the Greek Cypriot administration in Southern Cyprus, Greece, the Assad regime, and had minimal contact with Egypt's Sisi regime. Thus, the regional geoeconomics was formed in a manner that excluded Turkey. An exclusive economic zone agreement between Turkey and the Turkish Republic of Northern Cyprus (TRNC) in 2011 had already formed the basis of cooperation over the gas resources.[112] In January 2019, Greece, Israel, Cyprus, Egypt, and Jordan created the Eastern Mediterranean Gas Forum to enhance their regional cooperation in the supply and the marketing of the reserves from the region.[113] At this point, the exclusive economic zone agreement between Turkey and Libya, signed on November 27, 2019, provided legal support to Turkey's claim for energy resources in the Eastern Mediterranean.[114] One year after the initial Eastern Mediterranean Gas Forum, Israel, the Greek Cypriot administration in Cyprus and Greece formed the EastMed consortium to form the basis of a pipeline project that would carry the Israeli and Cypriot gas to Europe, ignoring the claims of Turkey and the TRNC.[115] Turkey also began to conduct seismic research and drilling operations in the area between Turkey and Cyprus, which caused a backlash from the EU.[116]

As discussed in chapter 2, access to the Mediterranean Sea has been a strategic aim for Russia for centuries and a source of contention between Russia, Turkey, and the West. Since Russia remained Turkey's number one natural gas supplier, the emergence of another significant potential gas supply would hurt Russia's commercial and strategic interests as it would diminish Turkey's reliance on Russia. Also, Russia and Turkey directly clashed with one another in Syria, Libya, and Greek Cypriot administration in Cyprus through the alliances they formed. To maintain its influence in the region and protect its commercial interest, Russia kept its military in Syria, gave lifeline support to Haftar, and signed defense agreements with the Greek Cypriot administration in Cyprus. Russia also offered to mediate between Turkey and Greece in the Eastern Mediterranean in September 2020.[117]

Cooperation and Conflict with Energy Projects

In this period, the energy cooperation between Turkey and Russia continued with the progress made in multiple projects. The TurkStream was completed, and the groundbreaking ceremony of Akkuyu NPP took place. The beginning of gas flow through the TANAP helped Turkey balance Russia's dominance of the region's energy geopolitics and diversify Turkey's energy supply. Meanwhile, Turkey also took additional steps toward reducing its energy reliance on Russia with drilling activities and LNG (liquid natural gas), particularly from the United States. Turkey's increasing purchase of LNG enabled Turkey to benefit from the diminishing LNG prices due to the pandemic, increase its energy security by storing LNG in several facilities around Turkey and diversify Turkey's energy supplies. This is important in the sense that such a move was a step toward reducing Turkey's dependence on Russia.

The completion of the TurkStream pipeline project created substantial geopolitical consequences. With continued political support, the subsea portion of the TurkStream pipeline was finished in late 2018. In January 2020, the TurkStream was officially launched with a ceremony that included Erdoğan, Putin, Serbian president Vucic, and the Bulgarian prime minister Borisov. The completion of the TurkStream project, along with the second line, increased Russia's influence in the European gas market while increasing Europe's reliance on Russia's supply of energy. The project also contributed to Turkey's regional geoeconomic power in the Balkans and Europe.

In April 2018, the groundbreaking ceremony of the Akkuyu Nuclear Power Plant took place in Turkey with the participation of Putin and Erdoğan. During the visit, Putin stated that the first block of the Akkuyu NPP will commence operation in 2023 and that the best Russian technologies will be used in the construction of the plant. In turn, Erdoğan stated the Akkuyu NPP would meet 10 percent of Turkey's electricity needs. In 2019, the construction works of Akkuyu NPP continued, with the number of workers in the construction of the facility reaching 4,500.[118] Meanwhile, some of the Turkish engineers who were educated in Russia began to work in Akkuyu NPP in late 2020.[119]

In this period, Turkey significantly diminished its natural gas dependence on imports from Russia. Turkey took the first step toward this direction after the Jet Crisis, by increasing LNG storage and regasification investments and continuing with additional facilities.[120] Turkey also diversified its energy supply by purchasing more gas from Azerbaijan and less from Russia. The data taken from Turkey's Energy Market Regulatory Authority demonstrates a sharp decrease in Russia's natural gas share in Turkey's energy supply.

The completion of the TANAP project strengthened Turkey's position in the regional geoeconomics vis-à-vis Russia. The ribbon-cutting ceremony for TANAP took place in July 2018, and TANAP's connection to the Trans-Adriatic Pipeline was completed in December 2019.[121] By increasing the flow of Azerbaijani gas to Turkey, TANAP helped Turkey to decrease its reliance on Russian gas and bolstered its role as an energy hub between the Caucasus and Europe.[122]

COOPERATION AT A GLOBAL LEVEL

Turkey and Russia's foreign policies and the deepening of bilateral partnerships between Turkey and Russia brought about significant global political consequences. Turkey's assertive actions in Syria, Libya, and Nagorno-Karabakh reinforced the erosion of Western influence in these regions. The cooperation between Turkey and Russia also signified the possibility of non-Western solutions to regional problems.

The election of Trump was a significant factor in encouraging Turkey and Russia to further advance their agenda beyond the U.S. security interests. Aside from facilitating Turkey and Russia to strengthen their partnerships, Trump's presidency also weakened the global context through which the United States used to put pressure on the two countries. The so-called liberal international order seemed not as essential as it had been, since the acting U.S. president, who is supposed to lead this order, was no longer acting accordingly. The regional and systemic impact of Russia's invasion of Ukraine are yet to be seen.

CONCLUSION

In this period, Turkey's increasing activism after the July 2016 coup attempt shaped the course of bilateral relations. While the resolution of the Jet Crisis paved the way for Turkey's rapprochement with Russia, Turkey's new foreign policy strategy strongly challenged Russia in multiple regions. The turbulence created by the further diminishing of U.S. activity in the Black Sea, the Middle East, and Europe under Trump, created a power vacuum in Central Eurasia. Against the backdrop of these dynamics, Turkey and Russia utilized their bilateral mechanisms to resolve their differences, while the positive trend in trade and energy continued.

Turkey's activism and the continued regional turbulence shaped the dynamics of cooperation and conflict between Turkey and Russia in different regions. The Syrian Civil War continued to be the most critical subject of their bilateral relations. As the U.S. military and political influence further diminished, Turkey and Russia played a significant role in shaping Syria's future through Turkey's military operations in Northern Syria and the Astana Process. The minimal U.S. involvement and inconsequential EU initiatives enabled Turkey and Russia to become the leading players to decide on Libya's future. In Nagorno-Karabakh, Turkey's daring involvement in the post-Soviet region, with its strong support toward Azerbaijan, was indicative of the changes in regional dynamics, Russian foreign policy, Turkish foreign policy, and Turkey-Russia relations. While Russia overlooked Turkey's activism, the way Russia set the terms of the cease-fire demonstrated its continued interest in keeping the region under control.

The two countries attempted to recover their bilateral trade relations from the impact of Russian sanctions on Turkey. Although bilateral trade relations recovered after the Jet Crisis, Turkey reduced the share of energy it imported from Russia per its "independent" foreign policy strategy. Turkey and Russia also continued to make progress in mutual energy projects. With Turkey's purchase of the S-400, the missile defense system from Russia, the two countries trade relations acquired a strategic edge. However, the bilateral trade volume began to diminish due to the COVID-19 outbreak and the increase of Turkey's shale gas purchased from the United States in place of Russian natural gas.

Conclusion

This book attempts to analyze the evolution of Turkey-Russia relations in 2001–2022, using an eclectic framework benefitting from various primary and secondary sources. Within the framework of the methodological approach and model used in this research, I have investigated the subject in three body chapters, focusing on different periods (2001–2009, 2009–2016, and 2016–2022).

This book comprehensively evaluates Turkey-Russia relations with a thorough analysis of the bilateral relations during the period between 2001 and 2022. The framework used in this research enabled me to consider factors that stem from different levels (systemic, regional, state, and individual) and different dimensions (strategic, economic, and normative). I argue that the most critical factors in shaping bilateral relations were the changes in the balance of power in the international system, in multiple regions (Middle East, Black Sea, Mediterranean, and Caucasus in particular), as they relate to the Turkey-Russia nexus. Therefore, I conclude that changes on bilateral, regional, and global levels influenced the prevailing dynamics of Turkey-Russia relations. And I consider the concept of "change in the balance of power" as not just a result of comparing the total resources of each country in a particular period. Instead, I argue, various factors can be influential in turning the tide in the balance of power. These resources can be economical, strategic, and even normative. Explaining the impact of various factors on bilateral relations in this context helps reveal the nature of the relations in the context in which they occur.

This work's primary contribution will be a comprehensive analysis to explain and interpret the transformation of Turkey-Russia relations within their regional and global contexts. It also examines the transformations of their domestic and foreign policies. In addition, it analyzes relevant primary and secondary sources in multiple languages using a working model and an eclectic framework. The cohesive explanation of Turkey-Russia relations provided here examines factors that operate at different levels (domestic, regional, and global) and varying dimensions (strategic, normative, and economic). By doing so, this book will be able to touch upon all the major dynamics that influence Turkey-Russia relations and provide its readers with a near-complete understanding of the bilateral affairs between Turkey and Russia.

Aside from its contribution to the literature on Turkey-Russia relations, this work also advances knowledge in several other research areas. First, the discussions on the emerging international structure generally focus on China's rise, changes in U.S. foreign policy, and the EU's future role in the global political system.[1] Yet, this literature often overlooks the Turkey-Russia nexus, even though the interactions between Turkey and Russia are creating far-reaching global consequences.[2] By pointing out the results of the peaks and troughs in Turkey-Russia relations, this work contributes to the studies on the emerging world order. In that sense, this book presents its readers with how the relations between Turkey and Russia interact and remake the contours of the emerging world order. Second, Turkey and Russia's activism in the twenty-first century and the changes in the Turkey-Russia nexus influence regional dynamics in multiple regions, including the Middle East, the Black Sea, and the Caucasus.[3] The insight provided in this work on how the Turkey-Russia nexus interacts with other regional dynamics contributes to understanding the contemporary dynamics in these regions. Third, this work uses an original model loosely based on Type-3 Neoclassical Realism.[4] With the help of my model, I look at how the changes in state power in normative and economic dimensions create international outcomes. This original theoretical framework can be helpful in other studies that examine bilateral relations between different countries.

In the first period, between 2001 and 2009, the most significant factor that shaped bilateral relations was the invasion of Iraq. This invasion had a transformative impact on the global balance of power by bringing about a rather multipolar world order compared to the 1990s. Although the global backlash against the U.S. invasion of Iraq did not have an immediate impact on the U.S. superiority in economic and strategic dimensions, the belief in the wise and moral leadership of the United States was significantly tarnished. This decay in U.S. normative power enabled Turkey to pursue a multidimensional foreign policy and encouraged Russia to foster a multipolar world order. The foreign policy approaches of the Putin administration in Russia and the AK Party government in Turkey fitted this trend. In such an environment, Turkey could consider Russia as more than an actor that used to be securitized within the framework of the regional competition between

Turkey and Russia, on the one hand, and the Cold-War era global securitization dynamics, on the other. In turn, Russia considered Turkey as an independent actor, which could assist Russia's attempts to foster a multipolar world order. Russia also aimed to pragmatically cooperate with Turkey in the areas of trade and energy. Therefore, during this period, Turkey and Russia increased their bilateral trade volume and strengthened their ties in the energy sector.

In the second period, between 2009 and 2016, the most significant factor shaping bilateral relations was the Syrian crisis. In this period, under the Obama administration, the United States attempted to restore its global leadership role by refraining from unnecessary military entanglements. However, the reverberations of the change in U.S. foreign policy had unintended consequences within the framework of the Syrian Civil War. In the initial phase of the Arab Uprisings, the U.S. support for the process helped the collapse of many autocratic regimes in the Middle East. In Syria, however, the situation required a concrete military response for any actor wishing to bring about a real change on the ground. In the absence of a U.S. military investment, Russia and Iran filled the vacuum and restored the Assad regime. On the other hand, Turkey continued to rely on the United States as a partner, one which, however, did not highly consider Turkey's security interests. Turkey's maladaptation to the changing conditions, which was also a liability, caused Turkey to lose ground to Russia in the Middle East and the Black Sea.

In the third period, between 2016 and 2022, the most significant factor in shaping bilateral relations was the July 2016 coup attempt in Turkey. Against the backdrop of the increasing frequency of terrorist attacks and domestic political instability, the coup attempt forced Turkey to consider it urgent to deal with the country's imminent security issues. During this period, Turkey would be prone to take risks and ignore institutional frameworks. At this juncture, the incompatibility between Turkey and the West pushed Turkey to consider a rapprochement with Russia. By encouraging Turkey's participation in regional orders, Russia enabled the amplification of Turkey's regional influence. Even though this development challenged Russia's interests in multiple regions, such a step made Russia a deal-breaker in the Middle East. Moreover, the change in Turkish foreign policy and Russia's increasing influence in the Middle East brought the global political system closer to multipolarity.

Within the framework of the absence of Cold War era securitization dynamics and the erosion of Western influence in Central Eurasia, Turkey and Russia were able to develop trade relations and strengthen regional institutions outside of the mentorship of the West. However, the domestic changes in Turkey and Russia complemented this process by increasing both countries' maneuvering areas. The consolidation of Erdoğan and Putin's power in their domestic realms enabled these two leaders to more comfortably adopt an independent foreign policy that counters the Western hegemonic influence in multiple regions as well as at the global level. In Turkey, Erdoğan gradually consolidated power over state institutions by prevailing over secular guardians of the bureaucracy and the Gülen Movement. The arming of the PYD by the United States and the harboring of the Gülen Movement in the United States convinced Erdoğan that the United States is not an actor that will help Turkey maintain its security. In his turn, for Putin, the invasion of Iraq and the U.S. support for the Color Revolutions demonstrated that Russia needs to counter the United States to realize its core strategic aims: restoring Russia's hegemony in the post-Soviet region and fostering a multipolar world order. As two significant powerhouses in Central Eurasia, Turkey and Russia strengthened their ties in the Black Sea, the South Caucasus, and in the Middle East, although their interests were often in conflict with one another.

I consider bilateral trade, energy, and people-to-people relations in the Turkey-Russia nexus as of secondary importance. That is, these dynamics generally follow the general trend and do not define the course of Turkey-Russia relations. The statist tradition in both countries brought about the developments in these sectors following the strategic issues, not vice versa. However, the trade relations also had their strategic dimension, through which they may become significant. For example, the extent to which Turkey is dependent on Russia in bilateral trade and who has the upper hand in this dimension may impact the course of their bilateral relations.

This book potentially contributes to different research topics in studies on multiple regions in Central Eurasia, to the scholarly attempts to explain the global political changes, and to theoretical attempts to explain state behavior. Primarily, this book provides a comprehensive analysis of Turkey-Russia relations between 2001 and 2022. Second, this work contributes to the studies that focus on the foreign policy making in Turkey and Russia, with its thorough examination of how both countries responded to the main regional and global events in 2001–2022. Third, by examining the interaction between Turkey and Russia with regional events, this book also contributes to the studies that attempt to explain the regional dynamics in the Middle East, the Black Sea, Central Asia, the South Caucasus, and the Eastern Mediterranean. Fourth, since it also analyzes the interaction between U.S. foreign policy and the regional dynamics in Central Eurasia, one might utilize this work to explain the consequences of U.S. foreign policy in different regions.

Using its original framework, this work contributes to explaining state behavior and international consequences. To create a comprehensive framework through which state behavior may be understood in the sophisticated context in which it takes place, I created an eclectic framework and model based on the Type-3 Neoclassical Realist framework. My model enables one to consider factors stemming from different levels and dimensions if appropriately applied. Such a model could be adapted to explain how states behave and how international consequences occur as a result of the interactions between more than one state. Its flexible and eclectic nature enables one to utilize various issues, including strategic culture, political psychology, and balance of power, when explaining state behavior and international consequences.

Notes

INTRODUCTION

1. Norrin M. Ripsman, Jeffrey W. Taliaferro, and Steven E. Lobell, *Neoclassical Realist Theory of International Politics* (New York: Oxford University Press, 2016), 80.

2. Suat Bilge, "An Analysis of Turkey-Russia Relations," *Perceptions* 2, no. 2 (1997): 66.

3. Lerna Yanık, "Allies or Partners? An Appraisal of Turkey's Ties to Russia, 1991–2007," *East European Quarterly* 41, no. 3 (Fall 2007): 363.

4. Mitat Çelikpala, "Rekabet ve İş Birliği İkileminde Yönünü Arayan Türkiye-Rusya İlişkileri" [Turkey-Russia Relations Looking for Its Direction in the Dilemma of Competition and Cooperation], *Bilig* 72 (Winter 2015): 139.

5. Fiona Hill and Ömer Taşpınar, "Turkey and Russia: Axis of the Excluded?" *Survival* 48, no. 1 (2006): 81.

6. Şener Aktürk, "Turkish–Russian Relations after the Cold War (1992–2002)," *Turkish Studies* 7, no. 3 (2006): 338.

7. Şener Aktürk, "Toward a Turkish-Russian Axis? Conflicts in Georgia, Syria, and Ukraine, and Cooperation over Nuclear Energy," *Insight Turkey* 6, no. 15 (2014): 21.

8. Şener Aktürk, "Relations between Russia and Turkey Before, During, and After the Failed Coup of 2016," *Insight Turkey* 21, no. 4 (2019): 97–113.

9. Tarık Oğuzlu, "Turkish Foreign Policy in a Changing World Order," *All Azimuth* 9, no. 1 (2020): 127–39.

10. Bülent Aras and Hakan Fidan, "Turkey and Eurasia: Frontiers of a New Geographic Imagination," *New Perspectives on Turkey* 40 (2009): 193.

11. Mohiaddin Mesbahi, "Eurasia Between Turkey, Iran and Russia," in *Key Players and Regional Dynamics in Eurasia: The Return of the "Great Game,"* ed. Marie Raquel Friere and Roger E. Kanet (London: Palgrave Macmillan, 2010), 175.

12. The works that are considered as Neoclassical Realist demonstrate how a systemic stimulus turns into a foreign policy strategy having passed through the dynamics of a domestic foreign policy decision-making process. Therefore, they reject Constructivism and Liberalism for downplaying the impact of the relative distribution of power in the system on state behavior. Yet they part ways with Structural Realism by including state-level factors in their explanations. Neoclassical Realism points out that various factors (misperception, lack of clarity of systemic signals, failure to mobilize state resources, irrationality, etc.) may condition the way states react to systemic signals. For more information about Neoclassical Realism, see Gideon Rose, "Neoclassical Realism and Theories of Foreign Policy," *World Politics* 51, no. 1 (October 1998): 144–72.

13. Ripsman et al. consider the first generation that attempts to explain anomalous foreign policy decisions as Type-1 and the emerging literature that focuses on why a foreign policy decision is taken as Type-2. See Ripsman et al., *Neoclassical Realist Theory*.

14. An important quality of Type-3 Neoclassical Realism is that the degree to which an intervening variable functionalizes in a particular situation depends on the clarity and quality of strategic environment. In restrictive strategic environments, when there is no adequate time to respond to a *systemic stimulus*, *domestic institutions* and *state-society relations* are unlikely to make a substantial impact on decision-making process. Since the imminence of the situation would call for immediate action, the decision is likely to be taken under the impact of *leader image* and *strategic culture*. In permissive high-clarity strategic environments, *domestic institutions* and *state-society relations* could be expected to impact the decision-making process along with the *strategic culture* since the state decision mechanism will have the luxury to evaluate the pros and cons of alternative responses. However, in permissive environments where the clarity of strategic environment is low, we could expect any of these four variables to be operational. Ripsman et al., *Neoclassical Realist Theory,* 95.

15. Ibid., 32

16. Ibid., 82.

17. Kenneth Waltz, *Theory of International Politics* (Long Grove, IL: Waveland Press, 1979), 106.

18. Ripsman et al., *Neoclassical Realist Theory*, 62.

19. While these variables could easily be proliferated, the scope of these four could easily explain the way systemic stimuli are responded to by individual states since these four variables potentially distort the policy implementation. Ripsman et al., *Neoclassical Realist Theory,* 58.

20. Robert Jervis, *System Effects: Complexity in Political and Social Life* (Princeton, NJ: Princeton University Press, 1997).

21. Ripsman et al., *Neoclassical Realist Theory,* 38.

22. Rose, "Neoclassical Realism," 147–48.

23. Please see Nicholas Kitchen, "Systemic Pressures and Domestic Ideas: A Neoclassical Realist Model of Grand Strategy Formation," *Review of International Studies* 36, no. 1 (January 2010): 117–43.

24. Ripsman et al., *Neoclassical Realist Theory,* 85.

25. Ibid., 36.
26. Ibid., 43.
27. Mohiaddin Mesbahi, "Free and Confined: Iran and the International System," *Iranian Review of Foreign Affairs* 2, no. 5 (Spring 2011): 11.
28. Ripsman et al., *Neoclassical Realist Theory,* 40.

CHAPTER 1

1. For an accessible account of the history of the Turksm, see Carter Findley, *Turks in World History* (New York: Oxford University Press, 2005), and Norman Stone, *Turkey: A Short History* (London: Thames & Hudson, 2017).

2. For more information about the history of the Mongols and their successor states, see Timothy May, *The Mongol Empire* (Edinburgh: Edinburgh University Press, 2018).

3. Such tribes were called *Uç beylikleri* (frontier principalities), political entities emerging across Anatolia in the late thirteenth century and strengthened as Ilkhanates declined.

4. For more about the Mongols' relations with the Turks in Asia Minor, see Sara Nur Yıldız, "Mongol Rule in Thirteenth-Century Seljuk Anatolia: The Politics of Conquest and History Writing, 1243–1282" (PhD dissertation, University of Chicago, 2006).

5. For more information about the early phase of the Ottomans, see Halil İnalcık, *The Ottoman Empire: The Classical Age 1300–1600* (New Haven: Phoenix Press, 2001).

6. Halil İnalcık, *Studies in Ottoman Social and Economic History* (London: Variorum Reprints, 1985), 78–79.

7. The name "Ottoman" comes from a false transliteration of Arabic *Uthman.*

8. *Ghaza,* the practice of fighting infidels in order to spread Islam, played a significant role in early Ottoman expansion. See Halil İnalcık and Donald Quatert, *An Economic and Social History of the Ottoman Empire:1300–1600* (New York: Cambridge University Press, 1997), 11.

9. For the political and social institutions of Tsarist Russia, see Richard Pipes, *Russia under the Old Regime* (New York: Charles Scribner's Sons, 1974).

10. Tatar was the name of one of the tribes that comprised the Mongol Empire.

11. During this first visit, the Russian envoy's disrespectful attitude in the palace resulted in his deposition. Only after a second visit were bilateral relations established. Since the Ottoman Sultans did not see Muscovite *knyazes* as equals, the Ottoman vassal—the Crimean Tatar Khanate—was chosen to act as mediator between the Ottoman palace and the Muscovites. For more information, see Halil İnalcık, *Osmanlı-Rus İlişkileri* [OttomanRussia Relations].

12. When the Golden Horde collapsed, the balance of power tilted in favor of the Crimean Khanate. Until the late sixteenth century, the Ottomans supported the Muscovites, considering them a natural ally against Poland. When the Muscovites

began to match the Crimeans' power, the Ottoman Empire began to back the Crimeans against the Russians.

13. The only plan the Ottoman Empire made in order to increase their control in the region is the Don-Volga canal project, which would connect the two rivers. Yet the developments in central Europe and Crimean opposition to the project prevented the plan from coming to fruition. For more information, please see Halil İnalcık, *Osmanlı–Rus Rekabetinin Menşei ve Don Volga Kanalı Teşebbüsü* [The Source of the Ottoman-Russian Competition and the Don-Volga Canal Venture] (Ankara: Türk Tarih Kurumu, 1948).

14. Stanford Shaw, *History of the Ottoman Empire and the Modern Turkey: Empire of Gazis—the Rise and Decline of the Ottoman Empire 1280–1808*, vol. 1 (New York: Cambridge University Press, 1997), 177.

15. For more information, see Hugh Ragsdale, "Evaluating the Traditions of Russian Aggression: Catherine II and the Greek Project," *The Slavonic and East European Review* 66, no. 1 (1988): 91–117.

16. Mehmet Ali Pasha was the commander of the Albanian troops in Egypt. Following the end of French rule there (1798–1801), Mehmet Ali secured the position of governor of Egypt, accumulated power for himself, and formed a new army with the help of the instructors he had imported from France.

17. Frank Edgar Bailey, *British Policy and the Turkish Reform Movement: A Study in Anglo-Turkish Relations, 1826–1853* (Cambridge: Harvard University Printing Office, 1942), 49–50.

18. Frederick Stanley Rodkey, "Lord Palmerston and the Rejuvenation of Turkey, 1830–41," *The Journal of Modern History* 1, no. 4 (December 1929): 573–77.

19. These movements differed in the means they used to achieve their objective and the systems they wanted to use to replace the Tsarist autocracy. Upon his defeat in the Crimean War, Tsar Alexander II (reign: 1855–1881) emancipated millions of serfs in Russia but could not satisfy the revolutionaries who wanted more radical changes. Alexander III (reign: 1881–1894) succeeded his father, who was assassinated by revolutionaries. The son conducted massive economic reforms in an attempt to attract international investments to Russia and connect Russia's periphery to the center.

20. Western-oriented Ottoman reforms began in the early nineteenth century under Selim III (reign: 1789–1808), who attempted to form a European-type army. Selim's successor, Mahmut II (reign: 1808–1839), introduced European-style reforms not only to the military but also to the legal and administrative structures of the Ottoman Empire. The *Tanzimat* [reforms] that were declared by Abdulmecid (reign: 1839–1861) in 1839 furthered Mahmut II's administrative and military reforms. More importantly, *Tanzimat* resulted in the emergence of a Westernized elite that was dedicated to changing the way the Empire functioned.

21. Erik J. Zürcher, *Turkey: A Modern History* (New York: I. B. Tauris, 2017), 83–87.

22. Ibid., 134.

23. Stanford Shaw and Ezel Kural Shaw, *History of the Ottoman Empire and Modern Turkey: Reform, Revolution, and Republic: The Rise of Modern Turkey, 1808–1975*, vol. 2 (New York: Cambridge University Press, 2005), 343.

24. Founder of the modern Turkish Republic, Mustafa Kemal (Atatürk) was an army commander in the Ottoman Army and fought in Çanakkale and Palestine during WWI.

25. To achieve this end, Turkey adopted a jacobinite state secularism and conducted major reforms, including imposition of a new dress code, the Latinization of the alphabet, introduction of a secular education system, and the abolition of the Caliphate reforms as well as a population exchange between Greece and Turkey.

26. Malik Mufti, *Daring and Caution in Turkish Strategic Culture: Republic at Sea* (New York: Palgrave, 2009), 18.

27. Leonard Schapiro, *The Communist Party of the Soviet Union* (New York: Random House, 1960), 62.

28. For a detailed yet accessible account of the process leading to the Russian Revolution, see Richard Pipes, *A Concise History of the Russian Revolution* (New York: Alfred A. Knopf, 1991).

29. Ibid., 286.

30. Robert H. Donaldson, Joseph L. Nogee, and Vidya Nadkarni, *The Foreign Policy of Russia: Changing Systems, Enduring Interests* (New York: Routledge, 2014), 51.

31. Fritz W. Ermarth, "Russia's Strategic Culture: Past, Present, and . . . in Transition?" in *Comparative Strategic Cultures Curriculum Project,* ed. Jeffrey A. Larsen, chapter 12 (Fort Belvoir, VA: Defense Threat Reduction Agency, 2006).

32. Despite this, the leadership cadre of the Turkish Communist Party (TCP), which adopted a Leninist program, was exiled to the Soviet Union and murdered off the coast. For more information, see Bülent Gökay, *Soviet Eastern Policy and Turkey, 1920–1991: Soviet Foreign Policy, Turkey and Communism* (London: Routledge, 2006).

33. In those years, within the framework of "Soviet Eastern Policy," the Soviet Union supported bourgeoisie-nationalist states like Turkish nationalists or the Chinese Guomintang to weaken British imperialism.

34. David Gyurgenovich Bdoyan, "Transformatsiya rossiysko-turetskikh otnosheniy v usloviyakh bor'by za regional'noye liderstvo (2002–2017 gg.)" [Transformation of Turkish-Russian Relations within the Framework of the Fight over Regional Leadership (2002–2017)] (Unpublished PhD dissertation, MGIMO, 2017), 40.

35. Onur İşçi and Samuel Hirst, "Smokestacks and Pipelines: Russian-Turkish Relations and the Persistence of Economic Development," *Diplomatic History* 44, no. 5 (November 2020): 835.

36. Ali Balcı, *Türkiye Dış Politikası İlkeler, Aktörler Ve Uygulamalar* [Turkey Foreign Policy: Principles, Actors and Practices] (İstanbul: Alfa Yayınları, 2017), 39–40.

37. Onur İşçi, *Turkey and Soviet Union during World War II* (London: I. B. Tauris, 2019), 25–27.

38. A. F. Miller, *Ocherki noveishei istorii turtsii* [Essays on the Recent History of Turkey] (Moscow: Akademiya Nauk SSSR, 1948), 184–85.

39. İşçi, *Turkey and Soviet,* 78–79.

40. Examples include Selim Deringil, *Turkish Foreign Policy during the Second World War: An "Active" Neutrality* (Cambridge: Cambridge University Press, 1989); Türkkaya Ataöv, *Türk Dış Politikası, 1939–1945* [Turkish Foreign Policy, 1939–1945] (Ankara: SBF, 1964); Petr Pavlovich Moiseev and Yuriy Nikolayevich Rozaliyev, *K istorii sovetsko-turetskikh otnosheniy* [Towards the History of Soviet-Turkish Relations] (Moscow: Politzdat, 1958), and Manvel Arsenovich Gasratan and Petr Pavlovich Moiseev, *SSSR i Turtsiya 1917–1979* [USSR and Turkey 1917–1919] (Moskva: Nauka, 1981). There were also sporadic essays and books on the relations between the Ottoman and Russian Empires produced during the Cold War: Akdes Nimet Kurat, *Türkiye ve Rusya* [Turkey and Russia] (Ankara: Kültür Bakanlığı, 1990); Akdes Nimet Kurat, *Rusya Tarihi: Başlangıçtan 1917'ye kadar* [Russian History from the Beginning until 1917] (Ankara: Türk Tarih Kurumu, 1987); Halil İnalcık, *Osmanlı-Rus Rekabetinin Menşei ve Don Volga Kanalı Teşebbüsü* [The Origins of the Ottoman-Russia Competition and the Initiative of Don-Volga Canal] (Ankara: Türk Tarih Kurumu, 1948), and Halil İnalcık, *Osmanlı-Rus İlişkileri 1492–1700* [Ottoman-Russia Relations 1492–1700] (Ankara: Kırım Türkleri Yardımlaşma Derneği, 2003). After the Cold War, this literature was enriched by a number of contributions, a fact that may be assessed from the rise in the volume of books published in Turkey on Russia. See Ayten Çelebi, "Türkiye'de Rusya'ya Dair Çıkan Kitaplar (1991–2016)" [Latest Books Published in Turkey on Russia (1991–2016)], *Marmara Türkiyat Araştırmaları Dergisi* 3, no. 2 (Sonbahar 2016): 251–80.

41. The authenticity of these talks is verified in Molotov's memoirs, where he stated that he was ordered by Stalin, but it was the wrong thing to do. See Albert Resis, ed., *Molotov Remembers: Inside Kremlin Politics* (Chicago: Ivan R. Dee, 1993), 96.

42. Harry S. Truman, *The Memoirs of Harry S. Truman: Years of Trial and Hope 1945–1953*, vol. 2 (Suffolk: Hodder and Stoughton, 1956), 102.

43. Melvyn P. Leffler, *A Preponderance of Power: National Security, the Truman Administration, and the Cold War* (Stanford, CA: Stanford University Press, 1992), 551.

44. Irene Gendzier, *Notes from the Minefield: United States Intervention in Lebanon 1945–1958* (New York: Columbia University Press, 2006), 28.

45. For his speech before the Congress related to this issue, see Harry S. Truman, "President Harry S. Truman's Address before a Joint Session of Congress, March 12, 1947," *Avalon Project at Yale Law School*, accessed November 23, 2020, https://avalon.law.yale.edu/twentieth_century/trudoc.asp.

46. Yılmaz Eylem and Pinar Bilgin, "Constructing Turkey's 'Western' Identity during the Cold War: Discourses of the Intellectuals of Statecraft," *International Journal* 61, no. 1 (2005): 41.

47. Dianne Kirby, "Divinely Sanctioned: the Anglo-American Cold War Alliance and the Defence of Western Civilization and Christianity, 1945–48," *Journal of Contemporary History* 35, no. 3 (July 2000): 385–412.

48. Amy Austin Holmes, *Social Unrest and American Military Bases in Turkey and Germany since 1945* (New York: Cambridge University Press, 2014), 47–49.

49. Feroz Ahmad, *The Turkish Experiment in Democracy 1950–1975* (Boulder, CO: Westview Press, 1977), 32.

50. Ömer Aslan, *The United States and Military Coups in Turkey and Pakistan: Between Conspiracy and Reality* (Cham: Palgrave, 2018), 119–21.

51. A period of relaxation of tensions in U.S.-Soviet relations following the Cuban Missile Crisis and lasting until the late 1970s.

52. Pınar Bilgin and Kıvanç Coş, "Stalin's Demands: Constructions of the Soviet Other in Turkey's Foreign Policy, 1919–1945," *Foreign Policy Analysis* 6 (2009): 45.

53. At this point, the Democrat Party of Turkey had come into power after the Republican elites enabled the transition to a multi-party regime. The DP paid special attention to U.S.-Turkey relations and enabled Turkey's joining NATO.

54. Lyndon Johnson, "Correspondence between President Johnson and Prime Minister Inonu," *Middle East Journal* 20, no. 3 (1966): 386–93.

55. Since Turkey's 1974 military operation, which took place as a result of a Greek-led coup d'etat in the island, Cyprus remained divided between the Turks and the Greeks.

56. The Iskenderun Iron and Steel Plant, Seydişehir Aluminum Factory, Aliağa Petroleum Refinery, Bandirma Acid Sulfur Plant, and Artvin Sheet Factory, which were constructed in Turkey with Soviet aid, made Turkey the country that received the highest amount of Soviet developmental assistance in the 1970s. Gu Guan-fu, "Soviet Aid to the Third World: An Analysis of Its Strategy," *Soviet Studies* 15, no. 1 (January 1983): 71–76.

57. Atay Akdevelioğlu and Ömer Korkçooğlu, "SSCB ile İlişkiler" [Relations with the USSR], in *Türk Dış Politikası: Kurtuluş Savaşı'ndan Bugüne Olgular, Belgeler; Yorumlar Cilt I: 1919–1980* [Turkish Foreign Policy: From the War of Independence until Today, Facts, Documents, Comments, Vol. 1: 1919–1980], ed. Baskın Oran (İstanbul: İletişim, 2009), 781.

58. Oran, *Turkish Foreign Policy,* 620.

59. Erel Tellal, "SSCB ile İlişkiler" [Relations with the USSR], in *Türk Dış Politikası: Kurtuluş Savaşı'ndan Bugüne Olgular, Belgeler; Yorumlar: 1980–2001 II* [Turkish Foreign Policy: From the War of Independence until Today, Facts, Documents, Comments, Vol. 2: 1980–2001], ed. Baskın Oran (İstanbul: İletişim, 2002), 165.

60. This initiative would sow the seeds of the Turkic Council, which was founded in 2009 after several summits.

61. Boris Yeltsin, "*Ukaz Prezidenta Rossiyskoy Federatsii ot 17 dekabrya 1997 goda № 1300*" [Decree by the President of the Russian Federation from December 17, 1997 no. 1300 *Prezident Rossii*], December 17, 1997, www.kremlin.ru/acts/bank /11782.

62. *Partiya Karkerên Kurdistanê* (Kurdistan Workers Party) was founded in 1978 by a group of leftist university students led by Abdullah Öcalan. Since its foundation, the PKK has conducted terrorist attacks in Southeastern Turkey, killing tens of thousands of soldiers and civilians. PKK is designated as a terrorist organization by Turkey, the United States, and the European Union. Öcalan was captured in Kenya

in 1998 by the Turkish Intelligence Agency. He has since been imprisoned in Turkey, but the PKK remains operative.

63. "Turkey´s Political Relations with the Russian Federation," Republic of Turkey Ministry of Foreign Affairs, accessed November 15, 2020, www.mfa.gov.tr/turkey_s-political-relations-with-russian-federation.en.mfa.

64. Duygu Bazoğlu-Sezer, "Turkish-Russian Relations: The Challenges of Reconciling Geopolitical Competition with Economic Partnership," *Turkish Studies* 1, no. 1 (2000): 73.

65. Erel Tellal, "Rusya ile İlişkiler" [Relations with Russia], in *Türk Dış Politikası: Kurtuluş Savaşı'ndan Bugüne Olgular, Belgeler; Yorumlar: 1980–2001 II* [Turkish Foreign Policy: From the War of Independence until Today, Facts, Documents, Comments, Vol. 2: 1980–2001], ed. Baskın Oran (İstanbul: İletişim, 2002), 544.

66. Mikhail Meyer, "Rossiya i Turtsiya na iskhode XX v" [Russian and Turkey in the Twentieth Century], in *Rossiya i Turtsiya na poroge XXI veka: Na puti v Evropu ili v Evraziyu* [Russia and Turkey at the Doorstep of the Twenty-First Century: Towards Europe or Eurasia], ed. Irina Korbinski and Sherman Garnett (Moscow: Carnegie Endowment for International Peace, 1997), 21.

67. Mensur Akgün and Turan Aydın, *Türkiye-Rusya İlişkilerindeki Yapısal Sorunlar ve Çözüm Önerileri* [Structural Problems in Turkey-Russia Relations and Suggestions for Solutions] (İstanbul: Tüsiad, June 1999), 129–32.

68. Dmitri Trenin, "Russia and Turkey: A Cure for Schizophrenia," *Perceptions* 2, no. 2 (1997): 57–65.

69. Nagorno-Karabakh, a place over which Armenia claims possession, is located inside Azerbaijan. In 1988 the decline of the USSR caused the local Soviet government to pass a resolution to unify with Armenia. In late 1992, the conflict in the region turned into a full-fledged war between the independent Azerbaijan and Armenia.

70. Thomas Goltz, "Letter from Eurasia: The Hidden Russian Hand," *Foreign Policy*, no. 92 (1993): 99–102.

71. Gareth Winrow, "Turkey and the Newly Independent States of Central Asia and the Transcaucasus," *Middle East Review of International Affairs* 1, no. 2 (July 1997).

72. Under the leadership of Russia, the United States, and France, the Minsk Group was established in 1994 to resolve the Nagorno-Karabakh conflict. Turkey often criticizes the Minsk Group's protection of the advantageous position that Armenia established through the war.

73. In the process of the disintegration of the USSR, the unofficial opposition in Chechnya assumed power and declared independence under the leadership of Soviet Air Force general Dzokhar Dudayev. Failed in their attempts to bring about a functioning government, Chechnya was faced with internal dissent. In late 1994, Russia launched a military campaign in Chechnya, during which thousands of civilians were killed and hundreds of thousands displaced.

74. For more information, see Robert Olson, "The Kurdish Question and Chechnya: Turkish and Russian Foreign Policies since the Gulf War," *Middle East Policy* 4, no. 3 (March 1996): 106–18.

75. Zeyno Baran, "The Baku-Tbilisi-Ceyhan Pipeline: Implications for Turkey," in *The Baku-Tbilisi-Ceyhan Pipeline: Oil Window to the West,* ed. S. Frederick Starr and Svante E. Cornell (Washington, DC: Central Asia-Caucasus Institute & Silk Road Studies Program, 2005), 115.

CHAPTER 2

1. The United States based the legitimacy of the invasion on the Saddam Hussein regime's harboring of international terrorists and having weapons of mass destruction. The Bush Administration securitized the Saddam regime as the Axis of Evil, together with North Korea and Iran. The international community neither accepted such legitimacy nor securitized the Saddam regime in this manner.

2. See Barry Buzan and Ana Gonzalez-Pealez, "'International Community' after Iraq," *International Affairs* 81, no. 1 (2005): 41–43.

3. United Nations Security Council (UNSC), *Annex to the Letter Dated 8 November 2002 from the Representatives of China, France and the Russian Federation to the United Nations Addressed to the President of the Security Council,* UN Doc S/RES/1373 (November 8, 2002).

4. "America's Image Further Erodes, Europeans Want Weaker Ties," *Pew Research Center,* March 18, 2003.

5. Iraq had the world's third most proven oil reserves until the discovery of more oil in Venezuela. See OPEC, "Annual Statistical Bulletin 2019," (2019).

6. "Costs of War Project Releases Updated Estimates of Human and Budgetary Costs of Post-9/11 Wars," Brown University, September 1, 2021.

7. Mitat Çelikpala, "Rusya Federasyonuyla İlişkiler," in *Türk Dış Politikası* 3 *(2001–2012),* ed. Baskın Oran (İstanbul: İletişim, 2013), 534.

8. TC Dışişleri Bakanlığı, *Yazılı Soru Önergesi 026.21/2003/SPGY/239371* (Ankara: Turkish Grand National Assembly, November 6, 2003).

9. "Alexander Lebedev ile Ropörtaj," *Cumhuriyet* (October 15, 2001).

10. Mohiaddin Mesbahi, "Eurasia between Turkey, Iran and Russia," in *Key Players and Regional Dynamics in Eurasia: The Return of the "Great Game,"* ed. Marie Raquel Friere and Roger E. Kanet, 164–92 (London: Palgrave Macmillan, 2010), 173.

11. Dmitri Trenin, "Really Burying the Hatchet: Russia and Turkey Find Themselves on the Same Side," *Insight Turkey* 4, no. 2 (April–June 2002): 25–32.

12. "Vladimir Putin provel vstrechu s liderom partii spravedlivosti i razvitiya Turtsii Redzhepom Tayipom Erdoganom, pribyvshim nakanune v Moskvu s dvukhdnevnym rabochim vizitom" [Vladimir Putin Met with the Leader of the Justice and Development Party of Turkey, Recep Tayyip Erdogan, Who Arrived in Moscow on a Two-Day Working Visit], *Prezident Rossii,* December 24, 2002, http://kremlin .ru/events/president/news/27890.

13. Mohamad Arafat and Luqman O. Mahmood Alnuaimy, "Turkish-Russian Relations in the Era Of AKP," *Afyon Kocatepe Üniversitesi, İİBF Dergisi* 3, no. 1 (2011): 111.

14. This agreement was renewed in 2009 under Medvedev's presidency. See "Türkiye Cumhuriyeti İle Rusya Federasyonu Arasındaki İlişkilerin Yeni Bir Aşamaya Doğru İlerlemesi Ve Dostluğun Ve Çok Boyutlu Ortaklığın Daha da Derinleştirilmesine İlişkin Ortak Deklarasyon, Moskova, 13 Şubat 2009" [Joint Declaration between the Republic of Turkey and the Russian Federation on Progress toward a New Stage in Relations and Further Deepening of Friendship and Multidimensional Partnership], Republic of Turkey Ministry of Foreign Affairs, February 13, 2009, www.mfa.gov.tr/joint-declaration-between-the-republic-of-tur-key-and-the-russian-federation-on-progress-towards-a-new-stage-in-relations-and-further-deepening-of-friendship-and-multidimentional-partnership_-moscow_-13-february-2009.en.mfa.

15. Çelikpala, "Rusya ile İlişkiler," 538.

16. A. A. Guriyev, "Partiya spravedlivosti i razvitiya Turtsii: tri goda u vlasti" [Justice and Development Party of Turkey: Three Years in Rule], *Institut Blizhnevo Vostoka*, November 30, 2005, www.iimes.ru/?p=3972.

17. Necmettin Erbakan founded the *Milli Görüş* (National Vision) movement in the late 1960s. His movement called for the inclusion of pious Muslims in Turkey's politics and an Islamic domestic and foreign policy. Milli Görüş formed five parties, but four of them were shut down.

18. In an attempt to cleanse the public sphere of religion, Turkish state elites had prevented pious Muslims from promotion to top bureaucratic positions, especially in critical institutions such as the military, judiciary, and foreign service. For decades these elites formed a cadre of the guardians of Turkey's secular regime.

19. When the AK Party was founded, Erdoğan was under a political ban due to a poem he recited at a public rally in 1997. He was also briefly imprisoned in 1999, which boosted his popularity. He could become prime minister in 2003 after the lifting of the ban and after being elected in a snap election in Siirt Province.

20. Yalçın Akdoğan, *Muhafazakar Demokrasi* [Conservative Democracy] (Ankara: AK Parti, 2003), 79.

21. The AK Party did face a closure case in 2008, when ten out of eleven members of the Constitutional Court ruled that the party had become the center of anti-laicist activities. The vote count in the Constitutional Court was only one vote short of closing the AK Party.

22. In response to the rumors about Gül's candidacy, the Turkish General Staff (TGF), as the powerhouse of Turkey's secular elite, released a memorandum on its website to take a stance against a nonsecular candidate. The main opposition party CHP joined the TGF and alleged that the election of the new president required the presence of two-thirds of the MPs, a proportion the AK Party could not reach. When the Supreme Court confirmed this, the AK Party called for early elections, which brought it another victory. Abdullah Gül was elected president in the newly formed Parliament.

23. The Gülen Movement is a religious cult. Fetullah Gülen, who is the head of the organization, was a preacher in İzmir province in the 1970s, when he opened several student houses, dormitories, and boarding schools across Turkey and then abroad. Then he advised his followers to infiltrate the Turkish bureaucracy and military over

the decades. Since it was not possible for practicing Muslims to hold high offices in the military or judiciary, he advised his followers to practice *taqiyeh* (hiding one's religious beliefs). The members of the Gülen Movement in the police and judiciary played a significant role in persecuting the non-Gülenist bureaucrats, businessmen and activists in late 2000s.

24. Ahmet Davutoğlu is an international relations professor. He became the chief advisor to the prime minister in 2002, foreign minister in 2009 and prime minister in 2014. In his book, where he outlines his vision for Turkish foreign policy, he argues that there is a lack of strategic vision and coordination between foreign policy institutions, and Turkey should make more use of its historical ties with the peoples of the Balkans and the Middle East. Ahmet Davutoğlu, *Stratejik Derinlik* [Strategic Depth] (İstanbul: Küre Yayınları, 2001), 49–53.

25. Zeynep Taydaş and Özgür Özdamar, "A Divided Government, an Ideological Parliament, and an Insecure Leader: Turkey's Indecision about Joining the Iraq War," *Social Science Quarterly* 94, no. 1 (2012): 229.

26. It should be noted that there is a left-Kemalist/nationalist/secularist intellectual political community in Turkey called *Ulusalcılar* [Nationalists]. They promote stronger relations between Turkey and Russia in Eurasia against the West and maintain close relations with the Russian Eurasianists. For more information, see Şener Aktürk, "The Fourth Style of Politics: Eurasianism as a Pro-Russian Rethinking of Turkey's Geopolitical Identity," *Turkish Studies* 16, no. 1 (2015): 54–79.

27. "Hükümete AB desteği" [Support for EU to the Government], *Hürriyet*, May 21, 2020, www.hurriyet.com.tr/gundem/hukumete-ab-destegi-148000.

28. Gül was one of the founders of the AK Party. He served as the prime minister following the party's election victory due to Erdoğan's political ban, which was lifted in 2003. Gül then became foreign minister until 2007, when he became the president.

29. Abdullah Gül, "New Horizons in Turkish Foreign Policy," May 22, 2004, Boğaziçili Yöneticiler Vakfı, İstanbul, Dedeman Hotel.

30. Vincent Boland and Daniel Dombey, "Turkey's EU Hopes Fade with Sarkozy," May 7, 2007, www.ft.com/content/55374310-fc82-11db-9971-000b5df10621.

31. The project was put forward by the Bush administration in 2004. It aimed to transform the region called "the Greater Middle East" in cooperation with regional actors through extension of U.S. military and economic influence.

32. Baskın Oran, ed., *Turkish Foreign Policy: 1919–2006*, trans. Mustafa Akşin (Salt Lake City: University of Utah Press, 2011), 921.

33. Meltem Müftüler-Baç, "Turkey and the United States," *International Journal* 61, no. 1 (March 2006): 77.

34. Unity was founded by a group of bureaucrats and politicians against *Otechestvo–Vsya Rossiya* [Fatherland-All Russia] before the 1999 legislative elections. One of the most distinctive differences between these two groups was their stance toward the centralization of power in Russia.

35. Robert Service, *A History of Russia: From Tsarism to the Twenty-First Century* (Cambridge: Harvard University Press, 2009), 545–47.

36. Donald Kelley, *Russian Politics and Presidential Power: Transformational Leadership from Gorbachev to Putin* (Los Angeles: CQ Press, 2016), 131.

37. Vladimir Putin, "Ukaz Prezidenta Rossiyskoy Federatsii ot 13.05.2000 g. № 849" [Decree of the President of the Russian Federation No. 849 of 13.05.2000], *Prezident Rossii,* May 13, 2000, http://kremlin.ru/acts/bank/15492.

38. Oligarchs who refused to play by the new rules of the game and continued to criticize the government through their media institutions found themselves in exile or in jail. Examples include Michael Khodorkovsyky, who was imprisoned and then ended up in exile, and Boris Berezovsky, who was eventually found dead in his London apartment in 2013. For the details of the meeting, see Vladimir Putin, *"Vladimir Putin vstretilsya s rukovoditelyami ryada kompaniy i kommercheskikh bankov Rossii"* [Vladimir Putin Met with the Heads of a Number of Russia's Largest Companies and Commercial Banks], *Prezident Rossii,* July 28, 2000, http://kremlin .ru/events/president/news/38471.

39. Kelley, *Russian Politics,* 126.

40. Vladimir Putin, "Ukaz Prezidenta Rossiyskoy Federatsii ot 25 marta 2004 g. № 400" [Decree of the President of the Russian Federation No. 640 of 30.11.2016], *Prezident Rossii,* March 25, 2004, http://kremlin.ru/acts/bank/20694.

41. Stephen White, *Russia's Authoritarian Elections* (New York: Routledge, 2014), 116.

42. Kelley, *Russian Politics,* 145–46.

43. Roger Kanet, "Russian: Strategic Culture, Domestic Politics and Cold War 2.0," *European Politics and Society* 20, no. 2 (2019): 193.

44. These goals were identified explicitly in the Russian National Security Document, which was one of the first legal documents signed by Putin as the acting president. See Vladimir Putin, *"Ukaz Prezidenta Rossiyskoy Federatsii ot 17.12.1997 g. № 1300"* [Decree of the President of the Russian Federation No. 1300 of 17.12.1997], *Prezident Rossii,* January 17, 2000, www.kremlin.ru/acts/bank/11782.

45. These points are explicitly made in the Foreign Policy Concept of Russia, which was promulgated in June 2000. See Vladimir Putin, "Kontseptsiya vneshney politiki Rossiyskoy Federatsii" [Foreign Policy Concept of the Russian Federation], *Tekhexpert,* June 28, 2000, http://docs.cntd.ru/document/901764263.

46. Andrey Tsygankov, *Russia's Foreign Policy: Change and Continuity* (London: Rowman and Littlefield, 2016), 20.

47. Russia was eager to appear in solidarity with the United States that the Russian Foreign Policy Council advised Putin to drop the emphasis on multipolarity. Susan Turner, "Russia, China and a Multipolar World Order: The Danger in the Undefined," *Asian Perspective* 33, no. 1 (2009), 165.

48. Thomas Ambrosio, "The Russo-American Dispute over the Invasion of Iraq: International Status and the Role of Positional Goods," *Europe-Asia Studies* 57, no. 8 (2005): 1200.

49. Evgeny Finkel and Yitzhak M. Brudny, "Russia and the Colour Revolutions," *Democratization* 19, no. 1 (2012): 15–36.

50. Julianne Smith, *The NATO-Russia Relationship: Defining Moment or Déjà Vu?* (Washington, DC: CSIS, 2008), 1.

51. Roger Kanet, "From the 'New World Order' to 'Resetting Relations': Two Decades of U.S.–Russian Relations," in *Russian Foreign Policy in the 21st Century,* ed. Roger E. Kanet (New York: Palgrave Macmillan, 2011), 205–6.

52. Dmitry Medvedev, "Kontseptsiya vneshney politiki Rossiyskoy Federatsii" [Foreign Policy Concept of the Russian Federation], *Prezident Rossii,* July 12, 2008, http://kremlin.ru/acts/news/785.

53. Magda Leichtova, *Misunderstanding Russia: Russian Foreign Policy and the West* (Farnham: Ashgate, 2014), 73.

54. Cenk Başlamış, "Putin'in Ankara zamanlaması" [Putin's Ankara Timing], *Deutsche Welle Türkiye,* December 7, 2004, www.dw.com/tr/putinin-ankara -zamanlaması/a-2525673.

55. Yasemin Bilgel, "Regional Power Politics after the Cold War" (Unpublished PhD dissertation, University of Chicago, 2014), 3.

56. Tsygankov, *Russia's Foreign Policy,* 150.

57. Thomas Freedman, "Russian Policy towards the Middle East under Putin: The Impact of 9/11 and the War in Iraq," *Alternatives* 2, no. 2 (Summer, 2003): 72.

58. For more information about the process of negotiations, see Deniz Bölükbaşı, *1 Mart Vakası: Tezkere Krizi ve Sonrası Sonrası* [The Incident on March 1 Bill: The Bill Crisis and Aftermath] (İstanbul: Doğan Kitap, 2003), and Murat Yetkin, *Tezkere* [The Bill] (İstanbul: Remzi Kitabevi, 2017).

59. Taydaş and Özdamar, "A Divided Government," 235.

60. Mesbahi, "Eurasia between Turkey," 173.

61. Hill and Taşpınar, "Turkey and Russia," 88.

62. Roger E. Kanet and Rémi Piet, "Shifting Priorities in Russia's Foreign and Security Policy," in *Shifting Priorities in Russia's Foreign and Security Policy,* ed. Roger E. Kanet and Rémi Piet (Farnham: Ashgate, 2014), 2.

63. Özgür Özdamar, "Security and Military Balance in the Black Sea Region," *Southeast European and Black Sea Studies* 10, no. 3 (September 2010): 345.

64. "Charter of the Organization of the Black Sea Economic Cooperation," BSEC, May 1, 1999, www.bsec-organization.org/UploadedDocuments/Charter /CHARTERweb080630.pdf.

65. Igor Torbakov, "Turkey Sides with Moscow against Washington on Black Sea Force," *Jamestown Foundation,* March 3, 2006, https://jamestown.org/program /turkey-sides-with-moscow-against-washington-on-black-sea-force.

66. Mustafa Aydın, "Contending Agendas for the Black Sea Region: A Regional Alternative," *Demokratizatsiya* 20, no. 1 (2012): 53.

67. Özkan Şenol, "Cooperative Security in the Black Sea Region" (Master's thesis, Bilkent University, 2003), 81.

68. Emel G. Oktay, "Türkiye'nin Avrasya'daki Çok Taraflı Girişimlerine Bir Örnek: Karadeniz Ekonomik İşbirliği Örgütü" [An Example for Turkey's Multilateral Initiatives: Organization for Black Sea Economic Cooperation], *Uluslararası İlişkiler* 3, no. 10 (Yaz 2006): 168.

69. Mikhail Saakashvili, who was elected as a result of the popular protests in 2004, aimed to make Georgia a member of NATO and change the status quo in Georgia's de facto independent regions of South Ossetia and Abkhazia. Following an

incident that involved armed clashes between South Ossetian and Georgian authorities in August 2008, the Russian military forces initiated an invasion on August 8, 2008, which lasted until the cease-fire on August 12, 2008.

70. Igor Torbakov, *The Georgia Crisis and Russia-Turkey Relations* (Washington, DC: Jamestown Foundation, 2008), 20–21.

71. Claire Bigg, "Turkey Revives 'Caucasus Initiative,' but Faces Obstacles," *Radio Free Europe/Radio Liberty,* September 5, 2008, www.rferl.org/a/Turkey _Caucasus_Initiative_Obstacles/1196703.html.

72. John C. K. Daly, "Montreux Convention Hampers Humanitarian Aid to Georgia," *Eurasia Daily Monitor,* September 3, 2008, https://jamestown.org/program /montreux-convention-hampers-humanitarian-aid-to-georgia.

73. "Turkey Agrees to Supply Georgia Electricity: Source," *Reuters,* August 8, 2008, www.reuters.com/article/us-georgia-turkey-electricity-idUSIST00224320 080808.

74. "Türkiye Cumhuriyeti İle Ermenistan Cumhuriyeti Arasında Diplomatik İlişkilerin Kurulmasına Dair Protokol" [Protocol for the Formation of Diplomatic Relations between the Republic of Turkey and the Republic of Armenia], Republic of Turkey Ministry of Foreign Affairs, October 10, 2009, www.mfa.gov.tr/site_media /html/zurih-protokolleri-tr.pdf.

75. Richard Weitz, "Russian-Turkish Relations: Steadfast and Changing," *Mediterranean Quarterly* 21, no. 3 (2010): 77.

76. Mitat Çelikpala, "From Immigrants to Diaspora: Influence of the North Caucasian Diaspora in Turkey," *Middle Eastern Studies* 42, no. 3 (May 2006): 439.

77. Fatma Aslı Kelkitli, *Turkish–Russian Relations Competition and Cooperation in Eurasia* (London: Routledge, 2017), 81.

78. Murat Yetkin, "Rusya ile sıkı işbirliği" [Intense Partnership with Russia], *Radikal,* July 21, 2005, http://m.radikal.com.tr/yazarlar/murat_yetkin/rusya_ile_siki _isbirligi-752569.

79. M. K. Ziganshin, "Rossiysko-Turetskiye otnosheniya na sovremennom etape" [Russian-Turkish Relations in Contemporary Era], in *Turtsiya v novykh geopoliticheskıkh usloviyakh (materialy kruglogo stola mart 2004 g.)* [Turkey in New Geopolitical Conditions (Materials of the Round Table, March 2004)], ed. N. Y. Ulichenko (Moscow: Institut Vostokovedeniya RAN, 2004), 7.

80. CTSO grew out of the CIS agreement as a military alliance between a number of post-Soviet countries. The treaty became operative in 1994.

81. Bayram Balcı, *Islam in Central Asia and the Caucasus Since the Fall of the Soviet Union,* trans. Gregory Elliott (New York: Oxford University Press, 2018), 38.

82. James A. Warhola and William A. Mitchell, "The Warming of Turkish-Russian Relations: Motives and Implications," *Demokratizatsiya* 14, no. 1 (Winter 2006): 127.

83. Özgür Ekşi, "İsrail yerine Ruslardan füze alıyoruz" [We Are Purchasing Missiles from Russia Instead of Israel], *Hürriyet,* April 4, 2008, www.hurriyet.com.tr /gundem/israil-yerine-ruslardan-fuze-aliyoruz-8672522.

84. Erel Tellal, "SSCB ile İlişkiler," 163.

85. *"Gluboi Potok"* [Blue Stream], Gazprom, accessed December 10, 2020, www .gazprom.ru/projects/blue-stream.

86. This step was taken at the expense of excluding cheaper Turkmen gas. See "Turkmenistan: Gas Industry Seeks Export Routes," Radio Liberty, October 9, 1999, www.rferl.org/a/1092410.html.

87. "Beyaz enerji davası açıldı" [White Energy Case Was Opened], NTV, April 20, 2001, http://arsiv.ntv.com.tr/news/78189.asp.

88. Şükrü Elekdağ, *"Mavi İhanet"* [Blue Treason], *Milliyet,* May 13, 2001, http://gazetearsivi.milliyet.com.tr/Arsiv/2001/05/13.

89. Douglas Frantz, "Russia's New Reach: Gas Pipeline to Turkey," *New York Times,* June 8, 2001, www.nytimes.com/2001/06/08/world/russia-s-new-reach-gas -pipeline-to-turkey.html.

90. Fiona Hill, "Beyond Co-Dependency: European Reliance on Russian Energy," Brookings Institution (July 1, 2005), 4–5, www.brookings.edu/wp-content /uploads/2016/06/hill20050727.pdf.

91. Alexandra Jarosiewicz, *The Southern Gas Corridor: How the Azerbaijani-Turkish Project Becomes Part of the Game between Russia and the EU* (Warsaw: Centre for Eastern Studies, 2015), 9.

92. Angel Saz-Carranza and Maria Vandendriessche, "Routes to Energy Security: The Geopolitics of Gas Pipelines between Europe and its Neighbors," in *The New Politics of Strategic Resources: Energy and Food Security Challenges in the 21st Century,* ed. David Steven (Washington, DC: Brookings Institution Press, 2015), 129.

93. Nuri Yeşilyurt, "Orta Doğu ile İlişkiler" [Relations with the Middle East], in *Kurtuluş Savaşı'ndan Bugüne Olgular, Belgeler; Yorumlar Cilt: 2001–2012,* vol. 3 [Turkish Foreign Policy: From the War of Independence until Today, Facts, Documents, Comments, Vol. 3: 2001–2012], ed. Baskın Oran (İstanbul: İletişim, 2013), 458.

94. Rafael Kandiyoti, *Powering Europe: Russia, Ukraine, and the Energy Squeeze* (New York: Palgrave Macmillan, 2015), 69.

95. It should also be noted that Putin's speech at the Munich security conference in 2007, where he called for disarmament and adherence to the basic principles of international law against making use of NATO and OSCE for promoting the interests of the West, was immediately put on the website of the Turkish general chief of staff. See "Putin'in Münih konuşması Genelkurmay'ın sitesinde" [Putin's Münih Speech on the Website of the Chief of Staff], *Hürriyet,* February 15, 2007, www.hurriyet.com .tr/gundem/putinin-munih-konusmasi-genelkurmayin-sitesinde-5956456.

96. Emre Erşen, "Turkish-Russian Relations in the New Century," in *Turkey in the 21st Century: Quest for a New Foreign Policy,* ed. Özden Zeynep Oktav (New York: Routledge, 2011), 103.

CHAPTER 3

1. Arab Uprisings began in Tunisia, when grassroots protests brought about the toppling of Tunisia's Zine el-abidine Ben Ali, in January 2011. This event created a

domino effect and spread to other Arab nations across North Africa and the Middle East, bringing the end to decades-old dictatorships in Egypt and Libya as well as sparking protests in Syria.

2. For more information about the way this strategy was framed, please see Colin Dueck, *The Obama Doctrine: American Grand Strategy Today* (New York: Oxford University Press, 2015), and Barack Obama, "National Security Strategy," Obama White House (May 11, 2010), 25, https://obamawhitehouse.archives.gov/sites/default /files/rss_viewer/national_security_strategy.pdf.

3. Barack Obama, "National Security Strategy."

4. Hillary Clinton, "America's Pacific Century," *Foreign Policy,* October 11, 2011, https://foreignpolicy.com/2011/10/11/americas-pacific-century.

5. Paul K. MacDonald and Joseph M. Parent, "Graceful Decline? The Surprising Success of Great Power Retrenchment," *International Security* 35, no. 4 (2011): 11.

6. From late 2012, AK Party embarked on what is called the "Reconciliation Process" to end Turkey's decades long problems with the Kurdish minority. The steps included direct negotiations with the PKK's leader Öcalan, launching of Kurdish-language broadcasting in state television and the desecuritization of the Kurdish identity. In return, the PKK was expected to leave Turkish territory. However, the process was damaged with the escalation of violence due to the rising expectations of the PKK, who benefitted from the power vacuum in Kurdish majority areas of Syria. For more information, see Talha Köse, "Rise and Fall of the AK Party's Kurdish Peace Initiatives," *Insight Turkey* 19, no. 2 (2017): 139–65.

7. The peaceful protests to prevent an urban development project in *Gezi Park*, which is in the central Taksim district of İstanbul, spread to several major cities in Turkey and took an anti-AK Party/Erdoğan form, contesting various issues ranging from the restrictions on alcohol selling after 10:00 p.m. to police brutality. The protests, which reflect the deep-seated resentment of Turkey's secular middle class, made a lasting negative impact to the AK Party's image in Turkey and abroad. For more information, see Tarık Oğuzlu, "The Gezi Park Protests and Their Impact on Turkey's Soft Power Abroad," *Orsam,* June 18, 2013, www.orsam.org.tr/en/the-gezi -park-protests-and-their-impact-on-turkey-s-soft-power-abroad.

8. In February 2012, a Gülenist prosecutor prepared an indictment against Hakan Fidan, the head of Turkey's intelligence agency, accusing him of assisting the PKK. Gülenist prosecutors prepared a trumped-up indictment that associated Fidan, Erdoğan and several AK Party figures with an Iran-based terrorist organization (!). In December 2013, Gülenist police officers, in collaboration with Gülenist prosecutors arrested several AK Party figures on corruption charges. Simultaneously, secretly taped phone conversations of AK Party officials, including one between Erdoğan and his son, were leaked and promoted in the Gülenist media. With these steps, the Gülenists aimed to discredit AK Party in the eyes of Turkish nationalists through revealing peace talks with the PKK, in the eyes of the United States through fabricating links with Iran, and in the eyes of the voter through corruption allegations. For more information about Gülen Movement's fixation with Iran, see Ali Balcı, "When Foreign Policy Matters: The Gülen Movement's Fight with the AK Party over Iran," *Insight Turkey* 17, no. 1 (2015): 9–18. For an

authoritative account of the Gülen Movement, see Bayram Balcı and Hakan Yavuz, *Turkey's July 15th Coup What Happened and Why* (Salt Lake City: University of Utah Press, 2018).

9. In October 2014, PKK sympathizers murdered forty-five civilians during the protests against Turkey's Syria policy. The tensions resumed with the murder of two police officers in their homes by the PKK in July 2015. In effect, the conflicts between the Turkish army and the PKK resumed in urban areas in the proceeding period. See Kumru F. Toktamış, "A Peace That Wasn't: Friends, Foes, and Contentious Re-entrenchment of Kurdish Politics in Turkey," *Turkish Studies* 19, no. 5 (2008): 697–722.

10. Erdoğan left his seat of prime minister and party leader to the foreign minister, Davutoğlu in 2014. In the upcoming months, however, tensions began to emerge between the two over the new presidential system. Unsatisfied with Davutoğlu's cooperation in paving the way for a system change, Erdoğan forced him to resign and replaced him with Binali Yıldırım, former minister of transportation in May 2016. Davutoğlu later founded *Gelecek Partisi* (Future Party) and joined the opposition to Erdoğan.

11. "Obama Says U.S., Turkey Can be Model for World," CNN, April 6, 2009, www.cnn.com/2009/POLITICS/04/06/obama.turkey.

12. Led by Massoud Barzani, who belongs to the Barzani family, the Kurdistan Regional Government was established in 2005 as an autonomous region within Iraq. While Turkey was initially very anxious about this development, within the framework of the desecuritization of the political and cultural aspiration of Kurds, Turkey, under the AK Party, enjoyed very good relations with the KRG, making Iraq one of its most important trading partners.

13. In 2010, Brazil and Turkey brokered a nuclear swap deal with Iran. Yet the United States responded to this deal with new sanctions on Iran through UNSC.

14. After the regime changes, Erdoğan visited Tunisia and Egypt to show support. It was curious that on his visit Erdoğan offered Turkish *laicite* as a working model for Muslim democracies. "Erdoğan'dan Mısır'a laiklik çağrısı" [Call for Laicism to Egypt from Erdoğan], *Dünya Bülteni,* September 13, 2011, www.dunyabulteni.net /afrika/erdogandan-misira-laiklik-cagrisi-h174406.html.

15. Medvedev's priorities were reflected in the "National Security Strategy of Russia until 2020," which he signed as president. In the document, economic issues were given emphasis and it was indicated that Russia will focus on "multi-vector diplomacy" instead of bloc confrontation. See Dmitry Medvedev, "Strategiya natsional'noy bezopasnosti Rossiyskoy Federatsii do 2020 goda" [National Security Strategy of the Russian Federation until 2020], *Prezident Rossii,* May 12, 2009, http://kremlin.ru/supplement/424.

16. Medvedev's priorities were reflected in the "National Security Strategy of Russia until 2020," which he signed as president. In the document, economic issues were given emphasis and it was indicated that Russia will focus on "multi-vector diplomacy" instead of bloc confrontation. Please see "Dmitri Medvedev, Strategiya natsional'noy bezopasnosti Rossiyskoy Federatsii do 2020 goda" [National Security Strategy of the Russian Federation until 2020], *Kremlin,* May 12, 2009.

17. "Gosduma Prinyala Zakon o Popravkakh k Konstitutsii RF" [Duma Accepted a Law on Amendment to the Constitution], *Kommersant,* November 14, 2008, www.kommersant.ru/doc/1061738.

18. Kelley, *Russian Politics,* 238.

19. Maria Snegovaya, "Anti-Western Sentiment as the Basis for Russian Unity," *Carnegie Moscow,* April 4, 2014, https://carnegie.ru/commentary/57115.

20. By then, the emphasis on multipolarity had been consolidated as one of the core principles of Russia's strategy. This could be seen in the National Security Concept of 2013 and 2016. See Vladimir Putin, "Ukaz Prezidenta Rossiyskoy Federatsii ot 30.11.2016 g. № 640" [Decree of the President of the Russian Federation No. 640 of 30.11.2016], *Prezident Rossii,* November 30, 2016, http://kremlin.ru/acts/bank/41451. The stronger rhetoric used in 2015 National Strategy Document was the reflection and harbinger of more assertive actions by Vladimir Putin, "Ukaz Prezidenta Rossiyskoy Federatsii ot 31.12.2015 g. № 683" [Decree of the President of the Russian Federation No. 683 31.12.2015], *Prezident Rossii,* December 31, 2015, http://kremlin.ru/acts/bank/40391.

21. Chris Dolan, *Obama and the Emergence of a Multipolar World Order: Redefining U.S. Foreign Policy* (Lanham, MD: Lexington Books, 2018), 99.

22. Medvedev commented that the Tunisia example should be a lesson for all the governments. "Prezident Rossii vystupil na otkrytii Vsemirnogo ekonomicheskogo foruma" [The Russian President Spoke at the Opening of the World Economic Forum], *Prezident Rossii,* January 26, 2011, http://kremlin.ru/events/president/news/10163/audios.

23. Weeks before the intervention, Erdoğan rejected a NATO intervention as a solution to the situation in Libya. This would cause the sidelining of Turkey in the NATO operation. Jonathan Head, "Libya: Turkey's Troubles with NATO and No-Fly Zone," BBC, March 25, 2011, www.bbc.com/news/world-africa-12864742. Russia enabled the operation by abstaining in the UNSC Resolution which authorized a no-fly zone on Libya. When the no-fly zone turned into an extensive military campaign led by France, Putin expressed his strong disapproval. Sergey Smirnov, "Medvedev nazval nedopustimymi slova Putina o Livii" [Medvedev Called Putin's Words about Libya Unacceptable], *Vedomosti,* March 21, 2011, www.vedomosti.ru/politics/articles/2011/03/21/medvedev_nazval_nedopustimymi_slova_putina_o_livii.

24. Christopher Phillips, *The Battle for Syria: International Rivalry in the Middle East* (New Haven, CT: Yale University Press, 2016), 59.

25. On March 6, 2011, a group of teenagers who painted anti-regime graffiti on a school wall were arrested and tortured. The brutal government crackdown on the protesting families further agitated the Syrians and protests spread to other cities. In the meantime, Assad took some steps for dialogue, such as giving citizenship to the Kurds in Northern Syria and allowing other political parties. Yet, these steps did not ease the tensions amid continued violent oppression of the protesters.

26. After a group of defecting soldiers labeled themselves as the Free Syrian Army (FSA) several groups of soldiers and militia began to nominally join FSA from mid-2011 onward. Yet the FSA lacked a line of command from the political

leadership to the military leadership to the militiamen, the fighters were undisciplined, and it never had a strong leader. Efforts to regulate the opposition into a more formal structure through the involvement of Turkey, Qatar, and exiled Syrian opposition also failed.

27. ISIS (Islamic State in Iraq and Sham, or simply ISIS) was born in Iraq as an AlQaeda affiliated terrorist organization in the mid-2000s and became popular through graphic execution videos circulated online. The Syrian Civil War provided an opportunity to expand Daesh's regional influence. At first, Daesh sent a cell in Syria to create Al-Nusra front in late 2011. Al-Nusra's strengthening itself in Syria as a separate force created tensions with Daesh, which entered to Syria in late 2012. Daesh prioritized taking the leadership of the insurgency and primarily attacked other insurgent groups. The Assad regime considered Daesh as an asset which weakens the opposition through military operations and tarnishing their image by misrepresenting them. About the regime's strategic avoidance of Daesh, see Cassandra Vinograd and Ammar Cheikh Omar, "Syria, ISIS Have Been 'Ignoring' Each Other on Battlefield, Data Suggests," *CBS News* (December 11, 2014). For more information about Daesh, please see Charles Lister, *The Syrian Jihad Al Qaeda the Islamic State and the Evolution of an Insurgency* (New York: Oxford University Press, 2016); Ufuk Ulutaş, *The State of Savagery: ISIS in Syria* (Ankara: SETA, 2016).

28. Formed in 2003 as a branch of the PKK, the PYD (*Partiya Yekîtiya Demokrat* —Democratic Union Party) is a political organization based in Syria. The YPG (Yekîneyên Parastina Gel—People's Protection Units) is the PYD's armed wing. The power of PYD was negligible at the beginning of the conflict. Its strength significantly increased in the subsequent phases of the conflict as a result of Assad regime's concentrating its efforts on opposition and leaving PYD to strengthen and disturb Turkey in Northern Syria, which is home to three Kurdish majority cities— Afrin, Ayn-el Arab, and Qamishli. PYD also had access to a formidable fighting force with clear command structure and discipline from PKK. After the emergence of Daesh, PYD presented itself as a secular actor to the United States to be used against Daesh. As a result of this cooperation, PYD gained legitimacy in the West and control over areas that stretches well beyond the Kurdish-majority regions in Syria. For more information about PYD please see Can Acun and Bünyamin Keskin, *The PKK's Branch in Northern Syria PYD-YPG* (Ankara: SETA Yayınları, 2016); Kayla Koontz, *Borders Beyond Borders: The Many (Many) Kurdish Political Parties of Syria* (Washington, DC: Middle East Institute, 2019); and Harriet Allsopp and Wladimir van Wilgenburg, *The Kurds of Northern Syria: Governance, Diversity and Conflicts* (New York: I.B. Tauris, 2019).

29. In late March 2011, the then–secretary of state, Hillary Clinton, emphasized the widespread image of Assad as a reformer in the U.S. Congress. Glenn Kessler, "Hillary Clinton's Uncredible Statement on Syria," *Washington Post*, April 4, 2011, www.washingtonpost.com/blogs/fact-checker/post/hillary-clintons-uncredible-statement-on-syria/2011/04/01/AFWPEYaC_blog.html. By August, this position was revised with Obama calling Assad to step aside. Macon Phillips, "President Obama: 'The Future of Syria Must Be Determined by Its People, but President Bashar al-Assad Is Standing in Their Way,'" White House President Barack Obama, August

18, 2011, https://obamawhitehouse.archives.gov/blog/2011/08/18/president-obama
-future-syria-must-be-determined-its-people-president-bashar-al-assad. In August
2012, with respect to the allegations about the chemical weapons usage by the regime
forces, Obama stated that chemical weapons usage by the regime would constitute
a "red line" and change his calculus. See Barack Obama "Remarks by the President
to the White House Press Corps," ed. James S. Brady, August 20, 2012, https://
obamawhitehouse.archives.gov/the-press-office/2012/08/20/remarks-president-white
-house-press-corps.

30. Phillips, *The Battle,* 76.

31. Turkey and Syria had several unresolved issues in their bilateral relations
until the early 2000s including water disputes and PKK camps in Syria, which ended
when Syria agreed to expel the PKK in the Adana Agreement in 1998. During the
2000s, Turkey-Syria relations significantly developed within the framework of AK
Party's zero problems with neighbors. The visa requirements were lifted, bilateral
trade significantly increased after the signing of free trade agreements and Turkey
mediated the rapprochement between Syria and Israel in 2008. In 2010, Turkey,
Lebanon, Jordan, and Syria signed the Quadripartite High-Level Cooperation council
for creating a zone of free movement of peoples and goods in Levant.

32. Throughout 2011, Turkey used diplomatic pressure to convince Assad to
negotiate with the opposition. The continuing brutality by regime forces and the
expectation that Assad's fall was inevitable turned Turkey against the Assad regime.
The escalation of tone in Turkey's consideration of the Syrian regime can be observed
from the press releases of the National Security Council throughout the year 2011.
See "2011 Yılı Basın Açıklamaları" [Press Releases of the Year 2011], *Milli Güvenlik
Kurulu Genel Sekreterliği,* October 21, 2015, www.mgk.gov.tr/index.php/2011-yili
-basin-aciklamalari.

33. When the increasing migration created instabilities in Europe, Turkey
accepted to re-admit the illegal immigrants in return for the abolition of the visa
regime for Turkish citizens and economic aid, with the EU Readmission Agreement
in 2013.

34. Since the beginning of the Syrian crisis, multiple cities of Turkey were targeted by bombing attacks several times between 2013 and 2016. The most major ones
of these were the 2013 Reyhanlı car bombing at a public market (fifty-three civilians
died; the perpetrator who was captured in Syria admitted his guilt and ties with the
Syrian regime), the 2015 Ankara bombing at a rally of leftist group (109 civilians
died; one of the suicide bombers was identified as an ISIS member), and 2016 Ankara
car bombing targeting public buses (thirty-eight civilians died; PKK affiliated TAK
claimed responsibility).

35. At that point, Syria began to use Soviet-era Scud missiles, which could represent a great security risk to Turkey especially if used with chemical warheads. See
"Turkey Requested NATO Missile Defences over Syria Chemical Weapons Fears,"
The Guardian, December 21, 2012, www.theguardian.com/world/2012/dec/02/turkey
-syria-chemical-weapons-fears.

36. Turkey and the United States agreed on the necessity of eradicating ISIS.
However, while the United States considered ISIS as the source of insecurity in Syria,

Turkey saw ISIS as a consequence of the chaos perpetuated by the Assad regime. More importantly, Turkey considered the PYD as a bigger threat to its national security while the United States began to provide military support to the YPG from late 2014 onward in an attempt to eradicate ISIS.

37. Syria was one of the most loyal allies of USSR during the Cold War. Yet, Russia only developed relations with Syria in the 2000s, when it became Syria's most important arms supplier. It is noteworthy that Syria was one of the handful of countries that supported Russia's military endeavor in Georgia in 2008. For more information, see Nikolay Kozhanov, "Russian Support for Assad's Regime: Is There a Red Line?" *The International Spectator* 48, no. 2 (June 2013): 25–31.

38. For more information, see Yulia Nikitina, "The 'Color Revolutions' and 'Arab Spring' in Russian Official Discourse," *Connections* 14, no. 1 (Winter 2014): 87–104.

39. Noah Bonsey, "More Chechnya, Less Afghanistan," *Foreign Policy*, December 10, 2015, https://foreignpolicy.com/2015/10/12/more-chechnya-less-afghanistan.

40. "UN Documents for Syria: Other," Security Council Report, accessed October 28, 2020, www.securitycouncilreport.org/un_documents_type/other-documents/?ctype=Syria&cbtype=syria.

41. Following the incident, Assad claimed that the plane was shot down on the suspicion that it was an Israeli jet and expressed his regret. See Loveday Morris, "Assad: We Shot Down Turkish Jet Thinking It Was Israeli," *Independent*, July 4, 2012, www.independent.co.uk/news/world/middle-east/assad-we-shot-down-turkish-jet-thinking-it-was-israeli-7906821.html.

42. "Erdoğan: Rusya Suriye'nin diliyle konuşuyor" [Russia Is Using Syria's Language], *Dünya Bülteni,* June 27, 2012, www.dunyabulteni.net/politika/erdogan-rusya-suriyenin-diliyle-konusuyor-h215963.html.

43. "Turkey Says Syrian Plane Contained Ammunition," *VOA News,* October 11, 2012, www.voanews.com/world-news/middle-east-dont-use/turkey-says-syrian-plane-contained-ammunition.

44. "Syria Plane Carried Radar Parts, Not Weapons—Russia," BBC, October 12, 2012, www.bbc.com/news/world-europe-19928139.

45. "Duvarda silah varsa piyesin sonunda patlar" [If You Have a Pistol Hanging on the Wall in the First Act, It Fires in the Last Act], *Hürriyet,* December 3, 2012, www.hurriyet.com.tr/gundem/duvarda-silah-varsa-piyesin-sonunda-patlar-22068771.

46. "Russians Strike Targets in Syria, but Not ISIS Areas," *New York Times,* September 30, 2015, www.nytimes.com/2015/10/01/world/europe/russia-airstrikes-syria.html.

47. Before the Jet Crisis, Russia's ambassador in Ankara was called in to the Republic of Turkey ministry of foreign affairs for this matter. "Türkmen'e bomba yağıyor" [Bombs Are Raining on Turkmen], *Hürriyet,* November 20, 2015, www.hurriyet.com.tr/dunya/turkmene-bomba-yagiyor-40016723. It is noteworthy that in the interview he gave to Oliver Stone, Putin noted that Turkey's sensitivity regarding the Turkmens was never brought to him. Vladimir Putin, interview by Oliver Stone, *Putin Interviews,* Showtime, February 26, 2016.

48. Vladimir Putin, "70-ya sessiya General'noy Assamblei OON" [70th Session of the UN General Assembly], *Prezident Rossii,* September 28, 2015, http://kremlin.ru/events/president/news/50385.

49. "Cumhurbaşkanı Erdoğan 3. Uluslararası Ombudsmanlık Sempozyumu'nda açıklamalarda bulundu" [President Erdoğan Made Statements in the Third Symposium of Ombudsmanship], *Anadolu Ajansı,* September 16, 2015, www.aa.com.tr/tr/turkiye/cumhurbaskani-erdogan-3-uluslararasi-ombudsmanlik-sempozyumunda-aciklamalarda-bulundu/54913. At this point, the activities of Russia were evaluated in Turkey's National Security Council, as an indication that Turkey was considering the issue at a strategic level. *Milli Güvenlik Kurulu Genel Sekreterliği* "21 Ekim 2015 Tarihli Toplantı" [Meeting on October 21, 2015], October 21, 2015, www.mgk.gov.tr/index.php/21-ekim-2015-tarihli-toplanti.

50. "Syria Conflict: Russia Violation of Turkish Airspace 'No Accident,'" BBC, October 6, 2015, www.bbc.com/news/world-europe-34453739.

51. Regarding the issue, Turkey and Russia have contesting accounts. While Turkey argues that the Russian pilot was warned upon the violation of airspace, Russia argues that the violation never occurred and there was no warning. For Turkey's account with the voice recordings of the warnings, see "Genelkurmay Rus uçağına yapılan uyarıların ses kaydını yayımladı" [Turkish Chief of Staff Released the Voice Recordings of the Warnings Made to the Russian Aircraft], *Anadolu Ajansı,* November 25, 2015, www.aa.com.tr/tr/turkiye/genelkurmay-rus-ucagina-yapilan-uyarilarin-ses-kaydini-yayimladi/481350. For Russia's account, see "V Sirii sbit rossiyskiy Su-24" [A Russian SU-24 Fell in Syria], *Interfax,* November 24, 2015, www.interfax.ru/world/481166.

52. Eliott C. McLaughlin, Don Melvin, and Jethro Mullen, "Turkey Won't Apologize for Downing Russian Warplane, Erdogan Says," CNN, November 26, 2015, www.cnn.com/2015/11/26/middleeast/syria-turkey-russia-warplane-shot-down/index.html.

53. "'Udar v spinu': Zayavleniya Vladimira Putina ob intsidente s Su-24," [Stab in the Back: Statement of Putin on the Incident of SU-24], *RIA Novosti,* November 24, 2015, https://ria.ru/20151124/1327592353.html.

54. "Statement by the NATO Secretary General after the Extraordinary NAC Meeting," NATO, November 24, 2015, www.nato.int/cps/en/natohq/news_125052.htm.

55. Putin, *Putin Interviews,* Showtime, February 26, 2016.

56. "PYD Opens Office in Moscow, Inauguration Attended by HDP Deputy," *Daily Sabah,* February 11, 2016, www.dailysabah.com/diplomacy/2016/02/11/pyd-opens-office-in-moscow-inauguration-attended-by-hdp-deputy.

57. Emre Erşen, "Evaluating the Fighter," 92.

58. Andrew Higgins and Peter Baker, "Russia Claims U.S. Is Meddling over Ukraine," *New York Times,* February 6, 2014, www.nytimes.com/2014/02/07/world/europe/ukraine.html.

59. The Crimean Tatars, one of the many Turkic communities across the Black Sea region, have lived in the Crimean Peninsula for centuries. The demography of the peninsula began to change after the Russian takeover in 1783. In the following

century, millions of Crimean Tatars were forced to migrate to Turkey to escape perse-cution. Following WWII, on Stalin's orders, all the people of Crimean Tatar descent were forcibly relocated to Central Asia. After decades of struggle under Soviet autoc-racy a portion of them could come back to the peninsula but they now make up only 10 percent of the population there.

60. Vitaly Shevchenko, "'Little Green Men' or 'Russian Invaders'?" BBC, March 11, 2014, www.bbc.com/news/world-europe-26532154.

61. Vladimir Peshkov, "The Donbas: Back in the USSR," *European Council on Foreign Relations,* September 1, 2016, https://ecfr.eu/article/essay_the_donbas_back _in_the_ussr.

62. For a list of sanctions applied to Russia by the U.S., see "Ukraine and Russia Sanctions," U.S. State Department, accessed November 2, 2020, www.state.gov /ukraine-and-russia-sanctions.

63. "EU Restrictive Measures in Response to the Crisis in Ukraine," European Council, accessed November 2, 2020, www.consilium.europa.eu/en/policies /sanctions/ukraine-crisis.

64. For more information about this process, see Ulrich Speck, *The West's Response to the Ukraine Conflict: A Transatlantic Success Story* (Washington, DC: Transatlantic Academy, 2016), 7–11.

65. Suzanne Loftus and Roger E. Kanet, "Growing Confrontation between Russia and the West: Russia's Challenge to the Post–Cold War Order," in *The Russian Challenge to the European Security Environment,* ed. Roger Kanet (Cham: Palgrave, 2017), 18.

66. Richard Connolly, *Russia's Response to Sanctions: How Western Economic Statecraft Is Reshaping Political Economy in Russia* (New York: Cambridge University Press, 2018), 192–95.

67. "Joint Statement of the NATO-Ukraine Commission," NATO, May 13, 2015, www.nato.int/cps/en/natohq/official_texts_119425.htm.

68. Igor Delanoe, "After the Crimean Crisis: Toward a Greater Russian Maritime Power in the Black Sea," *Southeast European and Black Sea Studies* 14, no. 3 (2014): 373.

69. For more information about the plight of Crimean Tatars, see Muhammet Koçak, *Crimea and the Crimean Tatars after Annexation by Russia* (Ankara: SETA, June 2014).

70. "Turkey Waiting for Russia, West on Ukraine Problem," *Hurriyet Daily,* May 12, 2014, www.hurriyetdailynews.com/turkey-waiting-for-russia-west-on-ukraine -problem-66311.

71. "Erdoğan: Biz Rafa Kaldırdık" [Erdoğan: We Shelved It], *Milliyet,* December 5, 2015, www.milliyet.com.tr/siyaset/erdogan-biz-rafa-kaldirdik -2158892.

72. In response to a claim by Russia's foreign minister, Sergey Lavrov, who claimed that a number of U.S. vessels extended their presence beyond the established limits, Turkey immediately denied Lavrov's claim and provided a detailed report about the presence of the mentioned vessels. See Serkan Demirtaş, "Turkey under NATO and Russia Pressure over Black Sea," *Hurriyet Daily,* April 5, 2014, www

.hurriyetdailynews.com/opinion/serkan-demirtas/turkey-under-nato-and-russia-pressure-over-black-sea-64579.

73. Recep Tayyip Erdoğan, "Suriye'de Tüm Kırmızı Çizgilerin Aşılmasına Rağmen Bir Adım Atılmadı" [No Step Was Taken Despite All the Redlines Were Crossed in Syria], TC Cumhurbaşkanlığı, May 11, 2016, www.tccb.gov.tr/haberler/410/43922/suriyede-tum-kirmizi-cizgilerin-asilmasina-ragmen-bir-adim-atilmadi.html.

74. "Ukraine, Turkey Armies Sign Military Cooperation Roadmap until 2020," *Kyiv Post,* May 16, 2016, www.kyivpost.com/article/content/ukraine-politics/ukraine-turkey-armies-sign-military-cooperation-roadmap-until-2020-413826.html.

75. "Kak Zhivut v Turtsii, 'Novyye Mukhadzhıry' iz Rossii: Migratsiya Rossiyskikh musul'man v 2000-ye gody" [How They Live in Turkey: New "Mukhadzhirs" from Russia: Russian Muslims in the 2000s], *Aziya i Afrıka Segodnya* 8 (2018): 63.

76. The Chechen fighters often quickly rose up the ranks within various organizations with one of them leading the attack which captured Iraq's Anbar province.

77. For more information, see I. Dobaev and O. Cherevkov, "Transformatsiya Radikal'nogo Islamistskogo Dvizheniya na Severnom Kavkaze: ot 'Imarata Kavkaz' k 'Vilayyatu Kavkaz'" [Transformation of the Radikal Islamic Movement in North Caucasus: From the "Emirate of Caucasus" to the "Wilayat of Caucasus"], *Rossiya i Musul'manskiy Mir* 9 (2017): 13–30.

78. Mairbek Vatchagaev, "Another Chechen Émigré Murdered in Turkey," *Eurasia Daily Monitor,* March 6, 2015, https://jamestown.org/program/another-chechen-emigre-murdered-in-turkey-2.

79. "Başbakan Ahmet Davutoğlu'ndan Putin'e Esad göndermesi: Kadirov arıyor" [An Allusion from the Prime Minister Ahmet Davutoğlu to Putin on Assad: He Is Looking for a Kadirov], *Hürriyet,* February 16, 2016, www.hurriyet.com.tr/gundem/basbakan-ahmet-davutoglundan-putine-esad-gondermesi-kadirov-ariyor-40055161.

80. "Erdoğan'dan Azerbaycan-Ermenistan açıklaması" [Azerbaijan-Armenia Statement from Erdoğan], *Yeni Şafak,* April 2, 2016, www.yenisafak.com/dunya/erdogandan-azerbaycan-ermenistan-aciklamasi-2444314.

81. "Turkey Must Stop Meddling in Other States' Affairs, End Support of Terrorism, Russia Says," *Reuters,* April 4, 2016, www.reuters.com/article/us-mideast-crisis-russia-syria-turkey-idUSKCN0X10XT.

82. Crisis Group, *Russia and Turkey in the Black Sea and the South Caucasus* (Brussels: Crisis Group, June 28, 2018), 20.

83. For more information about the curious backchannel diplomacy behind the letter that took place with the involvement of Nazarbayev, see Murat Yetkin "Türk-Rus krizini bitiren gizli diplomasinin öyküsü" [Story of the Secret Diplomacy That Ended the Turkish-Russian Crisis], *Hürriyet*, August 8, 2016, www.hurriyet.com.tr/yazarlar/murat-yetkin/turk-rus-krizini-bitiren-gizli-diplomasinin-oykusu-40185705.

84. "*Rusya Devlet Başkanı Putin, Ankara'da, Türkiye-Rusya arasında 100 milyar dolarlık dev anlaşma*" [Russian President Putin Is in Turkey, 100 Billion

Dollar Worth Deal between Turkey and Russia], *Habertürk,* December 1, 2014, www
.haberturk.com/ekonomi/is-yasam/haber/1014724-dev-anlasma-tamam.

85. The Council was summoned every year, in either Ankara or in Moscow,
with the participation of ministers from both countries. During the meetings, the
delegations of two countries worked together to explore new areas of cooperation
and strengthen the existing ties. Turkey had similar mechanisms with Greece, Serbia,
Pakistan, and Syria (until the Syrian Civil War). For more information, see Tekin
Aycan Taşlı, "Türkiye-Rusya İlişkileri ve Üst Düzey İşbirliği Konseyi (ÜDİK)"
[Turkey-Russia Relations and the High-Level Cooperation Council], *Kare* 8 (2019):
81–128.

86. Vladimir Putin, "Ukaz o merakh po obespecheniyu natsional'noy bezopasnosti Rossii i zashchite grazhdan Rossii ot prestupnykh i inykh protivopravnykh
deystviy i o primenenii spetsial'nykh ekonomicheskikh mer v otnoshenii Turtsii"
[Decree on Measures to Ensure the National Security of Russia and Protect Russian
Citizens from Criminal and Other Illegal Actions and on the Application of Special
Economic Measures against Turkey], *Prezident Rossii,* November 28, 2015, http://
kremlin.ru/events/president/news/50805.

87. "Vneseny izmeneniya v Ukaz o merakh po obespecheniyu natsional'noy
bezopasnosti i zashchite grazhdan Rossii ot protivopravnykh deystviy i o primenenii
spetsial'nykh ekonomicheskikh mer v otnoshenii Turtsii" [Amendments Were Made
to the Decree on Measures to Ensure National Security and Protect Russian Citizens
from Illegal Actions and on the Application of Special Economic Measures against
Turkey], *Prezident Rossii,* December 28, 2015, http://kremlin.ru/events/president
/news/51027.

88. "Antalya'nın 'Turizm Krizi'" [Antalya's Tourism Crisis], 140 Journos,
May 31, 2016, https://140journos.com/antalyanin-turizm-krizi-d83894c13ba8?gi
=6bb0b6d9ac03.

89. "Rusya gazı keserse kısa vadede ısınma, elektrik ve sanayide alternatif
zayıf" [Alternatives in Heating, Electricity, and Industry Are Weak in the Short-
Term if Russia Cuts the Gas], *Hürriyet,* December 3, 2015, www.hurriyet.com.tr
/ekonomi/rusya-gazi-keserse-kisa-vadede-isinma-elektrik-ve-sanayide-alternatif
-zayif-40022179.

90. "Russia to Stop Gas Delivery via Ukraine by 2019, Push Ahead with Turkish
Stream—Miller," *Russia Today,* April 13, 2015, www.rt.com/business/249273-gaz-
prom-ukraine-gas-transit.

91. Gareth Winrow, "Turkey and Russia: The Importance of Energy Ties,"
Insight Turkey 19, no. 1 (2017): 23.

92. Winrow, "Turkey and Russia," 24.

93. For the full timeline of the progression of the project, see "Akkuyu Nuclear
Power Plant," Turkish Atomic Energy Authority, accessed November 14, 2020, www
.taek.gov.tr/en/institutional/akkuyu-nuclear-power-plant.html.

94. Winrow, "Turkey and Russia," 24.

95. "Turkish PM Erdoğan to Putin: Take Us to Shanghai," *Hurriyet Daily,*
November 22, 2013, www.hurriyetdailynews.com/turkish-pm-erdogan-to-putin-take
-us-to-shanghai-58348.

96. Nuri Yeşilyurt, "Explaining Miscalculation and Maladaptation in Turkish Foreign Policy toward the Middle East during the Arab Uprisings: A Neoclassical Realist Perspective," *All Azimuth* 6, no. 2 (2017): 66.

CHAPTER 4

1. Stephan Walt, *The Hell of Good Intentions: America's Foreign Policy Elite and the Decline of U.S. Primacy* (New York: Farrar, Straus & Giroux, 2018), 92–93.

2. "Rusya" [Rusya], TC Cumhurbaşkanlığı, August 9, 2020, www.tccb.gov.tr/yurt-disi-ziyaretler/355/49958/rusya.

3. "Timeline of WHO's Response to COVID-19," WHO, September 9, 2020, www.who.int/news/item/29-06-2020-covidtimeline.

4. There is a lot of speculation regarding the level of involvement and culpability of the Gülen Movement and Fetullah Gülen himself. On this particular issue, please see Bayram Balcı and M. Hakan Yavuz, *Turkey's July 15th Coup What Happened and Why* (Salt Lake City: University of Utah Press, 2018); and Mert Hüseyin Akgün, *Fetö'nün Askeri Kanadı-Genelkurmay Çatı Davası* [FETÖ's Military Wing: The Case of the Chief of Staff] (Ankara: SETA Yayınları, 2020).

5. M. Hakan Yavuz and Rasim Koç, "The Gülen Movement vs. Erdoğan: The Failed Coup," in *Turkey's July 15th Coup What Happened and Why*, ed. Bayram Balcı and M. Hakan Yavuz (Salt Lake City: University of Utah Press, 2018), 87–89.

6. Recep Tayyip Erdoğan, "Olağanüstü Hal Kapsamında Alınan Tedbirlere İlişkin Kanun Hükmünde Kararname" [Decree Having the Force of Law on the Measures Taken within the Framework of the State of Emergency], *Resmi Gazete*, July 22, 2016.

7. Under the new constitution, the president of Turkey selects his own cabinet from outside of the Parliament without parliamentary approval. The office of prime minister was abolished and subsumed by the president. The president is also able to issue decrees having the force of law on certain issues. With a change in law Erdoğan was able to return to the AK Party as the head of the party. All in all, the system provided more power to the president while decreasing the relevance of the Parliament.

8. The system would come into force with simultaneous parliamentary and presidential elections in 2019. However, the elections were moved earlier after the NMP leader Devlet Bahçeli called for early elections. In the 2018 parliamentary elections, AK Party ran with MHP, which supported Erdoğan's presidency. Prior to the election, AK Party and MHP enabled the forming of preelection alliances. In accordance with this law, AK Party and MHP formed the People's Alliance (*Cumhur İttifakı*). The formation of the Nation Alliance (*Millet İttifakı*) by four major opposition parties completely transformed the Turkish body politic, transforming it into a competition between two big blocs. Later two parties led by former ministers in AK Party governments—Ali Babacan's Democracy and Progress Party and Ahmet Davutoğlu's Future Party—joined the Nation Alliance.

9. The letter was widely circulated as a letter of apology. However, the letter did not contain an apology. The letter contained the Russian word *izviniite*, which could be translated as "I am sorry" in Russian, specifically addressed to the family of the pilot.

10. As the coup attempt took place in Turkey, top U.S. officials avoided declaring their support for the elected government. The first U.S. reaction to the coup was when the U.S. state minister, John Kerry, emphasized the importance of continuity in Turkey's foreign engagements, in a manner that could easily be interpreted as a green light to the *putschists*.

11. It should be remembered that such feeling was discussed as a major component of Turkey's strategic culture in chapter 2.

12. Burhanettin Duran, "15 Temmuz Darbe Girişiminin Türkiye'nin İç Ve Dış Politikasina Etkisi" [The Impact of the July 15 Coup Attempt of Turkey's Domestic and Foreign Policy], in *Türk Dış Politikası Yıllığı 2017* [Yearbook of Turkish Foreign Policy 2017], ed. Burhanettin Duran, Kemal İnat, and Mustafa Caner (Ankara: SETA, 2018), 29.

13. "Erdoğan: Türkiye yanlış güvenlik anlayışını terk etmiştir" [Turkey Has Left the Wrong Understanding of Security], NTV, October 19, 2020, www.ntv.com.tr/turkiye/turkiye-yanlis-guvenlik-anlayisini-terk-etmistir,XQuseHLt2UW5dtuvV6m5oA.

14. For more information, see Berdal Aral, "'The World Is Bigger Than Five': A Salutary Manifesto of Turkey's New International Outlook," *Insight Turkey* 21, no. 4 (2019): 71–95.

15. Dilek Kütük, "Importance of Humanitarian Aid During Covid-19 for Turkey as a Status-Seeking Country," Belgrade Security Forum, May 16, 2020, www.belgradeforum.org/the-importance-of-humanitarian-aid-during-covid-19-for-turkey-as-a-status-seeking-country.

16. For more information about Turkey's pursuit of independence in defense industry, see Ismail Demir, "Transformation of the Turkish Defense Industry: The Story and Rationale of the Great Rise," *Insight Turkey* 22, no. 3 (2020): 17–40.

17. Can Kasapoğlu, "Turkey's Burgeoning Defense Technological and Industrial Base and Expeditionary Military Policy," *Insight Turkey* 22, no. 3 (2020): 116–17.

18. Andrew Brunson had lived in Turkey for over twenty years until his arrest in 2017 on terror charges and for his alleged connections with both FETÖ and PKK. U.S. president Trump was personally involved in pushing Turkey to release the pastor. When in August 2018 Trump raised the import taxes on Turkish steel, Turkish Lira lost 40 percent of its value in a day. For more information, see Jen Kirby, "The U.S.-Turkey Trade Spat, Explained," *Vox,* August 15, 2018, www.vox.com/world/2018/8/15/17687928/turkey-united-states-tariffs-lira-andrew-brunson.

19. Halkbank is a state-owned Turkish bank. The deputy head of Halkbank was arrested in 2017 at the U.S. border and faced a trial charging him for violating U.S. sanctions against Iran. It is noteworthy that the case was significantly supported by evidence provided by a former Turkish police officer, who was fired from his job due to his connections with FETÖ. See "U.S. Jury Finds Turkish Banker Hakan Atilla Guilty on Five Counts," *Hurriyet Daily,* January 3, 2018, www.hurriyetdailynews.com/turkish-banker-convicted-of-helping-iran-evade-us-sanctions-125198.

20. "Putin Says U.S. Knew about Turkey's July 15 Coup Attempt," *Yeni Şafak,* June 17, 2017, www.yenisafak.com/en/news/putin-says-us-knew-about-turkeys-july -15-coup-attempt-2725798.

21. Weizhen Tan, "Oil Prices Fall to 17-Year Low as Saudi Arabia–Russia Standoff Continues, Coronavirus Hits Demand," *CNBC,* March 30, 2020, www .cnbc.com/2020/03/30/oil-falls-amid-saudi-arabia-russia-price-war-coronavirus-hits -demand.html.

22. "Doverie Politikam" [Trust in Politicians], Levada Tsentr, October 8, 2018, www.levada.ru/2018/10/08/doverie-politikam-2.

23. These changes included social welfare measures, ensuring the supremacy of the Constitution over international law, securing the role of the State Council, enhancing the role of the Duma and strengthening the Constitutional Court. See "Kakiye Izmeneniya c Konstitutsiyu Podderzhany v Pervom Chtenii" [What Changes to the Constitution Were Supported in First Reading?], Gosudarstvennaya Duma Federal'nogo Sobraniya Rossiiskoy Federatsii, January 23, 2020, http://duma.gov.ru/ news/47599.

24. Vladimir Putin "Poslaniye Prezidenta Federal'nomu Sobraniyu" [Message from the President to the Federal Assembly], *Prezident Rossii,* January 15, 2020, http://kremlin.ru/events/president/news/62582.

25. The new Constitution enabled the president to dismiss the prime minister and to supervise strategic ministries. Yet, the president can appoint the prime minister only after receiving the approval of the State Duma and the upper house of the Parliament can now fire the members of the Constitutional Court.

26. Thomas Grove and Georgi Kantchev, "Discord in Kremlin Helps Putin Remain Russia's No. 1," *Wall Street Journal,* March 6, 2020, www.wsj.com/articles /putin-sows-discord-in-kremlin-to-remain-russias-no-1-11583424937.

27. "Gosduma Prinyala Zakon o Popravkakh k Konstitutsii RF" [Duma Accepted a Law on Amendment to the Constitution], *Interfax,* March 11, 2020, www.interfax .ru/russia/698543.

28. "Trump Says Putin 'a Leader Far More Than Our President,'" BBC, September 8, 2016, www.bbc.com/news/election-us-2016-37303057.

29. "Trump: I Said NATO Was Obsolete 'Not Knowing Much about NATO,'" *Business Insider,* April 24, 2017, www.businessinsider.com/trump-nato-obsolete -2017-4.

30. Dmitry Trenin, "The Relationship between the USA and Russia in the Trump Era," *Inside Over,* May 2, 2019, www.insideover.com/politics/the-relationship -between-the-usa-and-russia-in-the-trump-era.html.

31. Following the allegations about Russia's interference into the 2016 U.S. presidential elections, Trump's term was plagued with judicial investigations.

32. Andrew Osborn, "Putin Warns NATO against Closer Ties with Ukraine and Georgia," *Reuters,* July 19, 2018, www.reuters.com/article/us-russia-nato-putin/putin -warns-nato-against-closer-ties-with-ukraine-and-georgia-idUSKBN1K92KA.

33. Vladimir Putin, "Ukaz Prezidenta Rossiyskoy Federatsii ot 20.07.2017 g. № 327" [Decree of the President of the Russian Federation No. 327 of 20.07.2017], *Prezident Rossii,* July 20, 2017, http://kremlin.ru/acts/bank/42117.

34. Vladimir Putin, "Ukaz Prezidenta Rossiyskoy Federatsii ot 02.06.2020 g. № 355" [Decree of the President of the Russian Federation No. 355 of 02.06.2020], *Prezident Rossii,* June 2, 2020, www.kremlin.ru/acts/bank/45562.

35. Ufuk Ulutaş and Burhanettin Duran, "Türkiye'nin DEAŞ'la Mücadelesinin Kritik Dönemeci: Fırat Kalkanı Harekâtı," [The Critical Juncture of Turkey's Fight with ISIS: Operation Euphrates Shield], in *Türk Politikası Yıllığı 2016* [Yearbook of Turkish Foreign Policy 2016], ed. Burhanettin Duran, Kemal İnat, and Mustafa Caner (Ankara: SETA, 2019), 23.

36. "Remarks by Vice President Joe Biden and Turkish Prime Minister Binali Yildirim at a Press Availability," Obama White House, August 25, 2016, https://obamawhitehouse.archives.gov/the-press-office/2016/08/25/remarks-vice-president-joe-biden-and-turkish-prime-minister-binali.

37. "Syria Conflict: Russia and Turkey 'in First Joint Air Strikes on IS,'" BBC, January 18, 2017, www.bbc.com/news/world-middle-east-38667895.

38. "Telefonnyy razgovor s Prezidentom Turtsii Redzhepom Tayipom Erdoganom" [Telephone Conversation with Turkish President Recep Tayyip Erdogan], *Prezident Rossii,* February 9, 2017, http://kremlin.ru/events/president/news/53851.

39. "Battle of Aleppo Ends after Years of Bloodshed with Rebel Withdrawal," *Reuters,* December 13, 2016, www.reuters.com/article/us-mideast-crisis-syria-idUSKBN1420H5.

40. "Background Briefing on the Joint Statement by the President of the United States and the President of the Russian Federation on Syria," U.S. Department of State, November 11, 2017, www.state.gov/background-briefing-on-the-joint-state-ment-by-the-president-of-the-united-states-and-the-president-of-the-russian-federa-tion-on-syria.

41. "Lavrov ob"yasnil slozhivshuyusya v Afrine situatsiyu provokatsiyami SSHA" [Lavrov Explained the Situation in Afrin as a U.S. Provocation], *Interfax,* February 20, 2018, www.interfax.ru/world/600761.

42. "The Latest: Russia Warned Kurdish Officials of Turkey Attack," Associated Press, January 21, 2018, https://apnews.com/article/1ca16b2e78c944bbbb7d092554be906b.

43. "Turkey Refutes Russian Call for Syria's Afrin," *Hurriyet Daily,* April 10, 2018, www.hurriyetdailynews.com/turkey-refutes-russian-call-for-syrias-afrin-130097.

44. "Russia Says Evacuation from Syria's Eastern Ghouta to End within Days," TRT World, April 4, 2018, www.trtworld.com/mea/russia-says-evacuation-from-syria-s-eastern-ghouta-to-end-within-days-16463.

45. "Rebels Agree Withdrawal Deal for Enclave Near Syria's Homs," *Reuters,* May 2, 2018, www.reuters.com/article/us-mideast-crisis-syria-homs/rebels-agree-withdrawal-deal-for-enclave-near-syrias-homs-idUSKBN1I329Y.

46. "Syrian Army Continues Push into Quneitra amid Ongoing Evacuations," *Al Jazeera,* July 22, 2018, www.aljazeera.com/news/2018/07/22/syrian-army-continues-push-into-quneitra-amid-ongoing-evacuations.

47. "Rudskoy: Astana sürecinin garantör ülkeleri, İdlib'de gözlem noktası kurma çalışmalarını tamamladı" [Rudskoy: Guarantor States of the Astana Process

Completed Setting Up Observation Posts in Idlib], *Sputnik Türkiye,* May 23, 2018, https://tr.sputniknews.com/rusya/201805231033562557-rudskoy-astana-sureci-idlib.

48. The M4 highway connects Latakia and Aleppo, and the M5 highway connects Aleppo and Damascus.

49. "İdlib mutabakatı zaptının 10 maddesi" [10 Articles of Idlib Memorandum of Understanding], *Sputnik Türkiye,* September 19, 2018, https://tr.sputniknews.com/ortadogu/201809191035276132-idlib-mutabakat-zaptinin-on-maddesi.

50. Following the intensification of PKK attacks in Turkey in 1998, Turkey threatened Syria with a ground invasion if the latter did not expel PKK camps inside Syria. With Egypt's mediation, the Adana Agreement was signed between Turkey and Syria. Through the agreement Syria enabled Turkey to chase PKK militants 5 km deep into the Syrian territory.

51. "Turkish and U.S. Troops Begin Joint Patrols in Syria's Manbij," *Middle East Eye,* November 2, 2018, www.middleeasteye.net/news/turkish-and-us-troops-begin-joint-patrols-syrias-manbij.

52. Donald Trump (@realdonaldtrump), "After Historic Victories against ISIS, It's Time to Bring Our Great Young People Home!" Twitter, December 19, 2018, 06:10 PM, https://twitter.com/realDonaldTrump/status/1075528854402256896.

53. "U.S. Envoy to the Coalition against ISIS Resigns over Trump's Syria Policy," NPR, December 22, 2018, www.npr.org/2018/12/22/679535003/u-s-envoy-to-the-coalition-against-isis-resigns-over-trumps-syria-policy.

54. "Statement from the Press Secretary," White House, October 6, 2019, www.whitehouse.gov/briefings-statements/statement-press-secretary-85.

55. "Kurdish Forces Backed by U.S. Strike Deal with Syria's Assad, in Major Shift in 8-Year War," CNN, October 14, 2019, www.cnn.com/2019/10/14/middleeast/syria-turkey-kurds-civilians-isis-intl-hnk/index.html.

56. "FULL TEXT: Memorandum of Understanding between Turkey and Russia on Northern Syria," *The Defense Post,* October 22, 2019, www.thedefensepost.com/2019/10/22/russia-turkey-syria-mou.

57. "Dozens Killed as Russian, Syrian Air Attacks in Idlib Intensify," *Al Jazeera,* May 4, 2019, www.aljazeera.com/news/2019/05/04/dozens-killed-as-russian-syrian-air-attacks-in-idlib-intensify.

58. Sarp Özer, "İdlib'de askeri konvoya saldırı" [Attack on a Military Convoy in Idlib], *Anadolu Ajansı,* August 19, 2019, www.aa.com.tr/tr/turkiye/idlibde-askeri-konvoya-saldiri/1559639.

59. "Syria War: Russia Announces Ceasefire in Idlib Rebel Stronghold," BBC, August 30, 2019, www.bbc.com/news/world-middle-east-49527419.

60. Carlotta Gali, "Syrian Attacks Draw Turkey Deeper into Syrian War," *New York Times,* February 28, 2020, www.nytimes.com/2020/02/12/world/middleeast/syria-turkey-russia-war.html.

61. Fatima Tlis, "The Strike: Did Russia Knowingly Target Turkish Troops?" *Polygraph,* February 28, 2020, www.polygraph.info/a/turkey-russia-syria-fact-check/30460458.html.

62. "Bahar Kalkanı Operasyonu Kapsamında Rejim Kayıpları" [Losses of the Regime in the Spring Shield Operation], *Suriye Gündemi,* March 2, 2020, www.suriyegundemi.com/bahar-kalkani-operasyonu-kapsaminda-rejim-kayiplari.

63. "Üçlü Astana Zirvesi sona erdi" [Trilateral Astana Summit Ended], *TRT Haber,* July 1, 2020, www.trthaber.com/haber/gundem/uclu-astana-zirvesi-sona-erdi-497705.html.

64. "Why Turkey's Libya Commitment Angers Arab Nations," *Deutsche Welle,* January 18, 2020, www.dw.com/en/why-turkeys-libya-commitment-angers-arab-nations/a-52052924.

65. "A Small Price to Pay for Tripoli," *Meduza,* October 2, 2019, https://meduza.io/en/feature/2019/10/02/a-small-price-to-pay-for-tripoli.

66. Priyanka Boghani, "The Man at the Center of the Chaos in Libya: Khalifa Haftar," *PRI,* May 31, 2014, www.pri.org/stories/2014-05-31/man-center-chaos-libya-khalifa-haftar.

67. Mona Thakkar, "Russia and Turkey in Libya, Testing the Waters?" *International Policy Digest,* February 3, 2020, https://intpolicydigest.org/2020/02/03/russia-and-turkey-in-libya-testing-the-waters.

68. "Tripoli: UAE Drones Hit Residential Area, Injure Family," *Middle East Monitor,* September 22, 2019, www.middleeastmonitor.com/20190922-tripoli-uae-drones-hit-residential-area-injure-family.

69. "Libya's GNA Activates Security Deal with Turkey," *Anadolu Agency,* December 19, 2019, www.aa.com.tr/en/africa/libyas-gna-activates-security-deal-with-turkey/1678715.

70. Jo Becker and Eric Schmitt, "As Trump Wavers on Libya, an ISIS Haven, Russia Presses On," *New York Times,* February 7, 2018, www.nytimes.com/2018/02/07/world/africa/trump-libya-policy-russia.html.

71. "Trump Has Praise for Controversial Libyan Gen. Khalifa Haftar in Phone Call," Associated Press, April 19, 2019, https://apnews.com/article/7cc6cc853ab05d1adda72195b5f58d4c.

72. "Libya Conflict: Haftar 'Leaves' Moscow Ceasefire Talks without Deal," BBC, January 14, 2020, www.bbc.com/news/world-africa-51104846.

73. "EU Launches Operation IRINI to Enforce Libya Arms Embargo," European Council, March 31, 2020, www.consilium.europa.eu/en/press/press-releases/2020/03/31/eu-launches-operation-irini-to-enforce-libya-arms-embargo/#.

74. "Operation Irini: Turkey Slams EU Mission to Contain Arms to Libya," *Al Jazeera,* June 19, 2020, www.aljazeera.com/news/2020/6/19/operation-irini-turkey-slams-eu-mission-to-contain-arms-to-libya.

75. "The Azerbaijan-Armenia Conflict Hints at the Future of War," *Economist,* October 10, 2020, www.economist.com/europe/2020/10/10/the-azerbaijan-armenia-conflict-hints-at-the-future-of-war.

76. "Pashinyan Says He Twice Had Phone Calls with Russia's President but Thinks He Will Be Having More with the French President," *Aysor,* October 3, 2020, www.aysor.am/en/news/2020/10/03/pashinyan-phone/1751306.

77. "'Turkey Has a Clear Objective of Reinstating the Turkish Empire,' Armenian PM Says," France 24, October 2, 2020, www.france24.com/en/20201002-turkey-has-a-clear-objective-of-reinstating-the-turkish-empire-armenian-pm-says.

78. "Cumhurbaşkanı Erdoğan: Azerbaycanlı kardeşlerimizin yanlarındayız" [President Erdoğan: We Are with Our Azerbaijani Brothers], *TRT Haber,* October

1, 2020, www.trthaber.com/haber/gundem/cumhurbaskani-erdogan-azerbaycanli
-kardeslerimizin-yanlarindayiz-520086.html.

79. Sebastien Roblin, "Cheap Drones from China, Turkey and Israel Are Fueling
Conflicts Like Armenia and Azerbaijan's," *NBC News,* October 14, 2020, www
.nbcnews.com/think/opinion/cheap-drones-china-turkey-israel-are-fueling-conflicts
-armenia-azerbaijan-ncna1243246.

80. "Russia Deplores 'Political' Charges against Former Armenian Officials,"
Azatutyun, July 31, 2018, www.azatutyun.am/a/29401668.html.

81. "Russia to 'Assist' Armenia if Conflict with Azerbaijan Spreads beyond
Nagorno-Karabakh," *Deutsche Welle,* October 31, 2020, www.dw.com/en/russia
-to-assist-armenia-if-conflict-with-azerbaijan-spreads-beyond-nagorno-karabakh/a
-55457174.

82. UNSC Resolutions 822, 853, 874, and 884 of 1993 called for the Armenian
forces to evacuate the Azerbaijani territories. See Security Council, "Resolution 884,"
November 12, 1993, http://unscr.com/en/resolutions/doc/884.

83. Elena Teslova, "No One Can Say Turkey Flouted Int'l Law in Karabakh:
Putin," *Anadolu Agency,* November 17, 2020, www.aa.com.tr/en/azerbaijan-front
-line/no-one-can-say-turkey-flouted-intl-law-in-karabakh-putin/2047249.

84. "Nagorno-Karabakh: Turkey to Send Peacekeepers to Azerbaijan to Monitor
Truce," France 24, November 17, 2020, www.france24.com/en/europe/20201117
-nagorno-karabakh-turkey-to-send-peacekeepers-to-azerbaijan-to-monitor-truce.

85. "Ukrayna ile Türkiye arasında savunma sanayinde iş birliği" [Cooperation
Between Ukraine and Turkey in Industry], *Anadolu Ajansı,* July 4, 2018, www.aa.
com.tr/tr/dunya/ukrayna-ile-turkiye-arasinda-savunma-sanayinde-is-birligi-/11
95063.

86. Burak Ege Bekdil, "Turkey, Ukraine Seek to Jointly Produce 'Sensitive'
Defense Technology," *Defensenews,* September 16, 2020, www.defensenews.com
/unmanned/2019/09/16/turkey-ukraine-seek-to-jointly-produce-sensitive-defense
-technology.

87. "Türkiye'den, Gürcistan'a 17 milyon dolarlık askeri reform tahsisi" [17
Million Dollars' Worth of Grant for Military Reform from Turkey to Georgia],
Akşam, December 25, 2019, www.aksam.com.tr/guncel/turkiyeden-gurcistana-17
-milyon-dolarlik-askeri-reform-tahsisi/haber-1032779.

88. "Turkish Foreign Minister Calls for Enlarged NATO, Georgia Membership,"
Reuters, January 23, 2020, www.reuters.com/article/us-davos-meeting-turkey
-georgia/turkish-foreign-minister-calls-for-enlarged-nato-georgia-membership
-idUSKBN1ZM1HB.

89. Luke Harding, "Russia Has Enough Troops Ready to Take Kyiv, Says
Former Ukraine Defence Chief," *The Guardian*, February 6, 2022, www.theguardian
.com/world/2022/feb/06/russian-troops-ready-to-seize-ukrainian-capital-says-former
-defence-chief.

90. Christina Wilkie and Amanda Macias, "U.S. Intelligence Agencies Point to
Potential Russian Invasion of Ukraine within a Month's Time," *CNBC,* January 14,
2022, www.cnbc.com/2022/01/14/russia-could-invade-ukraine-within-next-month
-us-intelligence.html.

91. Adam Taylor, "Russia's Putin Bluffing on Ukraine? Allies in the United States and Europe Are Divided," *Washington Post*, January 25, 2022, www.washingtonpost.com/world/2022/01/25/russia-ukraine-putin-bluff.

92. Max Fisher, "Putin's Case for War, Annotated," *New York Times*, February 24, 2022, www.nytimes.com/2022/02/24/world/europe/putin-ukraine-speech.html.

93. UNHCR, "Refugees Fleeing Ukraine (since 24 February 2022)," March 13, 2022, https://data2.unhcr.org/en/situations/ukraine.

94. *Independent*, "Ukraine Says More Than 11,000 Russian Troops Killed since Invasion Began," March 13, 2022, www.independent.co.uk/news/world/europe/ukraine-invasion-russia-troops-killed-b2029556.html.

95. BBC, "Ukraine: Are Arms Shipments from the West Making a Difference?" March 8, 2022, www.bbc.com/news/world-60655349.

96. BBC, "What Sanctions Are Being Imposed on Russia over Ukraine Invasion?" March 12, 2022, www.bbc.com/news/world-europe-6012565.

97. Hilal Kaplan. "A Book Aged Well 'Turkey as a Stabilizing Power in an Age of Turmoil,'" *Daily Sabah*, April 1, 2022, www.dailysabah.com/opinion/columns/a-book-aged-well-turkey-as-a-stabilizing-power-in-an-age-of-turmoil.

98. White House, "Readout of President Biden's Call with President Recep Tayyip Erdogan of Turkey," March 10, 2022, www.whitehouse.gov/briefing-room/statements-releases/2022/03/10/readout-of-president-bidens-call-with-president-recep-tayyip-erdogan-of-turkey.

99. TRT World, "Türkiye to Russia: Ukraine 'War' Must Stop," March 16, 2022, www.trtworld.com/europe/türkiye-to-russia-ukraine-war-must-stop-55559.

100. Paul Stronski and Nicole Ng, *Cooperation and Competition Russia and China in Central Asia, the Russian Far East, and the Arctic* (Washington, DC: Carnegie, 2018), 10.

101. Seçkin Köstem, "Geopolitics, Identity and Beyond: Turkey's Renewed Interest in the Caucasus and Central Asia," in *Turkey's Pivot to Eurasia Geopolitics and Foreign Policy in a Changing World Order*, ed. Emre Erşen and Seçkin Köstem (London: Routledge, 2018), 118.

102. "Putin: Erdoğan'ın katkısı büyük" [Putin: Erdoğan's Contribution is Big], *Takvim*, September 28, 2017, www.takvim.com.tr/guncel/2017/09/28/putin-erdoganin-katkisi-buyuk.

103. "Turkey, Russia Seek New Ways to Reach $100B in Bilateral Trade," *Daily Sabah*, April 09, 2019, www.dailysabah.com/business/2019/04/09/turkey-russia-seek-new-ways-to-reach-100b-in-bilateral-trade.

104. "Rus ticaretinde TL'nin adı yok" [Turkish Lira Doesn't Have a Place in Russian Trade], Ekonomi Alla Turca, November 1, 2019, https://ugurses.net/2019/11/01/rus-ticaretinde-tlnin-adi-yok.

105. Aaron Mehta, "Turkey Officially Kicked Out of F-35 Program, Costing U.S. Half a Billion Dollars," *Defense News,* July 17, 2019, www.defensenews.com/air/2019/07/17/turkey-officially-kicked-out-of-f-35-program.

106. Joe Gould, "U.S. Could Buy Turkey's Russian-Made S-400 under Senate Proposal," *Defense News,* June 29, 2020, www.defensenews.com/congress/2020/06/29/us-could-buy-turkeys-russia-made-s-400-under-senate-proposal.

107. Valerie Insinna, Joe Gould, and Aaron Mehta, "Congress Has Secretly Blocked U.S. Arms Sales to Turkey for Nearly Two Years," *Defense News,* August 12, 2020, www.defensenews.com/breaking-news/2020/08/12/congress-has-secretly -blocked-us-arms-sales-to-turkey-for-nearly-two-years.

108. Jim Zanotti and Clayton Thomas, "Turkey: Background and U.S. Relations in Brief," *Congressional Research Service,* November 9, 2020, https://crsreports .congress.gov/product/pdf/R/R44000.

109. "The United States Sanctions Turkey under CAATSA 231," The U.S. Department of State, December 14, 2020, https://2017-2021.state.gov/the-united -states-sanctions-turkey-under-caatsa-231/index.html.

110. "Russia-Turkey Cross-Cultural Year Has Lots in Store, Says Russia's Ambassador to Turkey," *TASS,* February 10, 2019.

111. "Gas Fields and Tensions in the Eastern Mediterranean," *Euractiv,* October 26, 2020, www.euractiv.com/section/energy-environment/news/gas-fields-and -tensions-in-the-eastern-mediterranean.

112. "No. 216, 21 Eylül 2011 Türkiye—KKTC Kıta Sahanlığı Sınırlandırma Anlaşması İmzalanmasına İlişkin Dışişleri Bakanlığı Basın Açıklaması" [No. 216, September 21, 2011 Turkish Ministry of Foreign Affairs Press Release for the Signing of the Continental Shelf Agreement between Turkey and the TRNC], Republic of Turkey Ministry of Foreign Affairs, September 21, 2011, www.mfa.gov.tr/no_-216 _-21-eylul-2011-turkiye-_-kktc-kita-sahanligi-sinirlandirma-anlasmasi-imzalanma- sina-iliskin-disisleri-bakanligi-basin-ac_.tr.mfa.

113. "Eastern Mediterranean Countries to Form Regional Gas Market," *Reuters,* January 14, 2019, www.reuters.com/article/us-egypt-energy-gas-idUSKCN1P81FG.

114. Ariel Cohen, "Turkey-Libya Maritime Deal Upsets Mediterranean Energy Plan," *Forbes,* January 8, 2020, www.forbes.com/sites/arielcohen/2020/01/08/turkey -libya-maritime-deal-upsets-mediterranean-energy-plan/?sh=985e1bb6bee4.

115. "Greece, Israel, Cyprus Sign EastMed Gas Pipeline Deal," *Reuters,* January 2, 2020, www.reuters.com/article/us-greece-cyprus-israel-pipeline/greece-israel -cyprus-sign-eastmed-gas-pipeline-deal-idUSKBN1Z10R5.

116. "Turkey Spars with EU over Fresh Drilling off Cyprus," *Reuters,* January 19, 2020, www.reuters.com/article/us-turkey-cyprus/turkey-spars-with-eu-over-fresh -drilling-off-cyprus-idUSKBN1ZI0G0.

117. "Russia Ready to Mediate in Eastern Mediterranean Crisis: Lavrov," *Al Jazeera,* September 8, 2020, www.aljazeera.com/news/2020/9/8/russia-ready-to -mediate-in-eastern-mediterranean-crisis-lavrov.

118. "Akkuyu Nükleer Santrali inşaatı görüntülendi" [The Construction of Akkuyu Nuclear Power Plant Was Monitored], *Hürriyet,* July 23, 2019, www.hurriyet.com.tr /galeri-akkuyu-nukleer-santrali-insaati-goruntulendi-41281990/1.

119. Sezgin Pancar, "Eğitimlerini tamamlayan 53 Türk mühendis Akkuyu NGS'de işe başladı" [53 Turkish Engineers Who Completed Their Studies Started Work in Akkuyu NPP], *Anadolu Ajansı,* October 6, 2020, www.aa.com.tr/tr/turkiye /egitimlerini-tamamlayan-53-turk-muhendis-akkuyu-ngsde-ise-basladi/1872114.

120. "Turkey to Expand LNG Storage Capacity with 3rd FSRU," *Hurriyet Daily,* October 9, 2020, www.hurriyetdailynews.com/turkey-to-expand-lng-storage-capacity-with-3rd-fsru-158966.

121. "TANAP Is Ready to Deliver Natural Gas to Europe," TANAP, December 24, 2019, www.tanap.com/media/press-releases/tanap-is-ready-to-deliver-natural-gas-to-europe.

122. Kostis Geropoulos, "Reducing Dependence on Russia, Turkey Speeds Up TANAP Pipeline to EU," *New Europe,* February 20, 2018, www.neweurope.eu/article/reducing-dependence-russia-turkey-speeds-tanap-pipeline-eu.

CONCLUSION

1. The literature on the contours of the emerging world order became quite popular, with contributions from preeminent scholars who agree on the decline of the United States but have varied opinions on the dynamics of today's international system. See Richard Haas, "The Age of Nonpolarity," *Foreign Affairs* 87, no. 3 (May 2008): 44–56; Charles A. Kupchan, *No One's World: The West, the Rising Rest, and the Coming Global Turn* (New York: Oxford University Press, 2012); Fareed Zakaria, *The Post-American World* (New York: W. W. Norton, 2008); Amitav Acharya, *The End of American World Order* (Cambridge: Polity, 2018); and Barry Buzan, "The Inaugural Kenneth N. Waltz Annual Lecture: A World Order without Superpowers: Decentred Globalism," *International Relations* 25, no. 1 (2011): 3–25.

2. Şener Aktürk, "Turkish–Russian Relations after the Cold War (1992–2002)," *Turkish Studies* 7, no. 3 (2006): 337–64.

3. See "Russia and Turkey in the Black Sea and the South Caucasus," Crisis Group (June 28, 2018); Mohiaddin Mesbahi, "Eurasia between Turkey, Iran and Russia," in *Key Players and Regional Dynamics in Eurasia: The Return of the "Great Game,"* ed. Marie Raquel Friere and Roger E. Kanet, 164–92 (London: Palgrave Macmillan, 2010); and William Hale, "Turkey, the U.S., Russia, and the Syrian Civil War," *Insight Turkey* 21, no. 4 (Fall 2019): 25–40.

4. Norrin M. Ripsman, Jeffrey W. Taliaferro, and Steven E. Lobell, *Neoclassical Realist Theory of International Politics* (New York: Oxford University Press, 2016).

Bibliography

140 Journos. "Antalya'nın 'Turizm Krizi'" [Antalya's Tourism Crisis]. May 31, 2016. https://140journos.com/antalyanin-turizm-krizi-d83894c13ba8?gi=6bb0b6d9ac03.

Acharya, Amitav. *The End of American World Order*. Cambridge: Polity, 2018.

Acun, Can, and Bünyamin Keskin. *The PKK's Branch in Northern Syria PYD-YPG*. Ankara: SETA Yayınları, 2016.

Ahmad, Feroz. *The Turkish Experiment in Democracy 1950–1975*. Boulder, CO: Westview Press, 1977.

Akdevelioğlu, Atay, and Ömer Korkçooğlu. "SSCB ile İlişkiler" [Relations with the USSR]. In *Türk Dış Politikası: Kurtuluş Savaşı'ndan Bugüne Olgular, Belgeler; Yorumlar Cilt I: 1919–1980* [Turkish Foreign Policy: From the War of Independence until Today, Facts, Documents, Comments, Vol. 1: 1919–1980], edited by Baskın Oran, 169–83. İstanbul: İletişim, 2009.

Akdoğan, Yalçın. *Muhafazakar Demokrasi* [Conservative Democracy]. Ankara: AK Parti, 2003.

Akgün, Mensur, and Turan Aydın, *Türkiye-Rusya İlişkilerindeki Yapısal Sorunlar ve Çözüm Önerileri* [Structural Problems in Turkey-Russia Relations and Suggestions for Solutions]. İstanbul: Tüsiad, June 1999.

Akgün, Mert Hüseyin. *Fetö'nün Askeri Kanadı-Genelkurmay Çatı Davası* [Military Wing of FETÖ: Case of the Chief of Staff]. Ankara: SETA Yayınları, 2020.

Akşam. "Türkiye'den, Gürcistan'a 17 milyon dolarlık askeri reform tahsisi" [17 Million Dollars' Worth of Grant for Military Reform from Turkey to Georgia]. December 25, 2019. www.aksam.com.tr/guncel/turkiyeden-gurcistana-17-milyon -dolarlik-askeri-reform-tahsisi/haber-1032779.

Aktürk, Şener. "The Fourth Style of Politics: Eurasianism as a Pro-Russian Rethinking of Turkey's Geopolitical Identity." *Turkish Studies* 16, no. 1 (2015): 54–79.

———. "Relations between Russia and Turkey Before, During, and After the Failed Coup of 2016." *Insight Turkey* 21, no. 4 (2019): 97–113.

———. "Toward a Turkish-Russian Axis? Conflicts in Georgia, Syria, and Ukraine, and Cooperation over Nuclear Energy." *Insight Turkey* 6, no. 15 (2014): 12–22.

————. "Turkish–Russian Relations after the Cold War (1992–2002)." *Turkish Studies* 7, no. 3 (2006): 337–64.

Al Jazeera. "Dozens Killed as Russian, Syrian Air Attacks in Idlib Intensify." May 4, 2019. www.aljazeera.com/news/2019/05/04/dozens-killed-as-russian-syrian-air -attacks-in-idlib-intensify.

————. "Operation Irini: Turkey Slams EU Mission to Contain Arms to Libya." June 19, 2020. www.aljazeera.com/news/2020/6/19/operation-irini-turkey-slams -eu-mission-to-contain-arms-to-libya.

————. "Russia Ready to Mediate in Eastern Mediterranean Crisis: Lavrov." September 8, 2020. www.aljazeera.com/news/2020/9/8/russia-ready-to-mediate-in -eastern-mediterranean-crisis-lavrov.

————. "Syrian Army Continues Push into Quneitra amid Ongoing Evacuations." July 22, 2018. www.aljazeera.com/news/2018/07/22/syrian-army-continues-push -into-quneitra-amid-ongoing-evacuations.

Allsopp, Harriet, and Wladimir van Wilgenburg. *The Kurds of Northern Syria: Governance, Diversity and Conflicts.* New York: I.B. Tauris, 2019.

Ambrosio, Thomas. "The Russo-American Dispute over the Invasion of Iraq: International Status and the Role of Positional Goods." *Europe-Asia Studies* 57, no. 8 (2005): 1189–210.

Anadolu Agency. "Libya's GNA Activates Security Deal with Turkey." December 19, 2019. www.aa.com.tr/en/africa/libyas-gna-activates-security-deal-with-turkey /1678715.

Anadolu Ajansı. "Cumhurbaşkanı Erdoğan 3. Uluslararası Ombudsmanlık Sempozyumu'nda açıklamalarda bulundu" [President Erdoğan Made Statements in the Third Symposium of Ombudsmanship]. September 16, 2015. www.aa.com.tr/ tr/turkiye/cumhurbaskani-erdogan-3-uluslararasi-ombudsmanlik-sempozyumunda -aciklamalarda-bulundu/54913.

————. "Genelkurmay Rus uçağına yapılan uyarıların ses kaydını yayımladı" [Turkish Chief of Staff Released the Voice Recordings of the Warnings Made to the Russian Aircraft]. November 25, 2015. www.aa.com.tr/tr/turkiye/genelkurmay -rus-ucagina-Yapilan-uyarilarin-ses-kaydini-Yayimladi/481350.

————. "Ukrayna ile Türkiye arasında savunma sanayinde iş birliği" [Cooperation between Ukraine and Turkey in Industry]. July 4, 2018. www.aa.com.tr/tr/dunya /ukrayna-ile-turkiye-arasinda-savunma-sanayinde-is-birligi-/1195063.

Arafat, Mohamad, and Mahmood Alnuaimy. "Turkish-Russian Relations in the Era Of AKP." *Afyon Kocatepe Üniversitesi, İİBF Dergisi* 3, no. 1 (2011): 103–33.

Aral, Berdal. "'The World Is Bigger Than Five': A Salutary Manifesto of Turkey's New International Outlook." *Insight Turkey* 21, no. 4 (2019): 71–95.

Aras, Bülent, and Hakan Fidan. "Turkey and Eurasia: Frontiers of a New Geographic Imagination." *New Perspectives on Turkey* 40 (2009): 193–215.

Aslan, Ömer. *The United States and Military Coups in Turkey and Pakistan: Between Conspiracy and Reality.* Cham: Palgrave, 2018.

Associated Press. "The Latest: Russia Warned Kurdish Officials of Turkey Attack." January 21, 2018. https://apnews.com/article/1ca16b2e78c944bbbb7d092554be 906b.

————. "Trump Has Praise for Controversial Libyan Gen. Khalifa Haftar in Phone Call." April 19, 2019. https://apnews.com/article/7cc6cc853ab05d1adda7219 5b5f58d4c.

Ataöv, Türkkaya. *Türk Dış Politikası, 1939–1945* [Turkish Foreign Policy, 1939– 1945]. Ankara: SBF, 1964.

Aydın, Mustafa. "Contending Agendas for the Black Sea Region: A Regional Alternative." *Demokratizatsiya* 20, no. 1 (2012): 47–61.

————. "Kafkasya ve Orta Asya İle İlişkiler" [Relations with the Caucasus and the Central Asia]. In *Türk Dış Politikası: Kurtuluş Savaşı'ndan Bugüne Olgular, Belgeler; Yorumlar Cilt II: 1980–2001* [Turkish Foreign Policy: From the War of Independence until Today, Facts, Documents, Comments, Vol. 2: 1980–2001], edited by Baskın Oran, 463–531. İstanbul: İletişim, 2013.

Aysor. "Pashinyan Says He Twice Had Phone Calls with Russia's President but Thinks He Will Be Having More with the French President." October 3, 2020. www.aysor.am/en/news/2020/10/03/pashinyan-phone/1751306.

Azatutyun. "Russia Deplores 'Political' Charges against Former Armenian Officials." July 31, 2018. www.azatutyun.am/a/29401668.html.

Bailey, Frank Edgar. *British Policy and the Turkish Reform Movement: A Study in Anglo-Turkish Relations, 1826–1853*. Cambridge: The Harvard University Printing Office, 1942.

Balcı, Ali. *Türkiye Dış Politikası İlkeler, Aktörler Ve Uygulamalar* [Turkey Foreign Policy: Principles, Actors and Practices]. İstanbul: Alfa Yayınları, 2017.

————. "When Foreign Policy Matters: The Gülen Movement's Fight with the AK Party over Iran." *Insight Turkey* 17, no. 1 (2015): 9–18.

Balcı, Bayram. *Islam in Central Asia and the Caucasus since the Fall of the Soviet Union*. Translated by Gregory Elliott. New York: Oxford University Press, 2018.

Balci, Bayram, and M. Hakan Yavuz. *Turkey's July 15th Coup What Happened and Why*. Salt Lake City: University of Utah Press, 2018.

Baran, Zeyno. "The Baku-Tbilisi-Ceyhan Pipeline: Implications for Turkey." In *The Baku-Tbilisi-Ceyhan Pipeline: Oil Window to the West,* edited by S. Frederick Starr and Svante E. Cornell, 103–18. Washington, DC: Central Asia-Caucasus Institute & Silk Road Studies Program, 2005.

Başlamış, Cenk. "Putin'in Ankara zamanlaması" [Putin's Timing of Ankara]. *Deutsche Welle Türkiye,* December 7, 2004. www.dw.com/tr/putinin-ankara -zamanlaması/a-2525673.

Bazoğlu-Sezer, Duygu. "Turkish-Russian Relations: The Challenges of Reconciling Geopolitical Competition with Economic Partnership." *Turkish Studies* 1, no. 1 (2000): 59–82.

BBC. "Libya Conflict: Haftar 'Leaves' Moscow Ceasefire Talks without Deal." January 14, 2020. www.bbc.com/news/world-africa-51104846.

————. "Syria Conflict: Russia and Turkey 'in First Joint Air Strikes on IS.'" January 18, 2017. www.bbc.com/news/world-middle-east-38667895.

————. "Syria Conflict: Russia Violation of Turkish Airspace 'No Accident.'" October 6, 2015. www.bbc.com/news/world-europe-34453739.

———. "Syria Plane Carried Radar Parts, Not Weapons—Russia." October 12, 2012. www.bbc.com/news/world-europe-19928139.

———. "Syria War: Russia Announces Ceasefire in Idlib Rebel Stronghold." August 30, 2019. www.bbc.com/news/world-middle-east-49527419.

———. "Trump Says Putin 'a Leader Far More Than Our President.'" September 8, 2016. www.bbc.com/news/election-us-2016-37303057.

———. "Ukraine: Are Arms Shipments from the West Making a Difference?" March 8, 2022. www.bbc.com/news/world-60655349.

———. "What Sanctions Are Being Imposed on Russia over Ukraine Invasion?" March 12, 2022. www.bbc.com/news/world-europe-60125659.

Bdoyan, David Gyurgenovich. "Transformatsiya rossiysko-turetskikh otnosheniy v usloviyakh bor'by za regional'noye liderstvo (2002–2017 gg.)" [Transformation of Turkish-Russian Relations within the Framework of the Fight over Regional Leadership (2002–2017)]. Unpublished PhD dissertation, MGIMO, 2017.

Becker, Jo, and Eric Schmitt. "As Trump Wavers on Libya, an ISIS Haven, Russia Presses On." *New York Times,* February 7, 2018. www.nytimes.com/2018/02/07/world/africa/trump-libya-policy-russia.html.

Bekdil, Burak Ege. "Turkey, Ukraine Seek to Jointly Produce 'Sensitive' Defense Technology." *Defensenews,* September 16, 2020. www.defensenews.com/unmanned/2019/09/16/turkey-ukraine-seek-to-jointly-produce-sensitive-defense-technology.

Bigg, Claire. "Turkey Revives 'Caucasus Initiative,' but Faces Obstacles." *Radio Free Europe/Radio Liberty,* September 5, 2008. www.rferl.org/a/Turkey_Caucasus_Initiative_Obstacles/1196703.html.

Bilge, Suat. "An Analysis of Turkey-Russia Relations." *Perceptions* 2, no. 2 (1997): 66–92.

Bilgel, Yasemin. "Regional Power Politics after the Cold War." Unpublished PhD dissertation, University of Chicago, 2014.

Bilgin, Pınar, and Kıvanç Coş. "Stalin's Demands: Constructions of the Soviet Other in Turkey's Foreign Policy, 1919–1945." *Foreign Policy Analysis* 6 (2009): 43–60.

Boghani, Priyanka. "The Man at the Center of the Chaos in Libya: Khalifa Haftar." *PRI,* May 31, 2014. www.pri.org/stories/2014-05-31/man-center-chaos-libya-khalifa-haftar.

Boland, Vincent, and Daniel Dombey. "Turkey's EU Hopes Fade with Sarkozy." May 7, 2007. www.ft.com/content/55374310-fc82-11db-9971-000b5df10621.

Bölükbaşı, Deniz. *1 Mart Vakası: Tezkere Krizi ve Sonrası* [The Incident of March 1: The Bill Crisis and Aftermath]. İstanbul: Doğan Kitap, 2003.

Bonsey, Noah. "More Chechnya, Less Afghanistan." *Foreign Policy*, December 10, 2015. https://foreignpolicy.com/2015/10/12/more-chechnya-less-afghanistan.

Brown University. "Costs of War Project Releases Updated Estimates of Human and Budgetary Costs of Post-9/11 Wars." September 1, 2021. www.bu.edu/pardee/2021/09/02/costs-of-war-project-releases-updated-estimates-of-human-and-financial-costs-of-post-9-11-wars.

BSEC. "Charter of the Organization of the Black Sea Economic Cooperation." May 1, 1999. www.bsec-organization.org/UploadedDocuments/Charter /CHARTERweb080630.pdf.

Business Insider. "Trump: I Said NATO Was Obsolete 'Not Knowing Much about NATO.'" April 24, 2017. www.businessinsider.com/trump-nato-obsolete-2017-4.

Buzan, Barry. "The Inaugural Kenneth N. Waltz Annual Lecture: A World Order without Superpowers: Decentred Globalism." *International Relations* 25, no. 1 (2011): 3–25.

Buzan, Barry, and Ana Gonzalez-Pealez. "'International Community' after Iraq." *International Affairs* 81, no. 1 (2005): 31–52.

Çelebi, Ayten. "Türkiye'de Rusya'ya Dair Çıkan Kitaplar (1991–2016)" [Latest Books Published in Turkey on Russia (1991–2006)]. *Marmara Türkiyat Araştırmaları Dergisi* 3, no. 2 (Sonbahar 2016): 251–80.

Çelikpala, Mitat. "From Immigrants to Diaspora: Influence of the North Caucasian Diaspora in Turkey." *Middle Eastern Studies* 42, no. 3 (May 2006): 423–46.

———. "Rekabet ve İş Birliği İkileminde Yönünü Arayan Türkiye-Rusya İlişkileri" [Turkey-Russia Relations Looking for Its Direction in the Dilemma of Competition and Cooperation]. *Bilig* 72 (Winter 2015): 117–44.

———. "Rusya Federasyonuyla İlişkiler" [Relations with Russia]. In *Türk Dış Politikası: (2001–2012)* 3, edited by Baskın Oran. İstanbul: İletişim, 2013.

Clinton, Hillary. "America's Pacific Century." *Foreign Policy,* October 11, 2011. https://foreignpolicy.com/2011/10/11/americas-pacific-century.

CNN. "Kurdish Forces Backed by US Strike Deal with Syria's Assad, in Major Shift in 8-Year War." October 14, 2019. www.cnn.com/2019/10/14/middleeast/syria -turkey-kurds-civilians-isis-intl-hnk/index.html.

———. "Obama Says U.S., Turkey Can Be Model for World." April 6, 2009. www .cnn.com/2009/POLITICS/04/06/obama.turkey.

CNN Türk. "Türkiye'de tarihi gün! Türk Akımı vanasını dört lider çevirdi" [Historic Day in Turkey! Four Leaders Turned the Valve of the Turkish Stream]. January 8, 2020. www.cnnturk.com/turkiye/cumhurbaskani-erdogan-ve-putin-turkakiminin -acilisini-bugun-gerceklestirecek.

Cohen, Ariel. "Turkey-Libya Maritime Deal Upsets Mediterranean Energy Plan." *Forbes,* January 8, 2020. www.forbes.com/sites/arielcohen/2020/01/08/turkey -libya-maritime-deal-upsets-mediterranean-energy-plan/?sh=985e1bb6bee4.

Connolly, Richard. *Russia's Response to Sanctions: How Western Economic Statecraft Is Reshaping Political Economy in Russia.* New York: Cambridge University Press, 2018.

Crisis Group. "Russia and Turkey in the Black Sea and the South Caucasus." June 28, 2018.

Cumhuriyet. "*Alexander Lebedev ile Röportaj*" [Interview with Alexander Lebedev]. October 15, 2001.

Daily Sabah. "PYD Opens Office in Moscow, Inauguration Attended by HDP Deputy." February 11, 2016. www.dailysabah.com/diplomacy/2016/02/11/pyd -opens-office-in-moscow-inauguration-attended-by-hdp-deputy.

————. "Turkey, Russia Seek New Ways to Reach $100B in Bilateral Trade." April 09, 2019. www.dailysabah.com/business/2019/04/09/turkey-russia-seek-new-ways -to-reach-100b-in-bilateral-trade.

Daly, John C. K. "Montreux Convention Hampers Humanitarian Aid to Georgia." *Eurasia Daily Monitor*, September 3, 2008. https://jamestown.org/program /montreux-convention-hampers-humanitarian-aid-to-georgia.

Davutoğlu, Ahmet. *Stratejik Derinlik* [Strategic Depth]. İstanbul: Küre Yayınları, 2001.

The Defense Post. "FULL TEXT: Memorandum of Understanding between Turkey and Russia on Northern Syria." October 22, 2019. www.thedefensepost.com/2019 /10/22/russia-turkey-syria-mou.

Delanoe, Igor. "After the Crimean Crisis: Towards a Greater Russian Maritime Power in the Black Sea." *Southeast European and Black Sea Studies* 14, no. 3 (2014): 367–82.

Demir, Ismail. "Transformation of the Turkish Defense Industry: The Story and Rationale of the Great Rise." *Insight Turkey* 22, no. 3 (2020): 17–40.

Demirtaş, Serkan. "Turkey under NATO and Russia Pressure over Black Sea." *Hurriyet Daily,* April 5, 2014. www.hurriyetdailynews.com/opinion/serkan -demirtas/turkey-under-nato-and-russia-pressure-over-black-sea-64579.

Deringil, Selim. *Turkish Foreign Policy during the Second World War: An "Active" Neutrality.* Cambridge: Cambridge University Press, 1989.

Deutsche Welle. "Russia to 'Assist' Armenia if Conflict with Azerbaijan Spreads beyond Nagorno-Karabakh." October 31, 2020. www.dw.com/en/russia-to -assist-armenia-if-conflict-with-azerbaijan-spreads-beyond-nagorno-karabakh/a -55457174.

————. "Why Turkey's Libya Commitment Angers Arab Nations." January 18, 2020. www.dw.com/en/why-turkeys-libya-commitment-angers-arab-nations/a -52052924.

Dobaev, I., and O. Cherevkov. "Transformatsiya Radikal'nogo Islamistskogo Dvizheniya na Severnom Kavkaze: ot 'Imarata Kavkaz' k 'Vilayyatu Kavkaz'" [Transformation of the Radikal Islamic Movement in North Caucasus: From the "Emirate of Caucasus" to the "Wilayat of Caucasus"]. *Rossiya i Musul'manskiy Mir* 9 (2017): 13–30.

Dolan, Chris. *Obama and the Emergence of a Multipolar World Order: Redefining U.S. Foreign Policy.* Lanham, MD: Lexington Books, 2018.

Donaldson, Robert H., Joseph L. Nogee, and Vidya Nadkarni. *The Foreign Policy of Russia: Changing Systems, Enduring Interests.* New York: Routledge, 2014.

Dueck, Colin. *The Obama Doctrine: American Grand Strategy Today.* New York: Oxford University Press, 2015.

Dünya Bülteni. "Erdoğan: Rusya Suriye'nin diliyle konuşuyor" [Russia Is Using Syria's Language]. June 27, 2012. www.dunyabulteni.net/politika/erdogan-rusya -suriyenin-diliyle-konusuyor-h215963.html.

————. "Erdoğan'dan Mısır'a laiklik çağrısı" [Call for Laicism to Egypt from Erdoğan]. September 13, 2011. www.dunyabulteni.net/afrika/erdogandan-misira -laiklik-cagrisi-h174406.html.

Duran, Burhanettin. "15 Temmuz Darbe Girişiminin Türkiye'nin İç ve Dış Politikasina Etkisi" [The Impact of the July 15 Coup Attempt of Turkey's Domestic and Foreign Policy]. In *Türk Dış Politikası Yıllığı 2017* [Yearbook of Turkish Foreign Policy 2017], edited by Burhanettin Duran, Kemal İnat, and Mustafa Caner, 13–44. Ankara: SETA, 2018.

Economist. "The Azerbaijan-Armenia Conflict Hints at the Future of War." October 10, 2020. www.economist.com/europe/2020/10/10/the-azerbaijan-armenia-conflict -hints-at-the-future-of-war.

Ekonomi Alla Turca. "Rus ticaretinde TL'nin adı yok" [Turkish Lira Doesn't Have a Place in Russian Trade]. November 1, 2019. https://ugurses.net/2019/11/01/rus -ticaretinde-tlnin-adi-Yok.

Ekşi, Özgür. "İsrail yerine Ruslardan füze alıyoruz" [We Are Purchasing Missiles from Russia Instead of Israel]. *Hürriyet,* April 4, 2008. www.hurriyet.com.tr /gundem/israil-Yerine-ruslardan-fuze-aliyoruz-8672522.

Elekdağ, Şükrü. "Mavi İhanet" [Blue Treason]. *Milliyet,* May 13, 2001. http:// gazetearsivi.milliyet.com.tr/Arsiv/2001/05/13.

Erdoğan, Recep Tayyip. "Olağanüstü Hal Kapsamında Alınan Tedbirlere İlişkin Kanun Hükmünde Kararname" [Decree Having the Force of Law on the Measures Taken within the Framework of the State of Emergency]. *Resmi Gazete (Ankara),* July 22, 2016.

———. "Suriye'de Tüm Kırmızı Çizgilerin Aşılmasına Rağmen Bir Adım Atılmadı" [No Step Was Taken Despite All the Redlines Were Crossed in Syria]. TC Cumhurbaşkanlığı, May 11, 2016. www.tccb.gov.tr/haberler/410/43922/suriyede -tum-kirmizi-cizgilerin-asilmasina-ragmen-bir-adim-atilmadi.html.

Ermarth, Fritz W. "Russia's Strategic Culture: Past, Present, and . . . in Transition?" In *Comparative Strategic Cultures Curriculum Project,* edited by Jeffrey A. Larsen, chapter 12. Fort Belvoir, VA: Defense Threat Reduction Agency, 2006.

Erşen, Emre. "Evaluating the Fighter Jet Crisis in Turkish-Russian Relations." *Insight Turkey* 19, no. 4 (Fall 2017): 85–104.

———. "Turkish-Russian Relations in the New Century." In *Turkey in the 21st Century: Questor a New Foreign Policy*, edited by Özden Zeynep Oktav, 95–114. New York: Routledge, 2011.

Euractiv. "Gas Fields and Tensions in the Eastern Mediterranean." October 26, 2020. www.euractiv.com/section/energy-environment/news/gas-fields-and-tensions-in -the-eastern-mediterranean.

European Council. "EU Launches Operation IRINI to Enforce Libya Arms Embargo." March 31, 2020. www.consilium.europa.eu/en/press/press-releases/2020/03/31/eu -launches-operation-irini-to-enforce-libya-arms-embargo/#.

———. "EU Restrictive Measures in Response to the Crisis in Ukraine." Accessed November 02, 2021. www.consilium.europa.eu/en/policies/sanctions/ukraine -crisis.

Eylem, Yılmaz, and Pinar Bilgin. "Constructing Turkey's 'Western' Identity during the Cold War: Discourses of the Intellectuals of Statecraft." *International Journal* 61, no. 1 (2005): 39–59.

Findley, Carter. *Turks in World History.* New York: Oxford University Press, 2005.

Finkel, Evgeny, and Yitzhak M. Brudny. "Russia and the Colour Revolutions." *Democratization* 19, no. 1 (2012): 15–36.

Fisher, Max. "Putin's Case for War, Annotated." *New York Times,* February 24, 2022, www.nytimes.com/2022/02/24/world/europe/putin-ukraine-speech.html.

France 24. "Nagorno-Karabakh: Turkey to Send Peacekeepers to Azerbaijan to Monitor Truce." November 17, 2020. www.france24.com/en/europe/20201117 -nagorno-karabakh-turkey-to-send-peacekeepers-to-azerbaijan-to-monitor -truce.

———. "'Turkey Has a Clear Objective of Reinstating the Turkish Empire,' Armenian PM Says." October 2, 2020. www.france24.com/en/20201002-turkey -has-a-clear-objective-of-reinstating-the-turkish-empire-armenian-pm-says.

Frantz, Douglas. "Russia's New Reach: Gas Pipeline to Turkey." *New York Times,* June 8, 2001. www.nytimes.com/2001/06/08/world/russia-s-new-reach-gas-pipe-line-to-turkey.html.

Freedman, Thomas. "Russian Policy towards the Middle East under Putin: The Impact of 9/11 and the War in Iraq." *Alternatives* 2, no. 2 (Summer, 2003): 66–97.

Gali, Carlotta. "Syrian Attacks Draw Turkey Deeper into Syrian War." *New York Times,* February 28, 2020. www.nytimes.com/2020/02/12/world/middleeast/syria -turkey-russia-war.html.

Gasratan Manvel Arsenovich, and Petr Pavlovich Moiseev. *SSSR i Turtsiya 1917— 1979* [USSR and Turkey 1917–1919]. Moskva: Nauka, 1981.

Gazprom. "Gluboi Potok" [Blue Stream]. Accessed December 10, 2021. www .gazprom.ru/projects/blue-stream.

Gendzier, Irene. *Notes from the Minefield: United States Intervention in Lebanon 1945–1958.* New York: Columbia University Press, 2006.

Geropoulos, Kostis. "Reducing Dependence on Russia, Turkey Speeds Up TANAP Pipeline to EU." *New Europe,* February 20, 2018. www.neweurope.eu/article /reducing-dependence-russia-turkey-speeds-tanap-pipeline-eu.

Gökay, Bülent. *Soviet Eastern Policy and Turkey, 1920–1991: Soviet Foreign Policy, Turkey and Communism* London: Routledge, 2006.

Goltz, Thomas. "Letter from Eurasia: The Hidden Russian Hand." *Foreign Policy,* no. 92 (1993): 92–116.

Gosudarstvennaya Duma Federal'nogo Sobraniya Rossiiskoy Federatsii. "Kakiye Izmeneniya c Konstitutsiyu Podderzhany v Pervom Chtenii?" [What Changes to the Constitution Were Supported in First Reading?]. January 23, 2020. http://duma .gov.ru/news/47599.

Gould, Joe. "US Could Buy Turkey's Russian-Made S-400 under Senate Proposal." *Defense News,* June 29, 2020. www.defensenews.com/congress/2020/06/29/us -could-buy-turkeys-russia-made-s-400-under-senate-proposal.

Grove, Thomas, and Georgi Kantchev. "Discord in Kremlin Helps Putin Remain Russia's No. 1." *Wall Street Journal,* March 6, 2020. www.wsj.com/articles/putin -sows-discord-in-kremlin-to-remain-russias-no-1-11583424937.

Guan-fu, Gu. "Soviet Aid to the Third World: An Analysis of Its Strategy." *Soviet Studies* 15, no. 1 (January 1983): 71–76.

The Guardian. "Turkey Requested NATO Missile Defences over Syria Chemical Weapons Fears." December 21, 2012. www.theguardian.com/world/2012/dec/02 /turkey-syria-chemical-weapons-fears.

Gül, Abdullah. "New Horizons in Turkish Foreign Policy." May 22, 2004. Boğaziçili Yöneticiler Vakfı, İstanbul, Dedeman Hotel.

Guriyev, A. A. *"Partiya spravedlivosti i razvitiya Turtsii: Tri goda u vlasti"* [Justice and Development Party of Turkey: Three Years in Rule]. *Institut Blizhnevo Vostoka,* November 30, 2005. www.iimes.ru/?p=3972.

Haas, Richard. "The Age of Nonpolarity." *Foreign Affairs* 87, no. 3 (May 2008): 44–56.

Habertürk. "Rusya Devlet Başkanı Putin, Ankara'da, Türkiye-Rusya arasında 100 milyar dolarlık dev anlaşma" [Russian President Putin Is in Turkey, 100-Billion-Dollar Deal between Turkey and Russia]. December 1, 2014. www.haberturk.com /ekonomi/is-Yasam/haber/1014724-dev-anlasma-tamam.

Hale, William. "Turkey, the U.S., Russia, and the Syrian Civil War." *Insight Turkey* 21, no. 4 (Fall 2019): 25–40.

Harding, Luke. "Russia Has Enough Troops Ready to Take Kyiv, Says Former Ukraine Defence Chief." *The Guardian.* February 6, 2022. www.theguardian.com /world/2022/feb/06/russian-troops-ready-to-seize-ukrainian-capital-says-former -defence-chief.

Head, Jonathan. "Libya: Turkey's Troubles with NATO and No-fly Zone." BBC, March 25, 2011. www.bbc.com/news/world-africa-12864742.

Higgins, Andrew, and Peter Baker. "Russia Claims U.S. Is Meddling over Ukraine." *New York Times,* February 6, 2014. www.nytimes.com/2014/02/07/world/europe /ukraine.html.

Hill, Fiona. "Beyond Co-dependency: European Reliance on Russian Energy." Brookings Institution, July 1, 2005. www.brookings.edu/wp-content/uploads/2016 /06/hill20050727.pdf.

Hill, Fiona., and Ömer Taşpınar. "Turkey and Russia: Axis of the Excluded?" *Survival* 48, no. 1 (2006): 81–92.

Holmes, Amy Austin. *Social Unrest and American Military Bases in Turkey and Germany since 1945.* New York: Cambridge University Press, 2014.

Hürriyet. "Akkuyu Nükleer Santrali inşaatı görüntülendi" [The Construction of Akkuyu Nuclear Power Plant Was Monitored]. July 23, 2019. www.hurriyet.com .tr/galeri-akkuyu-nukleer-santrali-insaati-goruntulendi-41281990/1.

———. "Başbakan Ahmet Davutoğlu'ndan Putin'e Esad göndermesi: Kadirov arıyor" [An Allusion from the Prime Minister Ahmet Davutoğlu to Putin on Assad: He Is Looking for a Kadirov]. February 16, 2016. www.hurriyet.com.tr /gundem/basbakan-ahmet-davutoglundan-putine-esad-gondermesi-kadirov-ariyor -40055161.

———. "Duvarda silah varsa piyesin sonunda patlar" [If You Have a Pistol Hanging on the Wall in the First Act, It Fires in the Last Act]. December 3, 2012. www .hurriyet.com.tr/gundem/duvarda-silah-varsa-piyesin-sonunda-patlar-22068771.

———. "Hükümete AB desteği" [Support for EU to the Government]. May 21, 2020. www.hurriyet.com.tr/gundem/hukumete-ab-destegi-148000.

————. "Putin'in Münih konuşması Genelkurmay'ın sitesinde" [Putin's Münih Speech on the Website of the Chief of Staff]. February 15, 2007. www.hurriyet .com.tr/gundem/putinin-munih-konusmasi-genelkurmayin-sitesinde-5956456

————. "Rusya gazı keserse kısa vadede ısınma, elektrik ve sanayide alternatif zayıf" [Alternatives in Heating, Electricity and Industry Are Weak in the Short-Term if Russia Cuts the Gas]. December 3, 2015. www.hurriyet.com.tr /ekonomi/rusya-gazi-keserse-kisa-vadede-isinma-elektrik-ve-sanayide-alternatif -zayif-40022179.

————. "Türkmen'e bomba yağıyor" [Bombs Are Raining on Turkmen]. November 20, 2015. www.hurriyet.com.tr/dunya/turkmene-bomba-Yagiyor-40016723.

Hurriyet Daily. "Turkey Refutes Russian Call for Syria's Afrin." April 10, 2018. www.hurriyetdailynews.com/turkey-refutes-russian-call-for-syrias-afrin-130097.

————. "Turkey to Expand LNG Storage Capacity with 3rd FSRU." October 9, 2020. www.hurriyetdailynews.com/turkey-to-expand-lng-storage-capacity-with -3rd-fsru-158966.

————. "Turkey Waiting for Russia, West on Ukraine Problem." May 12, 2014. www.hurriyetdailynews.com/turkey-waiting-for-russia-west-on-ukraine-problem -66311.

————. "Turkish PM Erdoğan to Putin: Take Us to Shanghai." November 22, 2013. www.hurriyetdailynews.com/turkish-pm-erdogan-to-putin-take-us-to-shanghai -58348.

————. "US Jury Finds Turkish Banker Hakan Atilla Guilty on Five Counts." January 3, 2018. www.hurriyetdailynews.com/turkish-banker-convicted-of-helping-iran -evade-us-sanctions-125198.

İnalcık, Halil. "Osmanlı-Rus İlişkileri 1492–1700" [Ottoman-Russia Relations 1492– 1700]. Ankara: Kırım Türkleri Yardımlaşma Derneği, 2003.

————. Osmanlı–Rus Rekabetinin Menşei ve Don Volga Kanalı Teşebbüsü [The Origins of the Ottoman-Russia Competition and the Initiative of Don-Volga Canal]. Ankara: Türk Tarih Kurumu, 1948.

————. The Ottoman Empire: The Classical Age 1300–1600. New Haven, CT: Phoenix Press, 2001.

————. Studies in Ottoman Social and Economic History. London: Variorum Reprints, 1985.

İnalcık, Halil, and Donald Quatert, An Economic and Social History of the Ottoman Empire: 1300—1600. New York: Cambridge University Press, 1997.

Independent. "Ukraine Says More Than 11,000 Russian Troops Killed since Invasion Began." March 13, 2022. www.independent.co.uk/news/world/europe/ukraine -invasion-russia-troops-killed-b2029556.html.

Insinna, Valerie, Joe Gould, and Aaron Mehta. "Congress Has Secretly Blocked US Arms Sales to Turkey for Nearly Two Years." Defense News, August 12, 2020. www.defensenews.com/breaking-news/2020/08/12/congress-has-secretly-blocked -us-arms-sales-to-turkey-for-nearly-two-Years.

Interfax. "Gosduma Prinyala Zakon o Popravkakh k Konstitutsii RF" [Duma Accepted a Law on Amendment to the Constitution]. March 11, 2020. www.inter-fax.ru/russia/698543.

———. "Lavrov ob"yasnil slozhivshuyusya v Afrine situatsiyu provokatsiyami SSHA" [Lavrov Explained the Situation in Afrin as a US Provocation]. February 20, 2018. www.interfax.ru/world/600761.

———. "V Sirii sbit rossiyskiy Su-24" [A Russian SU-24 Fell in Syria]. November 24, 2015. www.interfax.ru/world/481166.

İşçi, Onur. *Turkey and Soviet Union during World War II*. London: I. B. Tauris, 2019.

İşçi, Onur, and Samuel Hirst. "Smokestacks and Pipelines: Russian-Turkish Relations and the Persistence of Economic Development." *Diplomatic History* 44, no. 5 (November 2020): 834–59.

Jarosiewicz, Alexandra. *The Southern Gas Corridor: How the Azerbaijani-Turkish Project Becomes Part of the Game between Russia and the EU*. Warsaw: Centre for Eastern Studies, 2015.

Jervis, Robert. *System Effects: Complexity in Political and Social Life*. Princeton, NJ: Princeton University Press, 1997.

Johnson, Lyndon. "Correspondence between President Johnson and Prime Minister Inonu." *Middle East Journal* 20, no. 3 (1966): 386–93.

Kandiyoti, Rafael. *Powering Europe: Russia, Ukraine, and the Energy Squeeze*. New York: Palgrave Macmillan, 2015.

Kanet, Roger. "From the 'New World Order' to 'Resetting Relations': Two Decades of US–Russian Relations." In *Russian Foreign Policy in the 21st Century*, edited by Roger E. Kanet, 204–27. New York: Palgrave Macmillan, 2011.

———. "Russian: Strategic Culture, Domestic Politics and Cold War 2.0." *European Politics and Society* 20, no. 2 (2019): 190–206.

Kanet, Roger E., and Rémi Piet. "Shifting Priorities in Russia's Foreign and Security Policy." In *Shifting Priorities in Russia's Foreign and Security Policy*, edited by Roger E. Kanet and Rémi Piet, 1–11. Farnham: Ashgate, 2014.

Kaplan, Hilal "A Book Aged Well 'Turkey as a Stabilizing Power in an Age of Turmoil.'" *Daily Sabah*, April 1, 2022. www.dailysabah.com/opinion/columns/a-book-aged-well-turkey-as-a-stabilizing-power-in-an-age-of-turmoil.

Kasapoğlu, Can. "Turkey's Burgeoning Defense Technological and Industrial Base and Expeditionary Military Policy." *Insight Turkey* 22, no. 3 (2020): 115–30.

Kelkitli, Fatma Aslı. *Turkish–Russian Relations Competition and Cooperation in Eurasia*. London: Routledge, 2017.

Kelley, Donald. *Russian Politics and Presidential Power: Transformational Leadership from Gorbachev to Putin*. Los Angeles: CQ Press, 2016.

Kessler, Glenn. "Hillary Clinton's Uncredible Statement on Syria." *Washington Post*, April 4, 2011. www.washingtonpost.com/blogs/fact-checker/post/hillary-clintons-uncredible-statement-on-syria/2011/04/01/AFWPEYaC_blog.html.

Kirby, Dianne. "Divinely Sanctioned: The Anglo-American Cold War Alliance and the Defence of Western Civilization and Christianity, 1945–48." *Journal of Contemporary History* 35, no. 3 (July 2000): 385–412.

Kirby, Jen. "The US-Turkey Trade Spat, Explained." *Vox*, August 15, 2018. www.vox.com/world/2018/8/15/17687928/turkey-united-states-tariffs-lira-andrew-brunson.

Kitchen, Nicholas. "Systemic Pressures and Domestic Ideas: A Neoclassical Realist Model of Grand Strategy Formation." *Review of International Studies* 36, no. 1 (January 2010): 117–43.

Koçak, Muhammet. *Crimea and the Crimean Tatars after Annexation by Russia.* Ankara: SETA, June 2014.

Kommersant. "Gosduma Prinyala Zakon o Popravkakh k Konstitutsii RF" [Duma Accepted a Law on Amendment to the Constitution]. November 14, 2008. www .kommersant.ru/doc/1061738.

Koontz, Kayla. *Borders Beyond Borders: The Many (Many) Kurdish Political Parties of Syria.* Washington, DC: Middle East Institute, 2019.

Köse, Talha. "Rise and Fall of the AK Party's Kurdish Peace Initiatives." *Insight Turkey* 19, no. 2 (2017): 139–65.

Köstem, Seçkin. "Geopolitics, Identity and Beyond Turkey's Renewed Interest in the Caucasus and Central Asia." In *Turkey's Pivot to Eurasia Geopolitics and Foreign Policy in a Changing World Order*, edited by Emre Erşen and Seçkin Köstem, 111–28. London: Routledge, 2018.

Kozhanov, Nikolay. "Russian Support for Assad's Regime: Is There a Red Line?" *The International Spectator* 48, no. 2 (June 2013): 25–31.

Kupchan, Charles A. *No One's World: The West, the Rising Rest, and the Coming Global Turn.* New York: Oxford University Press, 2012.

Kurat, Akdes Nimet. *Rusya Tarihi: Başlangıçtan 1917'ye kadar* [Russian History: From the Beginning until 1917]. Ankara: Türk Tarih Kurumu, 1987.

———. *Türkiye ve Rusya* [Turkey and Russia]. Ankara: Kültür Bakanlığı, 1990.

Kütük, Dilek. "Importance of Humanitarian Aid during Covid-19 for Turkey as a Status-Seeking Country." Belgrade Security Forum, May 16, 2020. www.bel-gradeforum.org/the-importance-of-humanitarian-aid-during-covid-19-for-turkey -as-a-status-seeking-country.

Kyiv Post. "Ukraine, Turkey Armies Sign Military Cooperation Roadmap until 2020." May 16, 2016. www.kyivpost.com/article/content/ukraine-politics/ukraine -turkey-armies-sign-military-cooperation-roadmap-until-2020-413826.html.

Leffler, Melvyn P. *A Preponderance of Power: National Security, the Truman Administration, and the Cold War.* Stanford, CA: Stanford University Press, 1992.

Leichtova, Magda. *Misunderstanding Russia: Russian Foreign Policy and the West.* Farnham: Ashgate, 2014.

Levada Tsentr. "Doverie Politikam" [Trust in Politicians]. October 8, 2018. www .levada.ru/2018/10/08/doverie-politikam-2.

Lister, Charles. *The Syrian Jihad Al Qaeda the Islamic State and the Evolution of an Insurgency.* New York: Oxford University Press, 2016.

Loftus, Suzanne, and Roger E. Kanet. "Growing Confrontation between Russia and the West: Russia's Challenge to the Post–Cold War Order." In *The Russian Challenge to the European Security Environment,* edited by Roger Kanet, 13–36. Cham: Palgrave, 2017.

MacDonald, Paul K., and Joseph M. Parent. "Graceful Decline? The Surprising Success of Great Power Retrenchment." *International Security* 35, no. 4 (2011): 7–44.

May, Timothy. *The Mongol Empire*. Edinburgh: Edinburgh University Press, 2018.

McLaughlin, Eliott C., Don Melvin, and Jethro Mullen. "Turkey Won't Apologize for Downing Russian Warplane, Erdogan Says." CNN, November 26, 2015. www .cnn.com/2015/11/26/middleeast/syria-turkey-russia-warplane-shot-down/index .html.

Meduza. "A Small Price to Pay for Tripoli." October 2, 2019. https://meduza.io/en /feature/2019/10/02/a-small-price-to-pay-for-tripoli.

Medvedev, Dmitry. "Kontseptsiya vneshney politiki Rossiyskoy Federatsii" [Foreign Policy Concept of the Russian Federation]. *Prezident Rossii*, July 12, 2008. http:// kremlin.ru/acts/news/785.

———. "Strategiya natsional'noy bezopasnosti Rossiyskoy Federatsii do 2020 goda" [National Security Strategy of the Russian Federation until 2020]. *Prezident Rossii*, May 12, 2009. http://kremlin.ru/supplement/424.

Mehta, Aaron. "Turkey Officially Kicked Out of F-35 Program, Costing US Half a Billion Dollars." *Defense News*, July 17, 2019. www.defensenews.com/air/2019/07 /17/turkey-officially-kicked-out-of-f-35-program.

Mesbahi, Mohiaddin. "Eurasia between Turkey, Iran and Russia." In *Key Players and Regional Dynamics in Eurasia: The Return of the 'Great Game,'* edited by Marie Raquel Friere and Roger E. Kanet, 164–92. London: Palgrave Macmillan, 2010.

———. "Free and Confined: Iran and the International System." *Iranian Review of Foreign Affairs* 2, no. 5 (Spring 2011): 9–34.

Meyer, Mikhail. "Rossiya i Turtsiya na Iskhode XX v" [Russian and Turkey in 20th Century]. In *Rossiya i Turtsiya na poroge XXI veka: Na puti v Evropu ili v Evraziyu* [Russia and Turkey at the Doorstep of the 21st Century: Towards Europe or Eurasia], edited by Irina Korbinski and Sherman Garnett, 10–21. Moscow: Carnegie Endowment for International Peace, 1997.

Middle East Eye. "Turkish and US Troops Begin Joint Patrols in Syria's Manbij." November 2, 2018. www.middleeasteye.net/news/turkish-and-us-troops-begin -joint-patrols-syrias-manbij.

Middle East Monitor. "Tripoli: UAE Drones Hit Residential Area, Injure Family." September 22, 2019. www.middleeastmonitor.com/20190922-tripoli-uae-drones -hit-residential-area-injure-family.

Miller, A. F. *Ocherki noveishei Istorii turtsii* [Essays on the Recent History of Turkey]. Moscow: Akademiya Nauk SSSR, 1948.

Milli Güvenlik Kurulu Genel Sekreterliği. "2011 Yılı Basın Açıklamaları" [Press Releases in the Year 2011]. Accessed March 2, 2022. www.mgk.gov.tr/index.php /2011-Yili-basin-aciklamalari.

———. "21 Ekim 2015 Tarihli Toplantı" [Meeting on October 21, 2015]. October 21, 2015. www.mgk.gov.tr/index.php/21-ekim-2015-tarihli-toplanti.

Milliyet. "Erdoğan: Biz Rafa Kaldırdık" [Erdoğan: We Shelved It]. December 5, 2015. www.milliyet.com.tr/siyaset/erdogan-biz-rafa-kaldirdik-2158892.

Moiseev, Petr Pavlovich, and Yuriy Nikolayevich Rozaliyev. *K Istorii sovetsko-turetskikh otnosheniy* [Towards the History of Soviet-Turkish Relations]. Moscow: Politzdat, 1958.

Morris, Loveday. "Assad: We Shot Down Turkish Jet Thinking It Was Israeli."
    Independent, July 4, 2012. www.independent.co.uk/news/world/middle-east/assad
    -we-shot-down-turkish-jet-thinking-it-was-israeli-7906821.html.

Mufti, Malik. *Daring and Caution in Turkish Strategic Culture: Republic at Sea.* New
    York: Palgrave, 2009.

Müftüler-Baç, Meltem. "Turkey and the United States." *International Journal* 61, no.
    1 (March 2006): 61–81.

NATO. "Joint Statement of the NATO-Ukraine Commission." May 13, 2015. www
    .nato.int/cps/en/natohq/official_texts_119425.htm.

———. "Statement by the NATO Secretary General after the Extraordinary NAC
    Meeting." November 24, 2015. www.nato.int/cps/en/natohq/news_125052.htm.

Neflyasheva, N. A. "Kak Zhivut v Turtsii «Novyye Mukhadzhıry» iz Rossii:
    Migratsiya Rossiyskikh musul'man v 2000-Ye gody" [How They Live in Turkey:
    New "Mukhadzhirs" from Russia: Russian Muslims in the 2000s]. *Aziya i Afrıka
    Segodnya* 8 (2018): 62–67.

Nikitina, Yulia. "The 'Color Revolutions' and 'Arab Spring' in Russian Official
    Discourse." *Connections* 14, no. 1 (Winter 2014): 87–104.

NPR. "U.S. Envoy to the Coalition against ISIS Resigns over Trump's Syria Policy."
    December 22, 2018. www.npr.org/2018/12/22/679535003/u-s-envoy-to-the-coali-
    tion-against-isis-resigns-over-trumps-syria-policy.

NTV. "Beyaz enerji davası açıldı" [White Energy Case Was Opened]. April 20, 2001.
    http://arsiv.ntv.com.tr/news/78189.asp.

———. "Erdoğan: Türkiye yanlış güvenlik anlayışını terk etmiştir" [Turkey Has
    Left the Wrong Understanding of Security]. October 19, 2020. www.ntv.com
    .tr/turkiye/turkiye-Yanlis-guvenlik-anlayisini-terk-etmistir,XQuseHLt2UW5dtu
    vV6m5oA.

New York Times. "Russians Strike Targets in Syria, but Not ISIS Areas." September
    30, 2015. www.nytimes.com/2015/10/01/world/europe/russia-airstrikes-syria.html.

Obama, Barack. "National Security Strategy." Obama White House, May 11,
    2010. https://obamawhitehouse.archives.gov/sites/default/files/rss_viewer/national
    _security_strategy.pdf.

———. "Remarks by the President to the White House Press Corps." Edited by
    James S. Brady. August 20, 2012. https://obamawhitehouse.archives.gov/the-press
    -office/2012/08/20/remarks-president-white-house-press-corps.

Obama White House. "Remarks by Vice President Joe Biden and Turkish Prime
    Minister Binali Yildirim at a Press Availability." August 25, 2016. https://
    obamawhitehouse.archives.gov/the-press-office/2016/08/25/remarks-vice
    -president-joe-biden-and-turkish-prime-minister-binali.

Oğuzlu, Tarık. "The Gezi Park Protests and Their Impact on Turkey's Soft Power
    Abroad." *Orsam,* June 18, 2013. www.orsam.org.tr/en/the-gezi-park-protests-and
    -their-impact-on-turkey-s-soft-power-abroad.

———. "Turkish Foreign Policy in a Changing World Order." *All Azimuth* 9, no. 1
    (2020): 127–39.

Oktay, Emel G. "Türkiye'nin Avrasya'daki Çok Taraflı Girişimlerine Bir
    Örnek:Karadeniz Ekonomik İşbirliği Örgütü" [An Example for Turkey's

Multilateral Initiatives: Organization for Black Sea Economic Cooperation]. *Uluslararası İlişkiler* 3, no. 10 (Yaz 2006), 168.

Olson, Robert. "The Kurdish Question and Chechnya: Turkish and Russian Foreign Policies since the Gulf War." *Middle East Policy* 4, no. 3 (March 1996): 106–18.

OPEC. "Iraq Had the World's Third Most Proven Oil Reserves until the Discovery of More Oil in Venezuela." Annual Statistical Bulletin, 2019. www.opec.org/opec _web/en/publications/202.htm.

Oran, Baskın. Ed. *Turkish Foreign Policy: 1919–2006.* Translated by Mustafa Akşin. Salt Lake City: University of Utah Press, 2011.

Osborn, Andrew. "Putin Warns NATO against Closer Ties with Ukraine and Georgia." *Reuters,* July 19, 2018. www.reuters.com/article/us-russia-nato-putin/putin-warns -nato-against-closer-ties-with-ukraine-and-georgia-idUSKBN1K92KA.

Özdamar, Özgür. "Security and Military Balance in the Black Sea Region." *Southeast European and Black Sea Studies* 10, no. 3 (September 2010): 341–59.

Özer, Sarp. "İdlib'de askeri konvoya saldırı" [Attack on a Military Convoy in Idlib]. *Anadolu Ajansı,* August 19, 2019. www.aa.com.tr/tr/turkiye/idlibde-askeri -konvoya-saldiri/1559639.

Pancar, Sezgin. "Eğitimlerini tamamlayan 53 Türk mühendis Akkuyu NGS'de işe başladı" [53 Turkish Engineers Who Completed Their Studies Started Work in Akkuyu NPP]. *Anadolu Ajansı,* October 6, 2020. www.aa.com.tr/tr/turkiye /egitimlerini-tamamlayan-53-turk-muhendis-akkuyu-ngsde-ise-basladi/1872114.

Peshkov, Vladimir. "The Donbas: Back in the USSR." *European Council on Foreign Relations,* September 1, 2016. https://ecfr.eu/article/essay_the_donbas_back_in _the_ussr.

Pew Research Center. "America's Image Further Erodes, Europeans Want Weaker Ties." March 18, 2003. www.pewresearch.org/global/2003/03/18/americas-image -further-erodes-europeans-want-weaker-ties.

Phillips, Christopher. *The Battle for Syria: International Rivalry in the Middle East.* New Haven: Yale University Press, 2016.

Phillips, Macon. "President Obama: "The Future of Syria Must Be Determined by Its People, but President Bashar al-Assad Is Standing in Their Way." White House President Barack Obama, August 18, 2011. https://obamawhitehouse.archives.gov /blog/2011/08/18/president-obama-future-syria-must-be-determined-its-people -president-bashar-al-assad.

Pipes, Richard. *A Concise History of the Russian Revolution.* New York: Alfred A. Knopf, 1991.

———. *Russia under the Old Regime.* New York: Charles Scribner's Sons, 1974.

Prezident Rossii. "Prezident Rossii vystupil na otkrytii Vsemirnogo ekonomichesk-ogo foruma" [The Russian President Spoke at the Opening of the World Economic Forum]. January 26, 2011. http://kremlin.ru/events/president/news/10163/audios.

———. "Telefonnyy razgovor s Prezidentom Turtsii Redzhepom Tayipom Erdoganom" [Telephone Conversation with Turkish President Recep Tayyip Erdogan]. February 9, 2017. http://kremlin.ru/events/president/news/53851.

———. "Vladimir Putin provel vstrechu s liderom partii spravedlivosti i razvitiya Turtsii Redzhepom Tayipom Erdoganom, pribyvshim nakanune v Moskvu s dvukhdnevnym rabochim vizitom." [Vladimir Putin Met with the Leader of the Justice and Development Party of Turkey, Recep Tayyip Erdogan, Who Arrived in Moscow on a Two-Day Working Visit]. December 24, 2002. http://kremlin.ru /events/president/news/27890.

———. "Vladimir Putin vstretilsya s rukovoditelyami ryada kompaniy i kommercheskikh bankov Rossii" [Vladimir Putin Met with the Heads of a Number of Russia's Largest Companies and Commercial Banks]. *Prezident Rossii*, July 28, 2000. http://kremlin.ru/events/president/news/38471.

———. "Vneseny izmeneniya v Ukaz o merakh po obespecheniyu natsional'noy bezopasnosti i zashchite grazhdan Rossii ot protivopravnykh deystviy i o primenenii spetsial'nykh ekonomicheskikh mer v otnoshenii Turtsii" [Amendments Were Made to the Decree on Measures to Ensure National Security and Protect Russian Citizens from Illegal Actions and on the Application of Special Economic Measures against Turkey]. December 28, 2015. http://kremlin.ru/events/president/news/51027.

Putin, Vladimir. "70-Ya sessiya General'noy Assamblei OON" [70th Session of the UN General Assembly]. *Prezident Rossii,* September 28, 2015. http://kremlin.ru /events/president/news/50385.

———. Interview by Oliver Stone. *Putin Interviews.* Showtime, February 26, 2016.

———. "Kontseptsiya vneshney politiki Rossiyskoy Federatsii" [Foreign Policy Concept of the Russian Federation]. *Tekhexpert,* June 28, 2000. http://docs.cntd.ru /document/901764263.

———. "Poslaniye Prezidenta Federal'nomu Sobraniyu" [Message from the Prezident to the Federal Assembly]. *Prezident Rossii,* January 15, 2020. http:// kremlin.ru/events/president/news/62582.

———. "Ukaz o merakh po obespecheniyu natsional'noy bezopasnosti Rossii i zashchite grazhdan Rossii ot prestupnykh i inykh protivopravnykh deystviy i o primenenii spetsial'nykh ekonomicheskikh mer v otnoshenii Turtsii" [Decree on Measures to Ensure the National Security of Russia and Protect Russian Citizens from Criminal and Other Illegal Actions and on the Application of Special Economic Measures against Turkey]. November 28, 2015. http://kremlin.ru/events /president/news/50805.

———. "Ukaz Prezidenta Rossiyskoy Federatsii ot 02.06.2020 g. № 355" [Decree of the President of the Russian Federation No. 355 of 02.06.2020]. June 2, 2020. www.kremlin.ru/acts/bank/45562.

———. "Ukaz Prezidenta Rossiyskoy Federatsii ot 13.05.2000 g. № 849" [Decree of the President of the Russian Federation No. 849 of 13.05.2000]. *Prezident Rossii,* May 13, 2000. http://kremlin.ru/acts/bank/15492.

———. "Ukaz Prezidenta Rossiyskoy Federatsii ot 17.12.1997 g. № 1300" [Decree of the President of the Russian Federation No. 1300 of 17.12.1997]. *Prezident Rossii,* January 17, 2000. www.kremlin.ru/acts/bank/11782.

———. "Ukaz Prezidenta Rossiyskoy Federatsii ot 20.07.2017 g. № 327" [Decree of the President of the Russian Federation No. 327 of 20.07.2017]. *Prezident Rossii,* July 20, 2017. http://kremlin.ru/acts/bank/42117.

———. "Ukaz Prezidenta Rossiyskoy Federatsii ot 25 marta 2004 g. № 400 Ob Administratsii Prezidenta Rossiyskoy Federatsii" [Decree of the President of the

Russian Federation No. 640 of 30.11.2016]. *Prezident Rossii,* March 25, 2004. http://kremlin.ru/acts/bank/20694.

———. "Ukaz Prezidenta Rossiyskoy Federatsii ot 30.11.2016 g. № 640" [Decree of the President of the Russian Federation No. 640 of 30.11.2016]. *Prezident Rossii,* November 30, 2016. http://kremlin.ru/acts/bank/41451.

———. "Ukaz Prezidenta Rossiyskoy Federatsii ot 31.12.2015 g. № 683" [Decree of the President of the Russian Federation No. 683 31.12.2015]. *Prezident Rossii,* December 31, 2015. http://kremlin.ru/acts/bank/40391.

Radio Liberty. "Turkmenistan: Gas Industry Seeks Export Routes." October 9, 1999. www.rferl.org/a/1092410.html.

Ragsdale, Hugh. "Evaluating the Traditions of Russian Aggression: Catherine II and the Greek Project." *The Slavonic and East European Review* 66, no. 1 (1988): 91–117.

Republic of Turkey Energy Market Regulatory Authority. "Doğal Gaz Piyasası Yıllık Sektör Raporu Listesi" [Natural Gas Market Yearly Sector Report List]. Accessed March 29, 2022. www.epdk.gov.tr/Detay/Icerik/3-0-94/yillik-sektor -raporu.

Republic of Turkey Ministry of Foreign Affairs. "No. 216, 21 Eylül 2011 Türkiye— KKTC Kıta Sahanlığı Sınırlandırma Anlaşması İmzalanmasına İlişkin Dışişleri Bakanlığı Basın Açıklaması" [No. 216, September 21, 2011 Turkish Ministry of Foreign Affairs Press Release for the Signing of the Continental Shelf Agreement between Turkey and the TRNC]. September 21, 2011. www.mfa.gov.tr/no_-216_ -21-eylul-2011-turkiye-_-kktc-kita-sahanligi-sinirlandirma-anlasmasi-imzalanma-sina-iliskin-disisleri-bakanligi-basin-ac_.tr.mfa.

———. "Turkey´s Political Relations with the Russian Federation." Accessed April 15, 2022. www.mfa.gov.tr/turkey_s-political-relations-with-russian-federation.en .mfa.

———. "Türkiye Cumhuriyeti İle Ermenistan Cumhuriyeti Arasında Diplomatik İlişkilerin Kurulmasına Dair Protokol" [Protocol for the Formation of Diplomatic Relations between the Republic of Turkey and the Republic of Armenia]. October 10, 2009. www.mfa.gov.tr/site_media/html/zurih-protokolleri-tr.pdf.

———. "Türkiye Cumhuriyeti İle Rusya Federasyonu Arasındaki İlişkilerin Yeni Bir Aşamaya Doğru İlerlemesi Ve Dostluğun Ve Çok Boyutlu Ortaklığın Daha da Derinleştirilmesine İlişkin Ortak Deklarasyon, Moskova, 13 Şubat 2009" [Joint Declaration between the Republic of Turkey and the Russian Federation on Progress towards a New Stage in Relations and Further Deepening of Friendship and Multidimensional Partnership]. February 13, 2009. www.mfa.gov.tr/joint-dec-laration-between-the-republic-of-turkey-and-the-russian-federation-on-progress -towards-a-new-stage-in-relations-and-further-deepening-of-friendship-and-multi-dimentional-partnership_-moscow_-13-february-2009.en.mfa.

Resis, Albert, ed. *Molotov Remembers: Inside Kremlin Politics.* Chicago: Ivan R. Dee, 1993.

Reuters. "Battle of Aleppo Ends after Years of Bloodshed with Rebel Withdrawal." December 13, 2016. www.reuters.com/article/us-mideast-crisis-syria-idUSKB N1420H5.

———. "Eastern Mediterranean Countries to Form Regional Gas Market." January 14, 2019. www.reuters.com/article/us-egypt-energy-gas-idUSKCN1P81FG.

———. "Greece, Israel, Cyprus Sign EastMed Gas Pipeline Deal." January 2, 2020. www.reuters.com/article/us-greece-cyprus-israel-pipeline/greece-israel-cyprus -sign-eastmed-gas-pipeline-deal-idUSKBN1Z10R5.

———. "Rebels Agree Withdrawal Deal for Enclave Near Syria's Homs." May 2, 2018. www.reuters.com/article/us-mideast-crisis-syria-homs/rebels-agree-with-drawal-deal-for-enclave-near-syrias-homs-idUSKBN1I329Y.

———. "Turkey Agrees to Supply Georgia Electricity: Source." August 8, 2008. www.reuters.com/article/us-georgia-turkey-electricity-idUSIST00224320 080808.

———. "Turkey Must Stop Meddling in Other States' Affairs, End Support of Terrorism, Russia Says." April 4, 2016. www.reuters.com/article/us-mideast-crisis -russia-syria-turkey-idUSKCN0X10XT.

———. "Turkey Spars with EU over Fresh Drilling off Cyprus." January 19, 2020. www.reuters.com/article/us-turkey-cyprus/turkey-spars-with-eu-over-fresh -drilling-off-cyprus-idUSKBN1ZI0G0.

———. "Turkish Foreign Minister Calls for Enlarged NATO, Georgia Membership." January 23, 2020. www.reuters.com/article/us-davos-meeting-turkey-georgia /turkish-foreign-minister-calls-for-enlarged-nato-georgia-membership -idUSKBN1ZM1HB.

RIA Novosti. "'Udar v spinu': Zayavleniya Vladimira Putina ob intsidente s Su-24" [Stab in the Back: Statement of Putin on the Incident of SU-24]. November 24, 2015. https://ria.ru/20151124/1327592353.html.

Ripsman, Norrin M., Jeffrey W. Taliaferro, and Steven E. Lobell. *Neoclassical Realist Theory of International Politics.* New York: Oxford University Press, 2016.

Roblin, Sebastien. "Cheap Drones from China, Turkey and Israel Are Fueling Conflicts Like Armenia and Azerbaijan's." *NBC News,* October 14, 2020. www.nbcnews.com/think/opinion/cheap-drones-china-turkey-israel-are-fueling -conflicts-armenia-azerbaijan-ncna1243246.

Rodkey, Frederick Stanley. "Lord Palmerston and the Rejuvenation of Turkey, 1830–41." *The Journal of Modern History* 1, no. 4 (December 1929): 573–77.

Rose, Gideon. "Neoclassical Realism and Theories of Foreign Policy." *World Politics* 51, no. 1 (October 1998): 144–72.

Russia Today. "Russia to Stop Gas Delivery via Ukraine by 2019, Push Ahead with Turkish Stream—Miller." April 13, 2015. www.rt.com/business/249273-gazprom -ukraine-gas-transit.

Saz-Carranza, Angel, and Maria Vandendriessche. "Routes to Energy Security: The Geopolitics of Gas Pipelines between Europe and Its Neighbors." In *The New Politics of Strategic Resources: Energy and Food Security Challenges in the 21st Century,* edited by David Steven. Washington, DC: Brookings Institution Press, 2015.

Schapiro, Leonard. *The Communist Party of the Soviet Union.* New York: Random House, 1960.

Security Council Report. "UN Documents for Syria: Other." Accessed October 28, 2021. www.securitycouncilreport.org/un_documents_type/other-documents /?ctype=Syria&cbtype=syria.

Security Council. "Resolution 884." November 12, 1993. http://unscr.com/en /resolutions/doc/884.

Şenol, Özkan. "Cooperative Security in the Black Sea Region." Master's Thesis, Bilkent University, 2003.

Service, Robert. *A History of Russia: From Tsarism to the Twenty-First Century.* Cambridge: Harvard University Press, 2009.

Shaw, Stanford. *History of the Ottoman Empire and the Modern Turkey: Empire of Gazis—the Rise and Decline of the Ottoman Empire 1280–1808.* Vol. 1. New York: Cambridge University Press, 1997.

Shaw, Stanford, and Ezel Kural Shaw. *History of the Ottoman Empire and Modern Turkey: Reform, Revolution, and Republic: The Rise of Modern Turkey, 1808–1975.* Vol. 2. New York: Cambridge University Press, 2005.

Shevchenko, Vitaly. "'Little Green Men' or 'Russian Invaders'?" BBC, March 11, 2014. www.bbc.com/news/world-europe-26532154.

Smirnov, Sergey. "Medvedev nazval nedopustimymi slova Putina o Livii" [Medvedev Called Putin's Words about Libya Unacceptable]. *Vedomosti,* March 21, 2011. www .vedomosti.ru/politics/articles/2011/03/21/medvedev_nazval_nedopustimymi _slova_putina_o_livii.

Smith, Julianne. *The NATO-Russia Relationship: Defining Moment or Déjà Vu?* Washington, DC: CSIS, 2008.

Snegovaya, Maria. "Anti-Western Sentiment as the Basis for Russian Unity." *Carnegie Moscow,* April 4, 2014. https://carnegie.ru/commentary/57115.

Speck, Ulrich. *The West's Response to the Ukraine Conflict: A Transatlantic Success Story.* Washington, DC: Transatlantic Academy, 2016.

Sputnik Türkiye. "İdlib mutabakatı zaptının 10 maddesi" [10 Articles of Idlib Memorandum of Understanding]. September 19, 2018. https://tr.sputniknews.com /ortadogu/201809191035276132-idlib-mutabakat-zaptinin-on-maddesi.

———. "Rudskoy: Astana sürecinin garantör ülkeleri, İdlib'de gözlem noktası kurma çalışmalarını tamamladı" [Rudskoy: Guarantor States of the Astana Process Completed Setting Up Observation Posts in Idlib]. May 23, 2018. https://tr .sputniknews.com/rusya/201805231033562557-rudskoy-astana-sureci-idlib.

Stern, Jonathan, Simon Pirani, and Katja Yafimava. *Does the Cancellation of South Stream Signal a Fundamental Reorientation of Russian Gas Export Policy?* Oxford: The Oxford Institute for Energy Studies, January 2015.

Stone, Norman. *Turkey: A Short History.* London: Thames & Hudson, 2017.

Stronski, Paul, and Nicole Ng. *Cooperation and Competition Russia and China in Central Asia, the Russian Far East, and the Arctic.* Washington, DC: Carnegie, 2018.

Suriye Gündemi. "Bahar Kalkanı Operasyonu Kapsamında Rejim Kayıpları" [Losses of the Regime in the Spring Shield Operation]. March 2, 2020. www.suriyegundemi .com/bahar-kalkani-operasyonu-kapsaminda-rejim-kayiplari.

Takvim. "Putin: Erdoğan'ın katkısı büyük" [Putin: Erdoğan's Contribution Is Big]. September 28, 2017. www.takvim.com.tr/guncel/2017/09/28/putin-erdoganin-kat-kisi-buyuk.

Tan, Weizhen. "Oil Prices Fall to 17-Year Low as Saudi Arabia–Russia Standoff Continues, Coronavirus Hits Demand." *CNBC,* March 30, 2020. www.cnbc.com /2020/03/30/oil-falls-amid-saudi-arabia-russia-price-war-coronavirus-hits-demand .html.

TANAP. "TANAP Is Ready to Deliver Natural Gas to Europe." December 24, 2019. www.tanap.com/media/press-releases/tanap-is-ready-to-deliver-natural-gas -to-europe.

Taşlı, Tekin Aycan. *"Türkiye-Rusya İlişkileri ve Üst Düzey İşbirliği Konseyi (ÜDİK)"* [Turkey-Russia Relations and the High-Level Cooperation Council]. *Kare,* no. 8 (2019): 81–128.

TASS. "Russia-Turkey Cross-Cultural Year Has Lots in Store, Says Russia's Ambassador to Turkey." February 10, 2019.

Taydaş, Zeynep, and Özgür Özdamar. "A Divided Government, an Ideological Parliament, and an Insecure Leader: Turkey's Indecision about Joining the Iraq War." *Social Science Quarterly* 94, no. 1 (2012): 217–41.

Taylor, Adam. "Russia's Putin Bluffing on Ukraine? Allies in the United States and Europe Are Divided." *Washington Post*, January 25, 2022. www.washingtonpost .com/world/2022/01/25/russia-ukraine-putin-bluff/.

TC Cumhurbaşkanlığı. "Rusya" [Russia]. August 9, 2020. www.tccb.gov.tr/yurt-disi -ziyaretler/355/49958/rusya.

TC Dışişleri Bakanlığı, *Yazılı Soru Önergesi 026.21/2003/SPGY/239371* [Written Parliamentary Question 026.21/2003/SPGY/239371]. Ankara: Turkish Grand National Assembly, November 6, 2003.

Tellal, Erel. "Rusya ile İlişkiler" [Relations with Russia]. In *Türk Dış Politikası: Kurtuluş Savaşı'ndan Bugüne Olgular, Belgeler; Yorumlar Cilt II: 1980–2001* [Turkish Foreign Policy: From the War of Independence until Today, Facts, Documents, Comments, Vol. 2: 1980–2001], edited by Baskın Oran, 540–50. İstanbul: İletişim, 2002.

Tellal, Erel. "SSCB ile İlişkiler" [Relations with the USSR]. In *Türk Dış Politikası: Kurtuluş Savaşı'ndan Bugüne Olgular, Belgeler; Yorumlar Cilt II: 1980–2001* [Turkish Foreign Policy: From the War of Independence until Today, Facts, Documents, Comments, Vol. 2: 1980–2001], edited by Baskın Oran, 158–66. İstanbul: İletişim, 2002.

Teslova, Elena. "No One Can Say Turkey Flouted Int'l Law in Karabakh: Putin." *Anadolu Agency,* November 17, 2020. www.aa.com.tr/en/azerbaijan-front-line/no -one-can-say-turkey-flouted-intl-law-in-karabakh-putin/2047249.

Thakkar, Mona. "Russia and Turkey in Libya, Testing the Waters?" *International Policy Digest,* February 3, 2020. https://intpolicydigest.org/2020/02/03/russia-and -turkey-in-libya-testing-the-waters.

Tlis, Fatima. "The Strike: Did Russia Knowingly Target Turkish Troops?" *Polygraph,* February 28, 2020. www.polygraph.info/a/turkey-russia-syria-fact -check/30460458.html.

Toktamış, Kumru F. "A Peace That Wasn't: Friends, Foes, and Contentious Re-entrenchment of Kurdish Politics in Turkey." *Turkish Studies* 19, no. 5 (2008): 697–722.

Torbakov, Igor. *The Georgia Crisis and Russia-Turkey Relations.* Washington, DC: Jamestown Foundation, 2008.

———. "Turkey Sides with Moscow against Washington on Black Sea Force." *Jamestown Foundation*, March 3, 2006. https://jamestown.org/program/turkey -sides-with-moscow-against-washington-on-black-sea-force.

Trenin, Dmitri. "Really Burying the Hatchet: Russia and Turkey Find Themselves on the Same Side." *Insight Turkey* 4, no. 2 (April–June 2002): 25–32.

———. "The Relationship between the USA and Russia in the Trump Era." *Inside Over,* May 2, 2019. www.insideover.com/politics/the-relationship-between-the -usa-and-russia-in-the-trump-era.html.

———. "Russia and Turkey: A Cure for Schizophrenia." *Perceptions* 2, no. 2 (1997): 57–65.

TRT Haber. "Cumhurbaşkanı Erdoğan: Azerbaycanlı kardeşlerimizin yanlarındayız" [President Erdoğan: We Are with Our Azerbaijani Brothers]. October 1, 2020. www.trthaber.com/haber/gundem/cumhurbaskani-erdogan-azerbaycanli -kardeslerimizin-Yanlarindayiz-520086.html.

———. "Üçlü Astana Zirvesi sona erdi" [Trilateral Astana Summit Has Ended]. July 1, 2020. www.trthaber.com/haber/gundem/uclu-astana-zirvesi-sona-erdi-497705 .html.

TRT World. "Russia Says Evacuation from Syria's Eastern Ghouta to End within Days." April 4, 2018. www.trtworld.com/mea/russia-says-evacuation-from-syria-s -eastern-ghouta-to-end-within-days-16463.

———. "Türkiye to Russia: Ukraine 'War' Must Stop." March 16, 2022. www .trtworld.com/europe/türkiye-to-russia-ukraine-war-must-stop-55559.

Truman, Harry S. *The Memoirs of Harry S. Truman: Years of Trial and Hope 1945–1953.* Vol. 2. Suffolk: Hodder and Stoughton, 1956.

———. "President Harry S. Truman's Address Before a Joint Session of Congress, March 12, 1947." Avalon Project at Yale Law School. Accessed September 23, 2022. https://avalon.law.yale.edu/20th_century/trudoc.asp.

Trump, Donald (@realdonaldtrump). "After Historic Victories against ISIS, It's Time to Bring Our Great Young People Home!" Twitter. December 19, 2018, 06:10 PM. https://twitter.com/realDonaldTrump/status/1075528854402256896.

Tsygankov, Andrey. *Russia's Foreign Policy: Change and Continuity.* London: Rowman and Littlefield, 2016.

Turkish Atomic Energy Authority. "Akkuyu Nuclear Power Plant." Accessed February 14, 2022. www.taek.gov.tr/en/institutional/akkuyu-nuclear-power-plant .html.

Turkish Ministry of Culture and Tourism. "*Sınır Giriş Çıkış İstatistikleri*" [Border Crossing Statistics]. Accessed March 30, 2022. https://yigm.ktb.gov.tr/TR-9854 /sinir-giris-cikis-istatistikleri.html.

Turkish Ministry of Trade. "Dış Ticaret İstatistikleri" [Foreign Trade Statistics]. Accessed April 10, 2022. https://ticaret.gov.tr/istatistikler/dis-ticaret-istatistikleri.

Turner, Susan. "Russia, China and a Multipolar World Order: The Danger in the Undefined." *Asian Perspective* 33, no. 1 (2009): 159–84.

Ulutaş, Ufuk. *The State of Savagery: ISIS in Syria.* Ankara: SETA, 2016.

Ulutaş, Ufuk, and Burhanettin Duran. "Türkiye'nin DEAŞ'la Mücadelesinin Kritik Dönemeci: Fırat Kalkanı Harekâtı" [The Critical Juncture of Turkey's Fight with ISIS: Operation Euphrates Shield]. In *Türk Politikası Yıllığı 2016* [Yearbook of Turkish Foreign Policy 2016], edited by Burhanettin Duran, Kemal İnat, and Mustafa Caner, 11–30. Ankara: SETA, 2019.

UNHCR. "Refugees Fleeing Ukraine (since 24 February 2022)." March 13, 2022. https://data2.unhcr.org/en/situations/ukraine.

United Nations Security Council (UNSC). *Annex to the Letter Dated 8 November 2002 from the Representatives of China, France and the Russian Federation to the United Nations addressed to the President of the Security Council.* UN Doc S/RES/1373, November 8, 2002.

U.S. Department of State. "Background Briefing on the Joint Statement by the President of the United States and the President of the Russian Federation on Syria." November 11, 2017. www.state.gov/background-briefing-on-the-joint-statement-by-the-president-of-the-united-states-and-the-president-of-the-russian-federation-on-syria.

———. "Ukraine and Russia Sanctions." Accessed January 2, 2022. www.state.gov/ukraine-and-russia-sanctions.

———. "The United States Sanctions Turkey under CAATSA 231." December 14, 2020. https://2017-2021.state.gov/the-united-states-sanctions-turkey-under-caatsa-231/index.html.

Vatchagaev, Mairbek. "Another Chechen Émigré Murdered in Turkey." *Eurasia Daily Monitor,* March 6, 2015. https://jamestown.org/program/another-chechen-emigre-murdered-in-turkey-2.

Vinograd, Cassandra, and Ammar Cheikh Omar. "Syria, ISIS Have Been 'Ignoring' Each Other on Battlefield, Data Suggests." *NBC News,* December 11, 2014. www.nbcnews.com/storyline/isis-uncovered/syria-isis-have-been-ignoring-each-other-battlefield-data-suggests-n264551.

VOA News. "Turkey Says Syrian Plane Contained Ammunition." October 11, 2012. www.voanews.com/world-news/middle-east-dont-use/turkey-says-syrian-plane-contained-ammunition.

Walt, Stephan. *The Hell of Good Intentions: America's Foreign Policy Elite and the Decline of U.S. Primacy.* New York: Farrar, Straus & Giroux, 2018.

Waltz, Kenneth. *Theory of International Politics.* Menlo Park: Addison-Wesley, 1979.

Warhola, James A., and William A. Mitchell. "The Warming of Turkish-Russian Relations: Motives and Implications." *Demokratizatsiya* 14, no. 1 (Winter 2006): 127–43.

Weitz, Richard. "Russian-Turkish Relations: Steadfast and Changing." *Mediterranean Quarterly* 21, no. 3 (2010): 61–85.

White House. "Readout of President Biden's Call with President Recep Tayyip Erdogan of Turkey." March 10, 2022. www.whitehouse.gov/briefing-room/statements-releases/2022/03/10/readout-of-president-bidens-call-with-president-recep-tayyip-erdogan-of-turkey.

———. "Statement from the Press Secretary." October 6, 2019. www.whitehouse
.gov/briefings-statements/statement-press-secretary-85.

White, Stephen. *Russia's Authoritarian Elections.* New York: Routledge, 2014.

WHO. "Timeline of WHO's Response to COVID-19." September 9, 2020. www.who
.int/news/item/29-06-2020-covidtimeline.

Wilkie, Christina, and Amanda Macias. "U.S. Intelligence Agencies Point to Potential
Russian Invasion of Ukraine within a Month's Time." *CNBC,* January 14, 2022.
www.cnbc.com/2022/01/14/russia-could-invade-ukraine-within-next-month-us
-intelligence.html.

Winrow, Gareth. "Turkey and Russia: The Importance of Energy Ties." *Insight
Turkey* 19, no. 1 (2017): 17–32.

———. "Turkey and the Newly Independent States of Central Asia and the
Transcaucasus." *Middle East Review of International Affairs* 1, no. 2 (July 1997):
1–12.

Yanık, Lerna. "Allies or Partners? An Appraisal of Turkey's Ties to Russia, 1991–
2007." *East European Quarterly* 41, no. 3 (Fall 2007): 349–71.

Yavuz, M. Hakan, and Rasim Koç. "The Gülen Movement vs. Erdoğan: The Failed
Coup." In *Turkey's July 15th Coup: What Happened and Why,* edited by Bayram
Balcı and Hakan Yavuz, 78–97. Salt Lake City: The University of Utah Press,
2018.

Yeltsin, Boris. "Ukaz Prezidenta Rossiyskoy Federatsii ot 17 dekabrya 1997 goda
№ 1300" [Decree by the President of the Russian Federation from December 17,
1997, no. 1300]. *Prezident Rossii,* December 17, 1997. www.kremlin.ru/acts/bank
/11782.

Yeni Şafak. "Erdoğan'dan Azerbaycan-Ermenistan açıklaması" [Azerbaijan-Armenia
Statement from Erdoğan]. April 2, 2016. www.yenisafak.com/dunya/erdogandan
-azerbaycan-ermenistan-aciklamasi-2444314.

———. "Putin Says US Knew about Turkey's July 15 Coup Attempt." June 17,
2017. www.yenisafak.com/en/news/putin-says-us-knew-about-turkeys-july-15
-coup-attempt-2725798.

Yeşilyurt, Nuri. "Explaining Miscalculation and Maladaptation in Turkish Foreign
Policy towards the Middle East during the Arab Uprisings: A Neoclassical Realist
Perspective." *All Azimuth* 6, no. 2 (2017): 66–85.

———. "Orta Doğu ile İlişkiler" [Relations with the Middle East]. In *Türk Dış
Politikası: Kurtuluş Savaşı'ndan Bugüne Olgular, Belgeler; Yorumlar Cilt III:
2001–2012* [Turkish Foreign Policy: From the War of Independence until Today,
Facts, Documents, Comments, Vol. 3: 2001–2012], edited by Baskın Oran, 401–
62. İstanbul: İletişim, 2013.

Yetkin, Murat. "Rusya ile sıkı işbirliği" [Intense Partnership with Russia]. *Radikal,*
July 21, 2005. http://m.radikal.com.tr/yazarlar/murat_yetkin/rusya_ile_siki
_isbirligi-752569.

———. *Tezkere* [The Bill]. İstanbul: Remzi Kitabevi, 2017.

———. "Türk-Rus krizini bitiren gizli diplomasinin öyküsü" [Story of the Secret
Diplomacy That Ended the Turkish-Russian Crisis]. *Hürriyet,* August 8, 2016.
www.hurriyet.com.tr/yazarlar/murat-Yetkin/turk-rus-krizini-bitiren-gizli-diploma-
sinin-oykusu-40185705.

Yıldız, Sara Nur. "Mongol Rule in Thirteenth-Century Seljuk Anatolia: The Politics of Conquest and History Writing, 1243–1282." PhD dissertation. University of Chicago, 2006.

Zakaria, Fareed. *The Post-American World.* New York: W. W. Norton, 2008.

Zanotti, Jim, and Clayton Thomas. "Turkey: Background and U.S. Relations in Brief." *Congressional Research Service,* November 9, 2020. https://crsreports .congress.gov/product/pdf/R/R44000.

Ziganshin, M. K. "Rossiysko-Turetskiye otnosheniya na sovremennom etape" [Russian-Turkish Relations in Contemporary Era]. In *Turtsiya v novykh geopoliticheskıkh usloviyakh (materialy kruglogo stola mart 2004 g.)* [Turkey in New Geopolitical Conditions (Materials of the Round Table, March 2004)], edited by N. Y. Ulichenko, 4–8. Moscow: Institut Vostokovedeniya RAN, 2004.

Zürcher, Erik J. *Turkey: A Modern History.* New York: I. B. Tauris, 2017.

Index

Page references for figures are italicized.

145

About the Author

Muhammet Koçak received his PhD in international relations from Florida International University. He is interested in international security with a focus on Russia and Turkey, and particularly in all aspects of Turkey-Russia Relations. He has written multiple academic articles and book chapters on Turkish foreign policy, Russian foreign policy, and Turkey-Russia relations. His articles on regional issues have appeared in major media outlets, including Middle East Eye, Al Sharq Forum, and TRT World. He regularly updates his website (mkocak.net) and shares his opinions on various issues related to his areas of research on his Twitter page: @muhammedkocak.

www.ingramcontent.com/pod-product-compliance
Lightning Source LLC
Chambersburg PA
CBHW031136270326
41929CB00011B/1648